The

NEGRO LEAGUES are MAJOR LEAGUES

BASEBALL REFERENCE

Essays and Research for Overdue Recognition

Edited by Sean Forman and Cecilia M. Tan
Associate Editors: Scott Bush, Adam Darowski,
Caitlin Moyer, Jacob Pomrenke

Society for American Baseball Research, Inc.
In collaboration with Sports Reference LLC

Copyright of individual articles may belong to individual contributors
and/or Sports-Reference.com.
Images: The Rucker Archive

ISBN 978-1-970159-62-2 ebook
ISBN 978-1-970159-63-9 paperback
Library of Congress Call Number 2021923521

Front cover art and design: Gary Cieradkowski, Studio Gary C
Interior design: Jennifer Bahl Hron
Interior font families: Sabon LT Pro & Forma DJR Micro

Society forAmerican Baseball Research (SABR)
Cronkite School at ASU
555 N. Central Ave. #416
Phoenix, AZ 85004
Phone: (602) 496-1460
www.sabr.org

Contents

The SABR Articles

Welcome
to The Negro Leagues are Major Leagues

by Sean Forman and Cecilia M. Tan

This book came to be because in 2020 a significant change took place in the way the Negro Leagues were viewed by the mainstream baseball establishment. A movement had been underway for some time at that point, with a vanguard of historians—notably Todd Peterson—making the case that the Negro Leagues were major leagues. The Society for American Baseball Research (SABR) convened a committee on the subject, which quickly concurred with Peterson and identified specific leagues and years that ought to be designated "major." Before that committee could announce its findings, Major League Baseball itself came independently to the same conclusion. In December 2020, Commissioner of Baseball Robert D. Manfred, Jr. announced a new MLB policy to recognize the Negro Leagues as major leagues.

To reflect the change, Baseball-Reference.com dramatically expanded coverage of the Negro Leagues and historical Black major league players on the site. Major Negro Leagues (from 1920 through 1948) are now listed alongside the National League and American League (and other historical major leagues such as the Federal League). In doing so, Baseball Reference did not bestow a new status on Negro League players or their accomplishments. The Negro Leagues have always been major leagues. Baseball Reference updated the site's presentation to properly recognize that fact. We would especially direct you to Gary Ashwill's piece on the building of the Seamheads database. This work forms the basis of the project and is a leap forward in the construction of a statistical record for Black baseball.

But the integration and presentation of Negro Leagues stats on the site were not the only update that took place. After all, the game and its players are not just their numbers. We commissioned articles from prominent Negro League historians, family members of Black baseball players, and others to explain the context behind the rise of Black baseball, how it operated, who was involved, and its part in the history of the game. We wanted to contextualize the numbers, and to recognize that the legend and lore of many of these players exist beyond stats.

The Negro Leagues data are not complete. While the quality of play in the Negro Leagues was on a major-league level, the wages, travel, playing conditions, press coverage, and record-keeping were more varied, primarily due to systemic racism. Additionally, Negro League teams played a shorter regular season schedule, but with an extensive amount of exhibitions and barnstorming games that made for seasons that often approached 200 or more games in total. These contests were not part of their league schedule and are therefore not included in this database. This is why Josh Gibson's Hall of Fame plaque says that he hit "almost 800 home runs" while his page on Baseball-Reference shows 165, and why presenting the numbers in context is a key part of our mission.

The fifteen articles commissioned for the site now comprise the bulk of this book, and are supplemented with some of the significant past works of Negro Leagues history from the SABR archives. In this way we are documenting not only the legacy of the Negro Leagues, but also the effort to rebuild the lost history that led to the current recognition that the Negro Leagues are major leagues.

The Baseball-Reference Essays

Negro Leagues By The Numbers by Bob Kendrick, President of the Negro Leagues Baseball Museum, with Joe Posnanski: A look at what the statistics of the Negro Leagues mean.

Negro Leagues = Major Leagues by Todd Peterson: An analysis of the quality of play of the Negro Leagues and the White major leagues.

A Love Story by Adam Jones, 14-year MLB veteran: What the Negro Leagues mean to a modern Black star.

The Black Boys of Summer: A Statistical Observation by Larry Lester: A look at how the Negro League stats were compiled and the effect on the record books.

Gibson Family Reflections on the Publication of Baseball Reference's Negro Leagues Statistics by Sean Gibson, great-grandson of Josh Gibson: What it means to family members of Negro League stars to see this update.

Women in the Negro Leagues by Leslie Heaphy: A discussion of the women who were executives and players the Negro Leagues.

A Black Baseball Legacy by Michael E. Lomax: The evolution of Black baseball from the 19th through the 20th century.

Turkey Stearnes and the Inclusive Grand Slam by Vanessa Ivy Rose, granddaughter of Turkey Stearnes: A reflection on the legacy of Hall of Famer Turkey Stearnes.

Building the Seamheads Negro Leagues Database by Gary Ashwill: A look at how the data that you see on the site today was collected.

Historiography of Black Baseball & Negro Baseball Leagues by Gary Gillette: A timeline of important Black baseball and Negro League histories and reference works.

Still Standing: Where to See Extant Negro League Ballparks by Gary Gillette: A look at which Negro League ballparks are still standing.

The Long Road to Jackie Robinson: Nineteenth Century Pioneers in Black Ball by Ryan Swanson: From Charles Douglass (son of Frederick) to Octavius Catto, all the way to Jackie Robinson.

Latinos in the Negro Leagues by Adrian Burgos, Jr.: The history of Latin stars in the Negro Leagues from Alex Pompez to Luis Tiant.

The Major Negro Leagues by Adam Darowski: A look at the seven major Negro Leagues.

The SABR Articles

The Negro Leagues Revisited, by Jules Tygiel: This 1986 article traces the history of literature and published sources of information about the Negro Leagues, from Sol White's seminal *Official Baseball Guide* to Robert Peterson's *Only the Ball was White* to John Holway's *Voices from the Great Black Baseball Leagues,* and a plethora of oral histories, interviews, and academic studies that followed in the 1970s and 1980s.

Rube Foster and Black Baseball in Chicago, by Jerry Malloy: Scholar Malloy, the namesake of SABR's annual Negro Leagues conference, here paints the picture of Chicago's Rube Foster, the "founding father" of the Negro Leagues, and goes on to detail how after the collapse of the leagues during the Great Depression, the resurgent leagues showcased their talent annually at Comiskey Park in the lavish East-West All-Star Game.

The Black Press and the Collapse of the Negro League in 1930, by David Hopkins: Tracing the effects of the Great Depression on the Negro National League through the spotty and sometimes contradictory coverage found in the *Pittsburgh Courier,* the Black weekly newspaper with the largest circulation.

Black Bluejackets: Great Lakes Negro Varsity team in 1944, by Jerry Malloy: As the Navy began to admit Black sailors to their ranks, they likewise admitted them to sports programs and teams that were important public relations and morale-building tools. The Great Lakes "Negro Varsity" would field numerous Negro League stars and pave the way for the eventual integration of baseball.

Pitching Behind the Color Line—Baseball, Advertising, and Race, by Roberta Newman: A look at representations of African Americans and baseball imagery in advertising in the 1930s and 1940s, in the Black weeklies, local newspapers, and, eventually, television.

Umpires in the Negro Leagues, by Leslie Heaphy: The history of umpires in the Negro Leagues, from the practice of using White umpires to pioneering Black umpires like Bob Motley and Julian Osibee Jelks.

Quebec Loop Broke Color Line in 1935, by Merritt Clifton: Eleven years before Jackie Robinson integrated the Montreal Royals en route to the Brooklyn Dodgers, a pitcher-outfielder named Alfred Wilson joined the Granby Red Sox of the Quebec Provincial League, an unaffiliated independent league.

The Double Victory Campaign and the Campaign to Integrate Baseball, by Duke Goldman: The two victories sought by the Double V campaign were to defeat Nazism abroad and racism at home. Launched by *The Courier*, the largest of the Black newspapers in the US, the campaign would ultimately score two victories: the desegregation of baseball and the US military.

It is important to remember that the history of Black baseball does not start in 1920 or end in 1948 and even from 1920-1948 our presentation is incomplete. There were hundreds of teams and thousands of players that would need to be included to make up a more complete and richer history of Black baseball. From 1920 though 1948 there were many star players and teams that found it more feasible to play a barnstorming schedule (not only in the United States, but also the Caribbean, Mexico, and Venezuela) rather than participate in leagues. These independent teams were often the equal of teams we are including as major league teams on the site now. The Baseball Reference complete register of baseball history contains a significant record of Independent and non-major Negro Leagues. For example, we have a page for the 1917 Chicago American Giants. Research on both the Negro Leagues and independent teams does not end here; this is but another step in the process.

Finally, we express our respect to the thousands of men and women who were involved in the Negro Leagues, with heartfelt acknowledgement to the very few who are still alive. Likewise, we express our respect to their descendants who keep the stories of their forebears alive—their struggles and also their accomplishments, not only on the field, but also off the field. We encourage our readers to seek out and support the likes of foundations and causes supported by the families of Satchel Paige, Josh Gibson, Buck Leonard, and others.

Acknowledgments

We would like to thank several partners who provided invaluable counsel and support during this project. Larry Lester, Gary Ashwill, Kevin Johnson and the team at Seamheads produced the vast majority of the statistical update that appears at Baseball-Reference. The Negro League Baseball Museum, especially President Bob Kendrick and Dr. Raymond Doswell, provided a significant amount of feedback and support as we worked to add this information to our site. Thanks also to Sean Gibson, Curtis Harris, and Caitlin Moyer for their insight and support. Ted Turocy performed the initial work necessary to merge the Seamheads database with the Baseball-Reference database. Thank you also to the Sports Reference team who worked on this project: Kenny Jackelen, Dan Hirsch, Mike Kania, Adam Darowski, Jaclyn Mahoney, Alex Bonilla, Jonah Gardner, Katie Sharp, Charlotte Eisenberg, Jay Hutchinson, Mike Lynch, Nick Pazoles, and Adam Wodon.

Thank you to the many researchers and historians who helped us by reviewing the update ahead of the launch, including Mark Armour, Mike Bates, Scott Bush, Jay Byland, Eric Chalek, Gary Joseph Cieradkowski, Philippe Cousineau, Chris Creamer, Nick Diunte, Raymond Doswell, Mischa Gelman, Gary Gillette, Tim Hagerty, Leslie Heaphy, Jay Jaffe, Adam Jones, Thomas Kern, Ted Knorr, Ben Lindbergh, Larry Lester, Andrew McCutchen, Rob Neyer, Alex Painter, Jim Passon, Todd Peterson, Jacob Pomrenke, Patrick Rock, Ryan Swanson, Tom Thress, Steve Treder, and Phil Williams.

Negro Leagues By the Numbers

by Bob Kendrick with Joe Posnanski

In 1994, a man named James A. Riley wrote an extraordinary book titled *The Biographical Encyclopedia of the Negro Baseball Leagues*. The book is almost 1,000 pages of stories and facts about the men and women who played Negro Leagues baseball. The research it took to put together such a masterpiece is mind-boggling; this was in the years before there was widespread study of the Leagues, before the beautiful Negro Leagues Baseball Museum on 18th and Vine in Kansas City was even built.

And the Encyclopedia has stats. Lots and lots of stats. Some examples:

"Satchel Paige estimated that in his career he pitched 2,000 games, 300 shutouts and 55 no-hitters."

"Josh Gibson was credited with 962 home runs in his seventeen year career."

"Cool Papa Bell once stole 175 bases in just under 200 games."

And so on.

Now, take a look at the career Negro Leagues stats of those three legendary players, here at Baseball Reference:

Satchel Paige: 90-49, 2.47 ERA, 1,150 strikeouts.

Josh Gibson: .374 average with 165 home runs.

Cool Papa Bell: .325 average with 285 stolen bases.

Obviously, these are significantly different. It's a long way from Gibson's 165 official home runs to his unofficial 962 home runs, right? It feels like the obvious question to ask: Where is the truth?

And the answer to that is there is more than one truth when it comes to the Negro Leagues. This is the story that the Negro Leagues Baseball Museum tells every day. Nothing at all is simple about a league that was built to combat and overcome hate, and yet was so much about joy and a love of the game.

Nothing at all is simple about counting statistics for players who traveled from town to town, regularly playing a dozen or more games per week against town teams and factory teams, in tournaments and exhibitions, all in addition to their official Negro Leagues games. Satchel Paige surely did pitch in thousands of games. Josh Gibson surely did hit close to 1,000 home runs, and Cool Papa Bell surely did steal at least as many bases as the great Josh hit homers.

And at the same time, the numbers that you will find online now are the work of dedicated and meticulous researchers who painstakingly went through box score after box score to log the totals these players had when playing top-level Negro Leagues baseball.

Each set of stats—the symbolic and the validated—offers insight into these amazing athletes when seen through the right context. For instance, look again at Gibson's official stats. Those 165 home runs, at first glance, might not seem as impressive as the much larger number Riley and so many others have thrown out there.

But consider now that they came in 2,511 plate appearances against the very best the Negro Leagues had to offer.

Babe Ruth got 10,626 plate appearances in his career. So, simple math, Ruth and Gibson hit home runs at remarkably similar rates—Ruth hit one homer every 14.88 plate appearances, Gibson hit one homer every 15.22 plate appearances. There's almost nothing between those numbers.

Projected over a similar length career to Ruth, Gibson would have hit 700 home runs himself. Now consider how much more difficult conditions were for Gibson, how many more games he had to play, how much more he had to endure, and you can see why Barry Bonds, when he broke the home run record himself, said he still considered Gibson to be the all-time home run king.

At the Negro Leagues Baseball Museum, we are thrilled that MLB has finally acknowledged what we already knew to be true—that the Negro Leagues were indeed major league. We are particularly happy that the numbers of these legendary players will become a part of the official record and, undoubtedly, people will become more curious about these players' stories.

And that's where we at the museum come in. The statistics offer an introduction to some of the greatest players in the history of the game: Oscar Charleston, Turkey Stearnes, the Devil Willie Wells, Bullet Rogan, Mule Suttles, Buck Leonard, the gloriously named Cristóbal Torriente, Leon Day, Hilton Smith, Martin Dihigo, Pop Lloyd and too many others to name. Go to their pages on Baseball Reference and learn a bit about them. Then come to Kansas City and discover the extraordinary full story.

As our friend Buck O'Neil used to say, "We could play, man!"

Oh, could they play.

Negro Leagues = Major Leagues

by Todd Peterson

The Negro Leagues were equal in quality of play to the White major leagues of their day. Thanks to the wealth of historical and statistical data now available, that fact can be demonstrated in a number of ways. The term "Negro Leagues" is used to describe a series of professional baseball organizations composed of African American and Latin American players that operated in the United States between 1920 and 1962. The designation is also applied to the many professional Black clubs that operated before the onset of league play or operated outside of their jurisdiction. The leagues themselves existed because, from 1899 until 1946, Black players were banned from "Organized Baseball," because of the color of their skin.[1]

The Seven Major Negro Leagues

Negro National League (I)	1920 - 1931
Eastern Colored League	1923 - 1928
American Negro League	1929
East-West League	1932
Negro Southern League	1932
Negro National League (II)	1933 - 1948
Negro American League	1937 - 1962

Source: Clark and Lester, *The Negro Leagues Book*, 1994.

Between 1866 and 1948, top-flight African American clubs played over 7,000 games with White semi-pro, college, minor league, and major league teams and beat them nearly 65 percent of the time. Drawing on statistics from these contests, games played in the Negro Leagues, and the events of post-integration baseball, several indisputable truths emerge.[2]

NLB vs. Other Classifications 1900-1948

Class	NLB					
	W	L	T	PCT	RF	RA
MLB	316	283	21	.527	4.29	4.07
MiLB	821	607	40	.573	5.22	4.45
Military	6	4	0	.600	4.30	2.70
Semi-Pro	2309	1014	69	.691	6.23	3.77
College	38	7	0	.844	8.18	3.64
Total	3490	1915	130	.642	5.76	3.98

Note: MiLB=Minor League Baseball.
Sources: Simkus, Outsider Baseball, 2014; Peterson NLB vs. MLB Database; Peterson NLB vs. MILB Database.

Negro League Teams Had a Winning Record against Major League Squads

The practice of African American outfits playing premier White players was an established tradition in cities such as New York, Philadelphia, Baltimore, Indianapolis, Chicago, St. Louis, Los Angeles, and San Diego. From the first year of the American League in 1900 through the last year of the second Negro National League in 1948, African American teams posted a record of 316-283-21 (.527) against White major league clubs and big-league All-Star aggregations. Against intact National, American, and Federal League teams, black squads posted a record of 47-60-8 (.443) However, from the inception of the Negro National League in 1920 through 1924, African American teams went 29-31-2 (.484) in head-to-head competition. Because the White mainstream press was often reluctant to print Black clubs' successes, the Negro Leaguers' overall tally is likely far better than what was recorded.[3]

NLB vs. MLB Head to Head 1900-1924

	W	PCT	R/9
NLB 1900- 1919	18	.396	4.03
MLB 1900- 1919	29	.604	4.42
NLB 1920- 1924	29	.484	4.58
MLB 1920- 1924	31	.516	4.70
NLB TOTAL	47	.443	4.34
MLB Total	60	.557	4.58

Sources: Peterson NLB vs. MLB Database; Holway, Johnson, and Borst, *The Complete Book of Baseball's Negro Leagues*, 2001.

In 1922, responding to the Black teams' continued success against American and National League squads, Commissioner of Baseball Kenesaw Mountain

Landis forbade big leaguers from appearing as under their team names or wearing their own uniforms, and insisted that they advertise themselves as All-Star teams, with only three individual teammates allowed to play together at any one time. Between 1900 and 1948, Black clubs defeated the best White batters, pitchers, and teams they were *allowed* to play nearly 55 percent of the time. The All-Star squads included in this tally were composed of five or more players with big league experience (including the starting pitcher) and at least three players who had appeared in the majors that particular season.[4]

NLB vs. MLB All-Stars 1900-1948

# Major Leaguers	W	L	T	PCT	NLBR/9	MLBR/9
Five	32	22	1	.591	3.93	3.44
Six	34	29	0	.540	4.71	4.52
Seven	39	31	4	.554	4.53	4.02
Eight	32	25	2	.559	4.09	4.00
Nine	91	86	3	.514	4.79	4.43
Total	269	223	13	.547	4.45	4.12

Sources: NLB vs. MLB Database; Holway with Johnson and Borst, *The Complete Book of Baseball's Negro Leagues*.

The number of big leaguers involved in many of these games was actually higher as the major leaguers often resorted to the use of aliases to avoid detection. As for the farfetched notion that the big leaguers were not giving their all, it should be noted that between 1900 and 1948, White major league squads racked up a record of 2640-897-71 (.742) against minor league, semi-pro, college and military teams—Only the Negro Leaguers had their number.[5]

MLB vs. Other Classifications 1900-1948

Class	MLB					
	W	L	T	PCT	RF	RA
NLB	283	316	21	.473	4.07	4.29
MiLB	1663	670	49	.708	6.55	3.97
Military	149	61	5	.705	7.11	4.04
Semi-Pro	687	155	17	.810	6.91	3.03
College	141	11	0	.928	9.87	2.57
Total	2923	1213	92	.702	6.39	3.77

Note: MiLB=Minor League Baseball.
Sources: Simkus, *Outsider Baseball*, 2014; Retrosheet.org; NLB vs. MLB Database; Peterson NLB vs. MILB Database.

When the combined results of 477 games between the Negro League squads and major league teams of varying composition are tabulated, the Black clubs are revealed to lead in almost every hitting, pitching, and fielding statistical category. Amazingly, both sides fielded at an identical .951 clip, but the Negro Leaguers turned more double plays. With the near disappearance of the African American pitcher from MLB in the twenty-first century, it is also interesting to note that the Black twirlers decisively outpaced their White big league counterparts in runs allowed, strikeouts, preventing base runners, and shut-outs.

NLB vs. MLB Batting Statistics 1900-1948

	SB	BA	OBP	SLG	OPS
NLB 1900-1919	136	.236	.285	.315	.601
MLB 1900-1919	176	.237	.306	.316	.622
MLB 1920-1948	315	.272	.321	.379	.701
MLB 1920-1948	175	.245	.307	.341	.648
NLB Total	451	.261	.310	.360	.670
MLB Total	351	.243	.307	.333	.640

NLB vs. MLB Pitching Statistics 1900-1948

	PCT	R/9	ERA	WHIP	K/9
NLB 1900-1919	.439	4.02	2.17	1.21	5.76
MLB 1900-1919	.561	3.53	1.85	1.10	6.25
MLB 1920-1948	.579	4.32	2.67	1.26	6.11
MLB 1920-1948	.421	5.04	3.24	1.33	5.78
NLB Total	.527	4.23	2.52	1.24	6.00
MLB Total	.463	4.56	2.76	1.25	5.93

NLB vs. MLB Fielding Statistics 1900-1948

	PO	A	E	FA	DP
NLB 1900-1919	3802	1678	341	.941	85
MLB 1900-1919	3633	1784	291	.949	60
MLB 1920-1948	8776	3205	552	.956	190
MLB 1920-1948	8397	3541	588	.953	183
NLB Total	12578	4883	893	.951	275
MLB Total	12030	5325	879	.951	243

Source for Tables: NLB vs. MLB Database.

The Negro Leagues Compare Favorably to the Major Leagues in Several Statistical Categories

Connie Mack once said that pitching makes up 70 percent of baseball. Historians John Thorn and Pete Palmer have asserted that the figure is more like 44 percent, but noted, "it is undeniably important." It is not a stretch then to say that a strong indicator of a baseball league's quality would be the strength of its pitching, and therefore those circuits with *lower* batting, slugging, and on-base percentages are superior to those with higher averages. For example, when comparing the hitting averages of the major leagues and those of the three highest minors—The International League, American Association, and Pacific Coast League—from 1912 (the year these three organizations were elevated to Double A status) until 1945 (the last season of segregation) the majors consistently posted lower batting totals.[6]

MLB and Class AAA Hitting Totals 1912-1945*

	BA	OBP	SLG	OPS
Major Leagues	.272	.336	.377	.713
Class AAA	.278	.340	.383	.723
% Difference	2.2	1.2	1.6	1.4

* The three Double A Leagues were reclassified Triple A in 1946.
Sources: Baseball-Reference; Snelling, *The Pacific Coast League: A Statistical History*, 1995; Wright, *The American Association Year-by-Year Statistics*, 1997; Wright, *The International League Year-by-Year Statistics*, 1998.

However when the White major league averages are compared to those of the Negro Leagues, a different truth emerges. Using statistics from the first season of the International League of Independent Professional Base Ball Clubs in 1906, through the last campaign of the Negro National League in 1948, the batting totals of the significant Black squads are noticeably *lower* than those of the Major Leagues.

NLB and MLB Hitting Totals 1906-1948

	BA	OBP	SLG	OPS
NLB	.266	.328	.360	.688
MLB	.268	.322	.369	.702
% Difference	0.7	1.2	2.5	2.1

Sources: Negro Leagues Researchers and Authors Group; Baseball-Reference; Seamheads.com Negro Leagues Database; *Center for Negro League Baseball Research;* Overmyer, *Black Ball and the Boardwalk: The Bacharach Giants of Atlantic City*, 2014.

Once Negro League play began in 1920, Blackball pitchers induced lower batting totals than their major league contemporaries in nearly every season until the early 1940s. Only the loss of manpower caused by player defections to Latin America, World War II, and integration, tilted the field back towards the White big leaguers.[7]

NLB and MLB Hitting Totals 1920-1948

	BA	OBP	SLG	OPS
NLB	.270	.332	.371	.704
MLB	.275	.340	.388	.728
% Difference	1.8	2.4	4.5	3.4

Sources: Negro Leagues Researchers and Authors Group; Baseball-Reference; Seamheads.com Negro Leagues Database; *Center for Negro League Baseball Research;* Overmyer, *Black Ball and the Boardwalk.*

In addition, Black hurlers annually allowed far fewer walks and hits than their AL or NL counterparts, and struck out many more batters. Although bases on balls were not as carefully documented by Negro Leagues scorekeepers as their AL/NL counterparts, the Blackball totals are certainly in the ballpark, and the similarly slighted strikeout totals are eye-popping enough as is.

NLB and MLB Pitching Totals 1906-1948

	WHIP	K/9
NLB	1.357	4.323
MLB	1.368	3.390
% Difference	0.8	24.2

NLB and MLB Pitching Totals 1920-1948

	WHIP	K/9
NLB	1.389	4.308
MLB	1.429	3.241
% Difference	2.8	28.3

Sources for Tables 2.19, 2.20, 2.21: Baseball-Reference; Seamheads.com Negro Leagues Database; *Center for Negro League Baseball Research;* Overmyer, *Black Ball and the Boardwalk.*

Negro League Clubs Were Markedly Better Than Minor League Teams

While Negro League teams more than held their own while playing major league squads, they absolutely dominated bush leaguers. From the turn of the twentieth century through 1948, Blackball clubs played well over 1400 games with minor league teams and All-Star outfits, beating them nearly 60 percent of the time.

NLB vs. MILB 1900-1948

Leagues	W	L	T	PCT	NLRPG	MLRPB
Low Minors	204	93	6	.683	6.34	4.20
Class A	125	111	8	.529	4.88	4.74
Class AA	168	156	7	.518	4.88	4.87
Class AAA	324	247	19	.565	4.98	4.31
Total	821	607	40	.573	5.22	4.45

Note: The minor leagues have been grouped according to their modern classifications. Prior to 1946, the leagues later considered Class AAA were called Double A; Class AA was A; Class A was B; and the remainder of circuits were either Class C or D.
Sources: Simkus, *Outsider Baseball*, 2014; NLB vs. MILB Database.

When the regular season batting records of the Negro Leagues and those of the three Double (later Triple A) Leagues are compared, the African American clubs posted lower batting averages (indicating a higher level of play) every year but four from the mid-teens until integration.

NLB and Class AAA Hitting Totals 1912–1948

	BA	OBP	SLG	OPS
NLB	.268	.330	.364	.695
AAA	.277	.341	.383	.724

Source: Authors Group; Baseball-Reference; Seamheads.com Negro Leagues Database; *Center for Negro League Baseball Research;* Overmyer, *Black Ball and the Boardwalk;* Snelling, *The Pacific Coast League;* Wright, *The American Association;* Wright, *The International League.*

Negro Leagues WHIP and K/9 pitching numbers also compare favorably to those of the high minors. From 1912 through 1948, Negro League pitchers struck out more batters than their Triple A brethren every single year, and allowed fewer base runners in every season but four. [8]

NLB and Class AAA Pitching Averages 1912-1948

	WHIP	K/9
NLB	1.374	4.328
AAA	1.464	3.662
% Difference	6.3	16.7

Sources: Negro Leagues Researchers and Authors Group; Baseball-Reference; Seamheads.com Negro Leagues Database; *Center for Negro League Baseball Research*; Overmyer, *Black Ball and the Boardwalk*; Snelling, *The Pacific Coast League*; Wright, *The American Association*; Wright, *The International League*.

Negro League Players Flourished After Entering Organized Baseball

During the fifteen years following Jackie Robinson's 1946 debut with the Montreal Royals, at least 333 former Negro Leaguers entered White affiliated baseball. Seventy-six of these players eventually made it to the major leagues, while 126 competed in the three Triple A circuits. Not every player was successful, but on the whole, and despite incredible hardships, the former Negro Leaguers out-performed their White counterparts. During the thirty years after integration, ex-Negro League players outhit their competition in both Triple A and the Major Leagues by a substantial margin.[9]

Negro Leaguers Class AAA Batting Totals 1946-1976

	BA	OBP	SLG	OPS
NLAAA	.286	.357	.433	.790
AAA	.264	.337	.386	.723
% Difference	7.7	5.6	10.9	8.3

Negro Leaguers MLB Batting Totals 1947-1976

	BA	OBP	SLG	OPS
NLMLB	.277	.361	.455	.815
MLB	.255	.324	.380	.704
% Difference	7.9	10.2	16.5	13.6

Sources for Tables: Clark and Lester, *The Negro Leagues Book*; Baseball-Reference.

Nine of the former Negro Leaguers who entered affiliated ball (formerly referred to as "Organized Baseball") were eventually elected to the National Baseball Hall of Fame, including Willie Mays and Hank Aaron, generally acknowledged as two of the five greatest players of all time. In 1952 alone, ex-Negro Leagues players topped the leaderboard in 46 minor league hitting and pitching categories. Beginning in 1955, former Negro Leaguers led the National

League in total bases for nine consecutive seasons. More dubiously, in 12 of the 13 years between 1949 and 1961, the player hit by the most pitches in the American League had gotten his start in the Negro Leagues.[10]

Negro League pitchers also performed well in integrated baseball. Forty-four of these Black hurlers made it as far as Triple A, while 21 of their number reached the majors. However, the majority of major league teams clung to their racist past. By the end of the 1951 season, five full years after Jackie Robinson signed with the Dodgers, only five out of the sixteen big league clubs had Black players on their rosters. Perversely, the organizations that *did* integrate strictly adhered to the unwritten "fifty-fifty" rule, wherein no more than four Black players could be in a team's lineup at any one time. The end result of this woefully slow integration process was that several qualified African Americans were left languishing in the minors until their opportunity to move up had passed them by.[11]

Negro Leaguers Class AAA Pitching Totals 1946-1975

	PCT	ERA	WHIP	K/9
NLAAA	.513	3.82	1.41	5.46
AAA	.500	3.92	1.45	5.29
% Difference	2.6	2.6	3.0	3.1

Negro Leaguers MLB Pitching Totals 1947-1969

	PCT	ERA	WHIP	K/9
NLMLB	.552	3.76	1.35	5.91
MLB	.500	3.91	1.35	4.89
% Difference	9.4	4.0	0	17.3

Sources for Tables: Clark and Lester, *The Negro Leagues Book*; Baseball-Reference.

As the former Negro Leaguers led the charge into White baseball, a new generation of Black players followed closely behind, bypassing the segregated circuits altogether. Sixty-eight members of this first wave got as far as Triple A during the first ten years of integration while 54 graduated to the major leagues by the close of the 1959 season. Although hampered by a rigid quota system, this "first generation" of Black players hit well above league average in both the major and high minor circuits.[12]

First Generation Black Players
Class AAA Batting Totals 1949-1975

	BA	OBP	SLG	OPS
BAAA	.276	.350	.415	.764
AAA	.263	.335	.385	.720
% Difference	4.7	4.3	7.2	5.8

First Generation Black Players MLB Batting Totals 1953-1980

	BA	OBP	SLG	OPS
BMLB	.273	.343	.422	.764
MLB	.255	.322	.380	.702
% Difference	6.6	6.1	10.0	8.1

Note: The term "First Generation," refers to black players who did not participate in the Negro Leagues and entered Organized Baseball during the first ten years of integration.
Sources for Tables: Moffi and Kronstadt, *Crossing the Line: Black Major Leaguers*, 1994; Baseball-Reference.

The new generation of Black pitchers also performed well when given the chance. Despite allowing fewer runs and base runners, while striking out more batters at both levels over a period of 30 years, the Black twirler became an endangered species due to institutional racism in big league front offices. By 1968 fewer than one in ten major league pitchers were Black. When the 1986 season started, only 5.7% of major league African Americans were pitchers.[13]

First Generation Black Players
Class AAA Pitching Totals 1952-1975

	PCT	ERA	WHIP	K/9
BAAA	.556	3.35	1.30	6.17
AAA	.500	3.83	1.43	5.54
% Difference	10.1	14.3	10.2	10.2

First Generation Black Players MLB Pitching Totals 1953-1976

	PCT	ERA	WHIP	K/9
BMLB	.522	3.55	1.31	5.67
MLB	.500	3.79	1.32	5.27
% Difference	4.2	6.8	0.8	7.1

Note: The term "First Generation," refers to black players who did not participate in the Negro Leagues and entered "Organized Baseball" during the first ten years of integration.
Sources for Tables: Moffi and Kronstadt, *Crossing the Line: Black Major Leaguers*, 1994; Baseball-Reference.

Black Players Have Dominated the Post-Segregation Era

In 1955 the initial wave of Black players won 23 Class B, C, or D minor league batting and pitching titles. During the 1959 season, this first generation led the three Triple A circuits in 14 different statistical categories. In 1962 a Black player led the National League in each of the following statistics: games played, at bats, runs, hits, doubles, triples, home runs, runs batted in, stolen bases, total bases, batting average, slugging percentage, and of course in being hit by pitches. In 1967, 40 Black players (5.57% of a total 718 big leaguers) accounted for more than half of the base hits made in the major leagues. Eleven out of the top 12 National League batters in 1969 were Black, along with four out of the top five hitters in the junior circuit. An African American failed to lead led the National League in slugging only twice between 1954 and 1978. In the 39 seasons from 1959 until 1997, a Black player won the National League batting crown 32 times. Since Jackie Robinson first captured the crown in 1947, through 2017 a non-Black player led the National League in stolen bases only *four* times. In the 52 seasons between 1965 and 2016, Black players captured 45 American League stolen base crowns.[14]

In the entire history of the American and National Leagues, only five batters have hit for 5,900 or more total bases, and four of them—Hank Aaron, Willie Mays, Barry Bonds, and Albert Pujols—are African or Latin American. Despite getting a 71-year late start, eight of the top ten all-time home run hitters are Black. Only Aaron, Mays, Pujols, and Alex Rodriguez have over 3,000 hits and 600 home runs. Not one of the four would have been allowed in the majors before 1947. From 1947 through 2013, African American players won 47 Most Valuable Player awards and Latinos 21: more than half of the 134 total.

Non-White players have contributed at least 1/3 of the yearly Wins Above Replacement in the big leagues since the early 1960s and have hovered around the 40 percent mark since 1990. From 1959 through 1985, the league with more Black players on their squad (i.e. the National) won 27 out of 31 All-Star games (with one tie). Between 1947 and 1973, big league Black hitters produced more hits, doubles, triples, and home runs, and stole more bases on average than White batters. During that same timeframe, Black pitchers struck out more hitters and allowed fewer base runners per inning. The legacy of the Negro Leagues is clear: Since integration, the best players in the major leagues have been Black. Evidence would indicate that the best baseball players have *always* been Black.[15]

White, Black, and Latin MLB
Batting and Pitching Averages 1947-1973

Years	Demo.	% AB	BA	SLG	% IP	WHIP	K/9
1947-1960	White	88.0	.261	.393	93.8	1.40	4.29
	Black	7.6	.280	.455	2.6	1.33	5.38
	Latin	4.6	.267	.384	3.6	1.39	4.59
1961-1968	White	64.0	.251	.380	87.8	1.28	5.69
	Black	22.0	.269	.421	5.9	1.27	6.45
	Latin	14.0	.267	.380	6.3	1.23	6.34
1969-1973	White	58.0	.251	.371	87.7	1.32	5.49
	Black	26.0	.270	.422	7.5	1.26	6.50
	Latin	18.0	.265	.366	4.8	1.30	5.35

Source: Yee and Wright, *The Sports Book*, 1975.

The Black Population of the Major Leagues has surpassed that of the Negro Leagues

Despite being a smaller part of the general population, African Americans have long dominated the upper echelons of United States amateur and professional sports. Between 1989 and 2017, for example, Blacks made up only 12.4% of the U.S. population and yet during those 29 years (the same duration as NLB's 1920–1948 peak period) 66.5% of the players in the National Football League and 76.5% of those in the National Basketball Association were African American. Due to expansion, there are now nearly twice as many major leaguers than there were during the segregated era (750 vs. 400). Perhaps not coincidentally, this player increase (350) is equal to the yearly average of Black major leaguers since 1969. In fact, in every season since 1995, the number of Black major leaguers has been the same or larger than the amount of *White* big leaguers during the segregated era.[16]

Black MLB Population 1969-2018

	BP	LP	B/L	BP %	LP %	B/L %
Average	141	213	354	13.5	19.9	33.38

Sources: Armour and Levitt, *Ethnicity Totals By Year, 1947-2014*; Lapchick, "The 2019 Racial and Gender Report Card: Major League Baseball," Tidesport.org, 2019.

Conversely, during the lifetime of the Negro Leagues, the rosters of Blackball clubs ranged anywhere from 14 to 20 players, although team photographs of the period rarely reveal squads larger than 16. Given that there were on average

13 league or league-associated franchises from 1920 until 1948, the average population of big-time Blackball on any given day was about 207 players. Even with a decline in African American participation, the number of Black major league players has been higher than the average population of the Negro Leagues in every season since 1969 and the apex of organized Blackball (around 377 players during the chaotic 1932 season) has been surpassed by Black big leaguers every year since 1995. Because at least 425 African Americans and Latinos currently play big league baseball every year, there are now more Black major leaguers annually than there ever were Negro League players. It is a safe assumption that the twentieth-century Blackball circuits with yearly populations that rarely exceeded 300 players were big league as well.[17]

NLB Population 1920-1948

	Teams	Player Limit	Player Total
Average	13	207	284

Note: Only league and league associated clubs were included. The player limit column reflects the team roster sizes set by the leagues before each season. The player total is the overall number of participants for that year.
Sources: Clark and Lester, *The Negro Leagues Book*; Dixon and Hannigan, *The Negro Baseball Leagues*; Seamheads.com Negro Leagues Database; Baseball-Reference; *Pittsburgh Courier*; *Chicago Defender*.

Major League Baseball Colonized the History and Culture of the Negro Leagues

A more subtle recognition of the Negro Leagues' quality occurred on the playing field. On August 3, 1994, at Kauffman Stadium in Kansas City, the hometown Royals defeated the Oakland Athletics, 9–5, while wearing replica uniforms of the 1924 Kansas City Monarchs. During the following 26 seasons, big league squads wore the throwback uniforms of Negro League teams—with the MLB emblem on their sleeves—nearly one hundred times.[18]

Historian Rob Neyer once postulated that a major league required "teams populated largely by the sport's best players," "playing a set and lengthy schedule." Because Blackball teams usually did not own their own ballparks, their schedules were more fluid than White baseball's. However, Negro League squads played *a lot* of games: Between 1920 and 1927 the Hilldale Club averaged 163 contests a season. Operating as an independent team in 1931, the Homestead Grays played 174 games. As for having the best players, African and Latin Americans have dominated the major leagues since 1947 and they now make up over one-third of MLB's yearly population. Negro Leaguers beat big league teams more than half the time in head-to-head contests, demonstrated better pitching in league play, and performed well above average when they were finally allowed in the majors. In other words, Negro Leagues = Major Leagues.[19]

Endnotes

1.   Dick Clark and Larry Lester, *The Negro Leagues Book* (Cleveland, OH: The Society For American Baseball Research, 1994), 159; *Omaha World Herald* (NE), July 30, 1962.

2.   *Philadelphia Press* (PA), September 9, 1866; Anthony DiFiore, "Advancing African American Baseball: The Philadelphia Pythians and Interracial Competition in 1869," in *Black Ball*, Volume 1, Number 1 (2008): 60-61, 64; Scott Simkus, *Outsider Baseball* (Chicago, IL: Chicago Review Press, 2014), 266.

3.   *Chicago Tribune* (IL), October 1, 1900; *Los Angeles Times* (CA), October 8, 1948. Although designated as a minor league, the 1900 American League contained a higher percentage of major-league caliber players than either the 1882 American Association or 1884 Union Association had in their inaugural major-league campaigns. Marshall D. Wright, *Nineteenth Century Baseball: Year-by-Year Statistics for the Major League Teams, 1871 through 1900*, (Jefferson, NC and London: McFarland & Company, Inc., Publishers, 1996), 318. After integration Negro League baseball declined precipitously in quality of play, leading to the demise of the NNL in 1948. By 1951 the surviving Negro American League was considered a Class C equivalent circuit. Scott Simkus, "Superstar Integration Model," *Outsider Baseball Bulletin*, Volume 2, Issue 27 (Number 57): 1-2, Outsiderbaseball.com, accessed August 25, 2015, http://www.i70baseball.com/wp-content/uploads/Outsider-Baseball-Bulletin-070611.pdf; *San Francisco Call* (California) March 20, 1913; John Holway, *Black Giants* (Springfield, VA: Lord Fairfax Press, 2010), 28; *New York Age* (NY), October 23, 1920; *Chicago Defender* (IL), July 27, 1918.

4.   Thomas Barthel, *Baseball Barnstorming and Exhibition Games* 1901-1962 (Jefferson, North Carolina: McFarland & Company, Inc. Publishers, 2007), 94, 102; Jules Tygiel, "Black Ball," in *Total Baseball*, John Thorn and Pete Palmer with David Reuther, editors (New York, NY: Warner Books, 1989), 555; Donn Rogosin, *Invisible Men: Life in Baseball's Negro Leagues* (New York, NY: Atheneum, 1983), 184; *New York Times* (NY), July 28, 1922.

5.   Robert Peterson, *Only the Ball Was White* (New York, NY; Oxford: Oxford University Press, 1992), 253; Simkus, *Outsider Baseball*, 265-266.

6.   John Thorn and Pete Palmer, *The Hidden Game Of Baseball: A Revolutionary Approach to Baseball and its Statistics* (Garden City, NY: Doubleday & Company, Inc., 1985), 177-178.

7.   Rob Ruck, *Raceball: How the Major Leagues Colonized the Black and Latin Game*, (Boston, MA: Beacon Press, 2011), 58, 69, 71, 93-96; Neil Lanctot, *Negro League Baseball: The Rise and Ruin of a Black Institution* (Philadelphia, PA: University of Pennsylvania Press, 2004), 144.

8.   TerryB, comment on jalbright, "Two Sources of Negro League Stats Online," Baseball Fever.com, accessed August 12, 2015; Peterson, *Only the Ball Was White*, 81; McNeil, *Baseball's Other All-Stars*, 189, 195-196; William F. McNeil, *The California Winter League: America's First Integrated Professional Baseball League* (Jefferson, NC: McFarland & Company, Inc. Publishers, 2002), 240, 306.

9.   Dick Clark and Larry Lester, editors, *The Negro Leagues Book*, (Cleveland, OH: The Society For American Baseball Research, 1994), 255-256, 262-336; Larry Moffi and Jonathan Kronstadt, *Crossing the Line: Black Major Leaguers, 1947-1959* (Jefferson, NC: McFarland & Company, Inc. Publishers, 1994), 105.

10.   Thorn and Palmer with Reuther, *Total Baseball*, "Total Baseball Ranking," 2041; ESPN.com, "ESPN's Hall of 100," accessed December 15, 2016, http://www.espn.com/mlb/feature/video/_/id/8652210/espn-hall-100-ranking-all-greatest-mlb-players; Baseball-Reference.com, "Baseball Hall of Fame Inductees," accessed December 15, 2016, http://www.baseball-reference.com/awards/hof.shtml; Phil Dixon with Patrick J. Hannigan, "Major and Minor League Titles 1946-1955," in *The Negro Baseball Leagues: A Photographic History* (Mattituck, NY: Amereon House, 1992); Clark and Lester, *The Negro Leagues Book*, 262-336; Baseball-Reference.com, "Yearly League Leaders & Records for Total Bases," accessed December 22, 2016, http://www.baseball-reference.com/leaders/TB_leagues.shtml; Baseball-Reference.com, "Yearly League Leaders & Records for Hit By Pitch," accessed December 22, 2016, http://www.baseball-reference.com/leaders/HBP_leagues.shtml; Zoss and Bowman, *Diamonds in the Rough*, 171; John Holway, *Black Diamonds: Life in the Negro Leagues from the Men Who Lived It* (New York, NY: Stadium Books, 1991), 72-73.

11.   Clark and Lester, *The Negro Leagues Book*, 313-336; Lee Lowenfish, "The Rise of Baseball's Quota System in the 1950s," *NINE: A Journal Of Baseball History And Culture*, Volume 16, Number 2 (Spring 2008): 53.

12.   Clark and Lester, *The Negro Leagues Book*, 255-256; 262-236; Moffi and Kronstadt, *Crossing the Line: Black Major Leaguers*, 3, 10; Tygiel, "Black Ball," in *Total Baseball*, 560-561; Joel Zoss and John Bowman, *Diamonds in the Rough: The Untold Story of Baseball* (Lincoln, NE and London: University of Nebraska Press, 2004), 187; Michael J. Haupert, "Pay, Performance, And Race During The Integration Era," *Black Ball*, Volume 2, Number 1 (Spring 2009): 50; Lee Lowenfish, "The Rise of Baseball's Quota System in the 1950s," *NINE: A Journal Of Baseball History And Culture*, Volume 16, Number 2 (Spring 2008): 53.

13.   Tygiel, "Black Ball," in *Total Baseball*, 561; Zoss and Bowman, *Diamonds in the Rough*, 188.

14.   Dixon with Hannigan, "Major and Minor League Titles 1946-1955," in *The Negro Baseball Leagues: A Photographic History*; Baseball-Reference.com, "1959 American Association Batting Leaders," accessed December 22, 2016, http://www.baseball-reference.com/register/leader.cgi?type=bat&id=ecc4882f; Baseball-Reference.com, "1959 International League Batting Leaders," accessed December 22, 2016, http://www.baseball-reference.com/register/leader.cgi?type=bat&id=2dece84d; Baseball-Reference.com, 1959 Pacific Coast League Batting Leaders," accessed December 22, 2016, http://www.baseball-reference.com/register/leader.cgi?type=bat&id=8363447e; Neft, Cohen, and Neft, *The Sports Encyclopedia: Baseball 2000*, 722-729; John Holway, *Voices from the Great Black Baseball Leagues* (Revised edition, New York, New York: Da Capo Press, 1992), 1; Baseball-Reference.com, "Yearly League Leaders & Records for Slugging %," accessed December 22, 2016, http://www.baseball-reference.com/leaders/slugging_perc_leagues.shtml: Baseball-Reference.com, "Yearly League Leaders & Records for Batting Average," accessed December 22, 2016, http://www.baseball-reference.com/leaders/batting_avg_leagues.shtml; Baseball-Reference.com, "Yearly League Leaders & Records for Stolen Bases," accessed May 15, 2021, http://www.baseball-reference.com/leaders/SB_leagues.shtml.

15.   Baseball-Reference.com, "Career Leaders & Records for Total Bases," accessed May 15, 2021, http://www.baseball-reference.com/leaders/TB_career.shtml; Baseball-Reference.com, "Career Leaders & Records for Home Runs," accessed May 15, 2021, http://www.baseball-reference.com/leaders/HR_career.shtml; Scott Boeck, "Albert Pujols Earns 3,000 Hit, Joining A-Rod, Hank Aaron, Willie Mays in Exclusive Club," USA Today.com, accessed May 24, 2018, https://www.usatoday.com/story/sports/mlb/2018/05/04/angels-albert-pujols-3000-hits-600-home-runs/557984002/; Mark L. Armour and Daniel R. Levitt, *In Pursuit Of Pennants: Baseball Operations from Deadball to Moneyball* (Lincoln, NE and London: University of Nebraska Press, 2015), 136-137; Mark Armour, "The Effects of Integration, 1947-1986," *The Baseball Research Journal,* Volume 36 (Cleveland, Ohio: The Society for American Baseball Research, Inc., 2007): 57; Frederick Ivor-Campbell, "The All-Star Game," in *Total Baseball*, 250-257; Min S. Yee, editor and Donald K. Wright, designer, *The Sports Book: An Unabashed Assemblage of Heroes, Strategies, Records, and Events* (New York, NY: Holt, Rinehart, and Winston, 1975), 39; Holway, *Voices from the Great Black Baseball Leagues*, 1.

16.   John Holway, e-mail message with author, September 9, 2015; Jim Overmyer, e-mail message with author, September 9, 2015; TerryB, September 28, 2013, comment on Jalbright, "Two Sources of Negro League Stats Online," Baseball Fever.com, September 4, 2013, accessed August 12, 2015, http://www.baseball-fever.com/showthread.php?39148-Negro-Leagues-vs-Major-Leagues&s=6086b28ebc6e705636848c4fc10aa990; Wikipedia.com, "Historical Racial and Ethnic Demographics of the United States," accessed December 8, 2016, https://en.wikipedia.org/wiki/Historical_racial_and_ethnic_demographics_of_the_United_States; Richard Lapchick with Craig Malveaux, Erin Davison and Caryn Grant, "The 2016 Racial and Gender Report Card: National Football League," Tidesport.org. September 28, 2016, accessed December 8, 2016, http://www.tidesport.org/nfl-rgrc.html; Richard Lapchick with Theren Bullock Jr, "The 2016 Racial and Gender Report Card: National Basketball Association," Tidesport.org. July 14, 2016, accessed December 8, 2016, http://www.tidesport.org/racial-and-gender-report-cards.html; Armour and Levitt, *Ethnicity Totals by Year, 1947-2014*; Richard Lapchick, "The 2019 Racial and Gender Report Card: Major League Baseball," Tidesport.org, 2017, accessed August 29, 2019, http://www.tidesport.org/mlb-rgrc.html.

17.   Lanctot, *Negro League Baseball*, 72, 156, 429; Peterson, *Only the Ball Was White*, 91; Clark and Lester, *The Negro Leagues Book*, 78, 98, 102, 116, 118, 126, 136, 138; Michael E. Lomax, *Black Baseball Entrepreneurs 1902-1931: The Negro National and Eastern Colored Leagues* (Syracuse, NY: Syracuse University Press, 2014), 223, 224, 226, 228, 229, 234, 235, 237, 238; Armour and Levitt, "Baseball Demographics, 1947-2012."

18.   *Kansas City Star* (MO), August 4, 1994, September 24, 2020; Bleacher Nation.com: "Wild Kyle Schwarber Slide Caps Six-Run 9th Inning for the Cubs," http://www.bleachernation.com/wp-content/uploads/2017/06/kyle-schwarber-slide-cubs-lelands-throwback-Photo-by-Justin-BerlGetty-Images.jpg.

19.   Rob Neyer, "Was the Federal League Really a Major League?" The National Pastime Museum.com, November 28, 2012, accessed August 26, 2015, http://www.thenationalpastimemuseum.com/article/was-federal-league-really-major-league; Lanctot, *Negro League Baseball*, 185, 188; Neil Lanctot, *Fair Dealing and Clean Playing: The Hilldale Club and the Development of Black Professional Baseball, 1910-1932*, (Syracuse, NY: Syracuse University Press, 2007), 232; Phil Dixon, *American Baseball Chronicles: Great Teams: The 1931 Homestead Grays Volume One*. (Bloomington, IN: Xlibris Corporation, 2009), 33, 326-338.

1936 Negro League All Stars

A Love Story

by Adam Jones

You know, it's true what they say. You never forget the first time you fell in love.

For me, it was on a warm summer evening at old Jack Murphy Stadium in 1995.

I was just nine years old, but I fell hard and I fell fast.

Sure, everybody played tee-ball growing up and that was fun for me, but that night, watching the Braves-Padres game with Lemuel Campbell, a close family friend, I truly fell in love with the game of baseball.

Lemuel introduced me to the game and while he was talking with me, he taught me a lot about not just what was going on in front of me, but also what happened *behind* me. He taught me why certain guys that were playing that night, guys like Fred McGriff, David Justice, Tony Gwynn... why those guys had the opportunities that they had...*because of other guys.*

We heard about Jackie Robinson in school, but Lemuel dug deeper into *why* Jackie got the opportunity, *how* he got that opportunity and *where* it came from. He taught me about the guys that made it possible for Jackie to break the color barrier in MLB. The guys that made it all possible for a lot of different guys.

I became interested in the Negro Leagues at a very young age because Lemuel was so instrumental in helping me learn about them and to understand that I was getting the opportunity to play this game because of the guys who paved the way for me. And, as I got older, I continued to learn more. It was just part of my education in the game. It would've been ignorant if I didn't study the reason why I was getting this opportunity. I recognized it was not just because of my talent, but also because of the sacrifices made by many others before me.

When I was a young, bright-eyed, fresh 22-year-old, I was with the Seattle Mariners. I remember going to play the Royals. Some of the older guys said they were going to take a trip to see the Negro Leagues Baseball Museum. This was my first time in Kansas City and I was excited because I had no idea the museum was there. I made sure that I got up early the next morning, caught that bus and went to the museum.

And... wow. When I arrived and got to meet Bob Kendrick, the museum's president, and heard him tell stories about the history of the game...I just sat there and my jaw just dropped. There were just so many things that I did not know, so many things I was intrigued by. And if you know Bob, you know how charismatic he is and how inspirational his stories are... I just sat there like I was that nine-year-old kid again, like, please tell me more. Just. Keep. Talking.

And as the years went by, every time I went to Kansas City, I made it a mission of mine to not just go back to the museum, but to also bring younger players with me. White, Black, Latino... It didn't matter to me. It was just important for me to take other players there so they could see other people's struggle and other people's grind, but at the same time, other people's passion and other people's love for the game. Other people's vigor and perseverance. Because those Negro League guys? They were tough.

People need to know about the perseverance of these men. They were willing to play in front of anyone who was willing to show up. But they couldn't go eat at local restaurants. They couldn't stay at local hotels.

Perseverance. If you did something like that now, in the current climate of the world, there'd be so much uproar. But back then, they just said, "Okay, we'll do what we gotta do. We came here to play ball, that's what we want to do and we will go and stay where we need to stay, be together, go eat a good meal and mind our own business."

But for me, thinking about all the things that they went through, it's a tough pill to swallow knowing that some people just see you as an entertainer and nothing more. It goes back to stories I've heard about Bob Gibson. We all know he's one of the best African American pitchers of all time. He could go and throw a shutout in St. Louis, yet he couldn't go out and enjoy a nice steak after the game. It's like, "You'll cheer me on when I'm entertaining you, but all I'm trying to do is have myself a nice dinner and I can't have that." That perseverance right there—and that understanding of "Okay, we know you don't want to see us as equals, but at the same time, we're not going to make an uproar about it"—is one of the toughest things I've learned about because I can only think of myself in those situations and I know that especially in today's climate, that stuff is not going to fly. People would film it and it would be all over social media. But back then, you didn't hear anything about it.

They just wanted to be a part of something bigger. And they were. Oh, how they were.

Over the years, I've made it my mission to educate not just myself but also other people. Because what's education? It's good for you to know something, but if you know something that's good and it's right and it's pure, why keep it to yourself? Why not share it? My relationship with Bob and the museum was a match made in heaven. I love Black history. I'm an African American. I love my history. I love learning more and more and more. And thankfully, during my time in MLB, a lot of other players were extremely receptive to visiting the museum with me and open to learning more as well.

You get in the locker room and it's literally a melting pot. You've got White, Black, Latin, Asian... and you should want to know about your teammates' backgrounds.

Right now, I'm playing in Japan and I want to know the history there. I ask my interpreter about it all the time. I got to play with guys like Ichiro, Kenji Johjima, Koji Uehara. It's very important that I learn about Japan's culture and their baseball history because I'd be a fool not to. That's the educational part that I think many are lacking... They don't have that desire to know more. To delve deeper like Lemuel and Bob did. And I think to myself, I have that desire and I want to share it. *Especially* with baseball. It's my passion, it's my love and I simply want to know more.

I think it's extremely important that *everyone* understands the history of the game and all the integral parts of it. It's just like with regular history. Black history is a very important part of history that is often forgotten and not taught as much as it should be. In baseball, I think many just skim over the major players of the Negro Leagues and don't take the time to delve into the actual heroes that formed the league and changed the lives for many, many people. Heroes like Buck O'Neil, who wanted all of us to share and understand that history. Buck was instrumental in preserving Negro Leagues history and establishing the museum's home in Kansas City. His lifetime of service to the game should be immortalized in Cooperstown, where he surely belongs among the game's legends.

There's so much history in the Negro Leagues and that's what has always interested me, way back to that day at the ballpark with Lemuel in San Diego. Society just dumbs it down to Jackie Robinson and leaves it at that. But there are the players who didn't have the chance to play in the American or National Leagues during their careers like Rube Foster, Cool Papa Bell, Buck Leonard, Leon Day and many, many more. And there are people who don't necessarily know about the Negro Leagues careers of players like Larry Doby, Satchel Paige, and Minnie Miñoso.

That's why I think the work that Bob and the museum have been doing all these years is amazing and that's why I think it's fantastic that Baseball Reference has now listed the Negro Leagues as major leagues. It's so important to have all of that information accessible to everybody. The more information that can be made available and the more visible that we can make it the better. It's the history of the *whole* game, not just part of it.

People are finally going to get to see both sides of the story and get to understand that the Negro Leagues were very, very important, the players were very important and, most importantly, they brought the community together with a common love. And they're important not just for Blacks, but for all people of color. There were a lot of early Latin American players and their stories also need to be told. All of these men—and some women, too, let's not forget about them—were very instrumental in the building of Major League Baseball and, like it or not, their stories need to be told.

I invite you to dive in and learn more with me, to share my passion and my love.

The Black Boys of Summer: A Statistical Observation

by Larry Lester

At times during our careers researching the Negro Leagues, the late Dick Clark, Wayne Stivers, and I felt like Sisyphus, the mortal of Greek mythology who was subjected to the dreadful punishment of hopeless labor, eternally rolling a rock to the top of a mountain, only to have the weight of the stone drag it back to ground zero. But with dedicated, persistent, and passionate efforts, the box score discovery project, though on-going, is nearly complete. For the 1920s, our teams of researchers often found more than 95% of the scheduled games. Finding the data for the games that took place during the aftermath of the Great Depression in the 1930s was more challenging, as leagues and teams often stuttered or folded in mid-season, while all citizens, especially African Americans, struggled in a depressed economy. A resurgence of sports coverage followed in the 1940s, as World War II and the fight against Naziism overseas brought an awakening of mindsets, with Americans and the liberal media challenging the justification for separate but profoundly unequal Black and White leagues.

After the big leagues welcomed Jackie Robinson, Larry Doby, Willard Brown, Hank Thompson, and Dan Bankhead, coverage by both the Black and White presses of Negro League games dwindled. For example, in October 1947, we find the lone sportswriter of a minority newspaper at a college football game (the second most popular sport in the country at the time) instead of attending the Negro World Series. Perhaps Black writers felt compelled to report on the trickling of ebony stars onto White major league teams. Likewise, Black fans quietly migrated to support their local White big-league team, to judge the success of their favorite Black player.

Coincidentally, judging the success of White players has never been without merit. The accuracy of the statistical record of the White major leagues is being challenged today by SABR statisticians. Who won the American League batting title in 1910, Nap Lajoie or Ty Cobb? Who holds the record for the most consecutive years leading the league in batting averages, Rogers Hornsby or Ty Cobb? In 1961, who really led the American League in RBIs, Roger Maris or Jim Gentile? Miscalculations, data omissions, mistakes made in box scores reported via telegram or telephone led to crowning the wrong seasonal or career leader more than once. Before technology, *The Sporting News* (the "Bible of Baseball") undertook data reconciliation while praying that the typesetters would put the reconciled digits into the printing presses correctly.

Behind the scenes, our team was faced with the same challenges with errors from data transmission. With courage and curiosity, the gang tackled the task of discovering box scores, analyzing, auditing, and repairing the printouts for database software entry. Below are the anomalies in examining the weight of the stone presented to the Sisyphus team of Clark, Stivers, and myself.

Box Score Anomalies
Irregularities, inconsistencies, and insanities

Box score information:

- Microfilmed Box scores are difficult to read because of a poor scan or print quality.
- Sometimes game dates are difficult to verify because the newspaper reported weekly.
- Two newspapers covering the same game report different results.
- Game text will mention players not listed in the box score.
- Game text will differ from the data provided in the box score.
- All nine positions are not listed; two players may be listed playing the same position.
- Misspelled names are common, especially Latin American names.
- Some names are spelled phonetically.
- Sometimes only a nickname is listed.
- As was the custom, no first names are listed in the lineup.
- Less than nine players are listed.

Batting:

- Total team hits do not equal total of individual hits.
- Total team hits do not equal hits given up by the opposing pitcher(s).
- Total team runs do not equal total of individual runs.
- Total team runs do not equal runs given up by the opposing pitcher(s).
- Sometimes At Bats are not listed.
- Sometimes individual Runs Scored are not listed.
- Sometimes individual RBIs are not credited.
- Sacrifice hits and sacrifice flies are not distinctively identified.
- Sometimes Sacrifices (hits and/or flies) are counted as At Bats.
- Sometimes no Hit Batsmen are listed [making it difficult to calculate walks].
- Sometimes extra base hits are not listed.
- Sometimes fielding errors are not listed.
- Sometimes stolen bases are not listed.
- Caught stealing is seldom listed in a box score or game text.
- Strikeouts of individual batters are not listed.

- Pinch hitters and pinch runners are sometimes missing.
- Breakdown of defensive innings for multi-positional players may not be available.
- Batting orders are not always sequential, as player substitutions could be listed at the bottom of the order. [This makes it difficult to calculate missing At Bats].

Pitching:

- Total team hits do not match total hits given up by pitcher(s).
- Total team runs do no match total runs given up by pitcher(s).
- Number of innings pitched not listed.
- Breakdown of innings pitched may not be listed.
- Breakdown of runs allowed may not be listed.
- Breakdown of earned runs may not be listed.
- Breakdown of hits allowed may not be listed.
- Breakdown of strikeouts may not be listed.
- Breakdown of walks may not be listed.
- Only the winning pitcher is listed.
- Starting pitchers may not be readily identified.
- Some box scores are void of pitching statistics; therefore one must rely on the game review.

PART II
The Negro Leagues –
Where baseball is as black as the Blues!

The bittersweet decision from Major League Baseball (MLB) to recognize the Negro Leagues as major leagues comes 100 years after the birth of Rube Foster's Negro National League in 1920, the first Black league to survive a full season. The genesis for the decision began with the Negro Leagues Researchers and Authors Group (NLRAG) in 2000. This MLB grant-funded group of scholars and historians generated an exhaustive database of statistics, starting with post-Civil War games from various colored leagues—leagues that existed because of the apartheid attitudes of White league power brokers. These leagues of color were patterned on a major-league blueprint of rules and regulations, with their own unique style of up-tempo play.

Overall, the NLRAG team found more than 14,000 full box scores, These have been entered into a Microsoft Access database for analysis, producing more than 200 customized reports that show the all-time pitching and batting leaders for 1) games, 2) seasons, or a 3) career. Tried and tested mathematical formulas have been developed to calculate the missing At Bats, Runs Batted In, Walks and Putouts, etc., for each performer. In a few cases, strikeouts and walks will be under-reported, due to the absence of information from the box score and printed storyline. Finally, data integrity checks are done to guarantee team batting and team pitching stats are balanced.

Some sample custom reports:
- What players from the Black leagues played all nine positions?
- How many players had six or more hits in a game?
- Which players hit for the cycle?
- What pitcher had the most games with double-digits strikeouts?
- Which pitchers recorded more complete games than wins?
- What third baseman or shortstop has the most career home runs, or doubles?
- What left-handed batter hit the most triples on the road?
- How well did Willie "the Devil" Wells hit on Sundays?

For each box score, it takes a researcher between 30 and 90 minutes to calculate missing RBIs, Runs Scored, At Bats, Innings Pitched, Earned Runs and identify first names. This labor of love is now in extra innings. As speculated, our Sisyphean efforts reveal that Negro League players were statistically as talented, or inept, as their White major-league counterparts.

Through a comparison of league batting and pitching records from the American League, National League, Eastern-based Negro Leagues, and Midwestern-based Negro Leagues, we found the aggregated totals (courtesy of Baseball-Reference in 2016) from 1920 to 1948, to be highly similar. See the summary table below.

League Totals, 1920 - 1948

	AVG	SLG	ERA
Major Eastern Negro Leagues	.268	.383	4.17
Major Midwestern Negro Leagues	.272	.383	4.16
Major National League	.274	.383	3.87
Major American League	.276	.392	4.16

Also note that during this period, Negro League teams played mostly on big league fields like Shibe Park, Comiskey Park, Yankee Stadium, the Polo Grounds, Municipal Stadium, Ruppert Stadium, and Griffith Stadium, among others, and not corn fields or cow pastures, as some cynics have reported. Teams often used Black and White minor league and ex-major league umpires. The players wore Wilson uniforms, used the Wilson W-150CC baseballs, gloves crafted by A.G. Spalding, and ordered their regulation lumber from the Louisville Slugger Factory—the same suppliers for the American and National Leagues. The distance between home plate and the pitching mound for each league was the same, and as well for the distances between the four stations. Furthermore, Black and White teams played under the same rules of engagement, mandated by the ever-evolving Knickerbocker Rules of 1845, up until 1949, when the official rules were re-codified into 10 sections.

Aside from the unmanicured playing fields, overuse of the Wilson baseballs and, in some cases, poorly lighted parks where Black teams competed, the infrastructure was identical. Consequently, it is a level playing field for comparative statistical analysis, and hence from 1920 through 1948, we found the Negro Leagues were the equivalent of the White major leagues in all facets of competition.

The newly recognized leagues are:
Negro National League (I), 1920 – 1931
Eastern Colored League, 1923 – 1928
American Negro League, 1929
East-West League, 1932
Negro Southern League, 1932
Negro National League (II), 1933 – 1948
Negro American League, 1937 – 1948

Part III

"Everything that divides men, everything that specified, separates, or pens them, is a sin against humanity." — José Martí, Cuban journalist and revolutionary philosopher.

On December 16, 2020, Major League Baseball (MLB) soared to new heights with the announcement that Negro League baseball stats from 1920 to 1948 would be included in the official national record and "elevated" to "major league" status. This American bald eagle of an institution is no longer flying with one wing.

So where do fans go from here? With the acknowledgement and acceptance of seven more major entities, what impact will blackball records have on the new and inclusive landscape of statistical excellence?

The final tallies will be available soon. It is doubtful that the career leader boards will change as the Negro Leaguers played fewer games than their White major league counterparts over the course of their careers. However, the leagues of colored players will produce some record shades of grays for games and seasons because of the newly endowed status.

Some noteworthy occurrences:

- Rickwood Field, built in 1910 and home of the Birmingham Black Barons from 1920 to 1948, is now the oldest major league ballpark in the country. Fenway Park in Boston is still the oldest stadium to field a White major league team.
- Owners Olivia Taylor of the Indianapolis ABCs, Henryene Green of the Baltimore Elite Giants, and Dr. Hilda Bolden Shorter of the Philadelphia Stars now join the Newark Eagles' Effa Manley, Marge Schott, Joan Payson, Joan Kroc, Jean Yawkey and other ladies as female owners of major league teams.
- No longer will New York Yankees pitcher Don Larsen be credited with the only World Series no-hitter (a perfect game in 1956 against the Brooklyn Dodgers). Thirty years earlier, in 1926, Claude "Red" Grier for the Bacharach (NJ) Giants hurled a no-no against the Chicago American Giants, and in the process became the first major league pitcher to throw a World Series no-hitter.
- And speaking of no-hitters, in 1927 Joe Strong of the Baltimore Black Sox lived up to his last name and pitched the longest no-hitter in major league history with an 11 inning, 2-1 victory over the Hilldale Club. Other no-hitters by Negro League aces came from Satchel Paige, Smokey Joe Williams, Andy Cooper, Willie Foster, and Hilton Smith, et al.
- Depending on the definition of independent league play by MLB, the new record books could show that Herbert "Rap" Dixon of the Baltimore Black Sox chain-smoked 14 consecutive hits in 1929. That is two more than the old major league record shared by three players: Johnny Kling of the 1902 Chicago Cubs, Pinky Higgins of the 1938 Boston Red Sox, and Walt Dropo of the 1952 Detroit Tigers.
- In 1929, the American Negro League batting champion was Chino Smith of the New York Lincoln Giants, hitting .451 in 66 games.
- In 1939, the Negro Leagues played two All-Star games, one in New York and another in Chicago. This came 20 years before the White major leagues would play two all-star games in the same season. MLB played its first All-Stars game at Pittsburgh's Forbes Field and the second game at Los Angeles's Memorial Coliseum.
- In 1941, catcher Frank Duncan, Sr. and pitcher Frank Duncan, Jr. of the Kansas City Monarchs become the first father and son—and the first father-and-son battery—to play for the same team in the same season. This is 50 years before the Ken Griffeys made ancestral history with the Seattle Mariners.
- In 1943, Al Gipson, pitching for the Birmingham Black Barons, struck out 20 Philadelphia Stars in nine innings. In the process, he joins aces Max Scherzer of the Washington Nationals, Kerry Wood (Chicago Cubs) and Roger Clemens (Boston Red Sox, twice) in the record books.

- At some point in our conversations, we will agree that Leon Day of the Newark Eagles pitched an Opening Day no-hitter in 1946, just like Bob Feller of the Cleveland Indians did in 1940.
- For the *Jeopardy* buffs: In 1947, he became the only player to hit a home run in both the Negro Leagues (with the Kansas City Monarchs) and in the White big leagues (with the St. Louis Browns) in the same season. Who is Willard "Home Run" Brown? With the inclusion of Negro League stats, Brown adds 13 seasons and roughly five dozen home runs and 450 RBIs, along with almost 100 stolen bases, to his major league totals.
- A look at a few notable players reveals that Monte Irvin will add 10 seasons, an estimated 60 home runs, and 340 RBIs while raising his lifetime batting average to over .300. Larry Doby will add five seasons, 20 more home runs, and 130 RBIs, while raising his batting average five points. Roy Campanella spent nine seasons in the darker leagues. His batting average goes up eight points plus he adds 30 or more home runs and 240 or more RBIs to his major league totals.
- Satchel Paige greatly benefits with the inclusion of 18 seasons, adding roughly 115 wins, with more than 1500 strikeouts.
- According to the NL's official stat keeper, Howe News Bureau, Artie Wilson of the Birmingham Black Barons of the Negro American League batted .402 in 1948, making the slap hitter the last major leaguer to hit over .400.
- For comparative purposes of gauging the worthiness of Negro Leagues players to enter the record books, we can show that Satchel Paige's strikeouts per nine innings rate is comparable to Nolan Ryan's career 9.5 K/9. A similar argument can be made that Josh Gibson's home run per At Bat ratio lands between Barry Bonds's 1-per-13 and Hank Aaron's 1:16 ratio.

Folklore and embellished truths have long been a staple of the Negro Leagues narrative. Those storylines will always be entertaining, but now our dialogues can be quantified and qualified to support the authentic greatest of these athletes. As baseball re-invents itself, every fan should welcome this statistical restitution towards social reparation. Play Ball!

Satchel Paige with Josh Gibson.

Gibson Family Reflections on the Publication of Baseball Reference's Negro Leagues Statistics

by Sean Gibson

The last 12 months have been a whirlwind for the descendants of those who played in the Negro Leagues and for the Gibson family in particular.

In the summer of 2020, a movement within the Baseball Writers Association of America (BBWAA) led to the removal of the name of Commissioner Kenesaw Mountain Landis from the American and National League MVP trophies. A growing number of past MVP winners and others in the game supported this initiative due to Landis's central role in barring Black baseball players from MLB-affiliated baseball. Among those whose names have been suggested to replace Landis on the trophy were Branch Rickey, Frank Robinson, and Josh Gibson.

The Gibson family was honored by the suggestion that the trophy be named for Josh. Renaming the MVP Award in memory of Josh Gibson (who likely would have won a couple of MVP awards himself, had he been in the major leagues) would do more than just honor a great baseball player. It would remind people of some of the many victims of Landis's racism—the players who were denied their lifelong dreams of playing ball at the highest level. For all those who came before Jackie Robinson, the "Josh Gibson MVP Award" would be an act of redemption. And poetic justice.[1]

Then, last December, MLB announced it would add the Negro Leagues to its official records of "major leagues." According to Commissioner Rob Manfred, "We are now grateful to count the players of the Negro Leagues where they belong: as major leaguers within the official historical record." Our family was struck by one phrase in Commissioner Manfred's press release—"the long overdue recognition" that this announcement will lead to. Recognition is an interesting word. It means *appreciate, respect, acknowledge.* And these are good words. However, there are stronger words that resonate with us and remain our beacon for honoring the legacy of the Negro Leagues. Words like *validation, redemption, justice.* In a word, Negro League ballplayers already knew they were major leaguers. It is just that the rest of the world did not.

If you would ask me again on how I felt about MLB's announcement, I would say, it's a journey. The Negro Leagues were about a commitment to excellence within the Black community when it had no choice but to engage in segregated business, sports, and community building.

Fast forward to the work of Sports Reference and its Baseball Reference platform that will publish a comprehensive statistical picture of the Negro Leagues, their teams, and the players who competed. We are immensely grateful to Sean Forman and his colleagues who labored diligently in conjunction with Seamheads and the Society of American Baseball Research (SABR) to build this platform. For those with little or no knowledge of the Negro Leagues and the era in which they played, the story must be told. We know there is more research to be done as we build on the significant work now in place. We appreciate Sports Reference for being a part of this process.

It is important to recognize the tireless of efforts of the families of Negro Leaguers who have kept the players front and center for many years. Some, like my family, established non-profits to honor their family's Negro League player, but also to do good for the community, often with a focus on disadvantaged youth through the prism of sports and education. We are grateful to all who have supported our efforts and have made a difference in the lives of others. I know Josh and his counterparts are smiling down on us from heaven when they see our work, much of which has taken place out of the spotlight and media glare.

What about Josh, since it is his story that is one of the many that are lifted up by Sports Reference's work?

Gibson was born in Buena Vista, Georgia, on December 21, 1911. The Gibson family moved north when Josh's father found work in Pittsburgh's steel mills. Josh grew up playing ball and gained the attention of local businessman and sports enthusiast Gus Greenlee, who signed Josh to his semipro team the Crawfords, a team that would emerge in the 1930s as one of the powerhouse squads in the Negro Leagues.

The story of Gibson's 1930 debut for the Homestead Grays is one for the ages. Judy Johnson, manager of the Grays and eventual Hall of Famer himself, needed a catcher after his was injured in a game at Forbes Field against the storied Kansas City Monarchs. Johnson saw Gibson in the stands (he knew of his local sandlot play) and invited him to catch. According to Johnson, "Here we are, Forbes Field is packed. Josh Gibson was sitting in the stands, him and a bunch of boys who played sandlot baseball. I asked if he would catch. 'Yes sir, Mr. Johnson!' I had to hold up the game, let him go in the clubhouse and put on a suit."

Gibson's career would quickly take off. Over a seventeen-year career, his play for the Crawfords and Grays, along with stints in the Caribbean, would be punctuated by mammoth home runs, a high batting average (BA), and an out-of-this-world On-Base plus Slugging (OPS) percentage. According to Seamheads, the recognized statistical source for the Negro Leagues, his career figures were a .365 BA, .690 Slugging, and 1.139 OPS.

Gibson played on two of the best Negro League teams ever—the 1931 Homestead Grays and the 1935 Pittsburgh Crawfords—and then went on to anchor a Grays team that were League champions every year but one from 1937 to 1945, playing in four Negro League World Series, winning two.

In a February 12, 1938, article in the *Pittsburgh Courier*—one of the premier African American newspapers of the day—Pittsburgh Pirates owner William E. Benswanger was quoted as saying, "If the question of admitting colored ballplayers into organized baseball becomes an issue, I would be heartily in favor of it. I think that colored people should have an opportunity in baseball just as they have an opportunity in music or anything else." In response to a request for his assessment of Josh Gibson who played next door, Benswanger responded "Well I saw Gibson about two years ago and he certainly looked like big league timber to me." The question remained, what would it take to make admitting Black ballplayers into "an issue?" Owners were complicit, if not cowed by Landis's racism. The doormat Pirates could have benefited from signing some players from those 1938 Grays—Gibson, Buck Leonard, and Ray Brown among them—but Benswanger lacked the courage to blaze the trail a decade before Rickey and the Brooklyn Dodgers eventually did (not coincidentally after Landis's passing).

Imagine for a moment if the National and American Leagues were integrated when Gibson began his career in the early 1930s. It is worth asking what difference it might have made and how Black ballplayers would have performed alongside White players. By comparison, from 1948 to 1962, the first fifteen years following Robinson's debut with the Dodgers, the National League awarded 11 of its 15 MVPs to Black ballplayers. (Half of the American League teams did not begin integrating their squads until September 1954 and trailed the senior circuit in the infusion of talent). It was not a question of skill; it was the matter of the lack of equal opportunity that had thwarted Black ballplayers from competition. The 1930s were a special time for the Negro Leagues and players like Buck Leonard, Jud Wilson, Willie Wells, Ray Dandridge, Judy Johnson, Oscar Charleston, Mule Suttles, Leon Day, Hilton Smith—in addition to Paige and Gibson—would have helped anchor or round out many a team lineup.

In the storied history of Negro League Baseball, it was Josh Gibson who personified baseball superstardom the likes of which should have been performed for all to see alongside his 1930s and 1940s contemporaries: Babe Ruth, Lou Gehrig, Jimmie Foxx, Joe DiMaggio, and Ted Williams. If the barriers between the races did not exist, Major League Baseball would have been all the richer for the competition, the storylines, and the sheer drama and pinnacle of play that the likes of Gibson would have brought to the national game. But like so much of American society in the first half of the twentieth century, MLB chose and countenanced division, separation, and justice for some, but not all. As recent incidents have shown, it is a price we continue to pay even now. But this is not a conversation about what might have been, but about redemption.

The convergence of Landis and Gibson is worth unpacking to explain why Josh's name should replace Landis's on the MVP trophy for a league in which he never played. Named Commissioner in 1920, Landis brought with him his legal background, an undying love for the game, and a bitter, relentless racism that would serve him well in thwarting any attempts by team owners to sign Black ballplayers and even banning teams from competing against them. When it came to the latter, Landis continually tried to prohibit or limit postseason barnstorming by major leaguers to control the sport's product. These prohibitions became equally useful when it meant preventing Black ballplayers from competing on the field against their White counterparts, often besting them in the process, to the chagrin of segregationists.

Despite playing in the shadow of so-called "Organized Baseball,"[2] Negro League stars such as Josh were so good such that White America paid them the "compliment" of comparisons with White baseball stars. Monikers like "Rube" Foster (earned from a pitching matchup when he beat Rube Marquard), "the Black Honus Wagner" (John Henry "Pop" Lloyd), "the Black Lou Gehrig" (Oscar Charleston), and yes, "the Black Babe Ruth" (Josh Gibson) all spoke to White America recognizing the greatness of these Black players.

Josh Gibson's hitting and power was second to none and, coupled with his catching, he helped lead his teams to numerous first-place finishes. A 1972 Hall of Fame inductee (along with Buck Leonard, making for the second and third Negro Leaguers enshrined after Satchel Paige), Gibson was a true baseball superstar. His illness and then tragic death at the age of 35 stole from all of us what likely would have been one of the greatest baseball careers ever.

I used the word *journey* earlier. Breaking the baseball color barrier, the eventual, retrospective recognition of the premier talent from the Negro Leagues in the Hall of Fame, and overcoming the stigmas attached to race—this is our journey. "Long overdue recognition" of Negro League statistics by MLB is further proof that is bound to attract more attention than we could have hoped for. Shining a light on this history, as Sports Reference is now helping to do, well, that is priceless. That all being said, if we are never again to fall prey to the prejudices that checker our history, we must always retain an appreciation for what happened and what our better angels call on us to be.

Endnotes

1. The MVP awards are nameless in the 2021 season and will be renamed at a later date.

2. "Organized Baseball"—a term created to include the American and National Leagues and their associated minor leagues to the exclusion of the Negro Leagues, implying that Negro baseball was less "organized."

Women in the Negro Leagues

by Leslie Heaphy

When Major League Baseball (MLB) made the decision to add seven Negro Leagues to those considered to be "major leagues," the door opened for over three thousand players and other baseball personnel to be added to the roster of those granted major league status. This change not only opened the doors for many men to see their stories and records added, but the same is true for a number of women. Most of these women will be new to the vast majority of baseball fans. For many, the only woman from the Negro Leagues that they may recognize is Newark Eagles owner Effa Manley. A few more may have heard the names Toni Stone, Connie Morgan, or Mamie Johnson, who played in the 1950s. Although that is usually where the story ends, now we can add a number of other women's names to the roster of those involved with (or who played against) major Negro League teams.

Effa Manley owned the Newark Eagles with her husband Abe. She was elected to the National Baseball Hall of Fame in 2006, the first woman ever, in recognition of her many accomplishments, working to elevate and support her team and Black players in general. She owned the Eagles when they won the Negro League World Series in 1946 and she pushed to get American and National League teams to pay for the Black players they signed after Jackie Robinson. But Manley was not the first woman to own a Negro League team. That distinction belongs to Olivia Taylor who owned the Indianapolis ABCs from 1922 to 1924. Taylor took over ownership after the death of husband C.I. Taylor. Taylor now belongs to a relatively small group of female owners of major league teams, and becomes the second woman owner of a major league team following Helene Hathaway Britton, who owned the St. Louis Cardinals from 1911-1916. In addition to her involvement with the ABCs, Taylor became president of the local NAACP chapter. She helped bring the national convention to Indianapolis in 1925, and became the first female to ever head the national convention.

We can also add to the list of female owners the names of Henryene Green and Dr. Hilda Bolden Shorter. Green took over the Baltimore Elite Giants after the death of her husband Vernon in 1949, and Shorter took over the reins for the Philadelphia Stars from 1950 through 1952. Green and Shorter owned teams not yet considered "major league" since the leagues chosen for the designation go through the 1948 season, but opening the doors means more research and interest should be generated in the Negro Leagues and Black baseball in general, and additional league-seasons may be added by MLB in the future.

Ethel Truman Posey became part of the management team for the Homestead Grays after her husband's death in 1946. Though she did not take an active role in the team, she was still listed as owning a share. In 1932 and 1933 Isabelle Baxter played second base for the Cleveland Giants who became a Negro National League team in the second half of the 1933 season. Baxter was no longer on the roster by then, but she had the chance to play with and alongside major-league players for the Giants.

Adding the names and stories for these women also opens the doors for people to learn about other women who worked in Black baseball and likely had opportunities to interact with and play against the now-major Negro League ballclubs. For example, Fabiola Wilson and Gloria Dymond , who played in the outfield for the New Orleans Creoles in 1948, or Lucille Bland, who coached for the Creoles of the Negro Southern League in 1947, or Georgia Williams, who pitched for the Creoles in 1945. Clara Jones is listed as the president in 1935 of the Boston ABCs, a local independent club that played Negro League competition that year. Billie Harden served as an officer for the Atlanta Black Crackers 1938–1948 and Maude Semler (wife of James "Soldier Boy" Semler) served a similar role for the New York Black Yankees 1947–1948. Due to the large role that barnstorming played in the history of the Negro Leagues, many of the independent and minor league Black teams often played exhibition games against the now major-league teams in the Negro National League and Negro American League.

With the addition of statistics and biographies of those involved in the seven leagues now considered major by MLB, the names Olivia Taylor, Ethel Posey, and Maude Semler will officially be included with Effa Manley. How many other women's stories will be brought to the forefront now? Did the Baltimore Black Sox Bloomer girls ever play any Negro men's teams in 1921 and 1922? Did the Creoles play any major Negro League teams between 1945 and 1948 when a number of women were hired by Allan Page? When Harriet Smith pitched for the Pullman Porters, who were their opponents? With the increased interest and research into Black baseball in general and the Negro Leagues specifically, these questions may soon be answered.

Toni Stone

A Black Baseball Legacy

by Michael E. Lomax

In the late nineteenth and early twentieth centuries, baseball had been a special game among African Americans. The sport's institutional and organizational development evolved as part of African American community building in the pre-Civil War era. Baseball served as a response to the health problems and high mortality rate brought on by the urban pathology affecting US cities. At the same time, African Americans utilized the sport to further the ultimate goal of integration into mainstream America. The Philadelphia Pythians' attempt to become a member of the National Association of Base Ball Players (NABBP) exemplified the African American effort to assimilate into US society.

The Pythians' effort ended in failure, but Black baseball's institutional and organizational development took root. The Black game was transformed into a commercialized amusement by a generation of African Americans who attempted to work within the parameters of a segregated institutional structure. These entrepreneurs operated their segregated enterprises (Black baseball teams) within the fabric of the mainstream economy (professional baseball). Several Black baseball clubs established a symbiotic business relationship with White professional and semiprofessional teams when the latter struggled to place their game on a sound economic footing. Simultaneously, Black baseball club operators established their own rivalries and constructed an unconventional playing style that made their game uniquely African American.

Black baseball magnates acknowledged that in order for them to conduct business they would have to negotiate with the White power structure, which meant dealing with the new industry that became "Organized Baseball" as well as a host of unaffiliated semiprofessional teams and leagues. These Black club operators utilized a business practice known as economic cooperation that had its roots in the late eighteenth century. Early Black baseball entrepreneurs recognized that any success would only occur by pooling their economic resources collectively. Therefore, consolidating resources served to establish business enterprises.

The Cuban Giants emerged as the most successful Black baseball club of the late nineteenth century—a direct result of economic cooperation. The Giants' development was the result of consolidating three Black teams into a top-level independent club. The Cubans formed a partnership with a wealthy White businessman and during the week played their home games in Trenton, New Jersey, and barnstormed Connecticut, New Jersey, New York, and Pennsylvania for weekend games. During the winter months, the Cubans traveled south and established a home base in St. Augustine, Florida. The players were hired as waiters, but their primary responsibility was to entertain the guests with their ballplaying skills. The Cuban Giants became the model that other Black clubs endeavored to emulate.

The Gorhams of New York exemplified the Black team operating in the late nineteenth century. They were formed in Manhattan at a time when New York's Black middle class resided there. The Gorhams did not established a home base of operation, resulting in them barnstorming the nation for gate receipts. Several attempts were made to establish a home base, however, most of them turned out to be bad business decisions. The Gorhams would, nevertheless, develop a rivalry with the Cuban Giants in the form of a Colored Championship series, designed to stimulate interest in the Black game. There were no substantial Black enclaves that could sustain a commercialized amusement of that type, resulting in the Cuban Giants and Gorhams marketing their games to a White clientele.

The Cubans and Gorhams faced several hurdles that hindered their efforts to operate in the White baseball world. White player hostility made it problematic to maintain continuity in scheduling games. Some club owners in White baseball struggled to place their game on a sound economic footing, making it difficult to sustain consistent business relations. With the exception of Chicago, Illinois, in most large metropolitan cities the semiprofessional teams and leagues did not develop stability.

Simultaneously, Black baseball clubs benefited from White professional and semiprofessional baseball's fledgling existence. Black teams created a demand for themselves once their caliber of play equaled or surpassed White teams. Playing one exhibition game with either the Cuban Giants or Gorhams could result in a struggling White club meeting its payroll and expenses. Black baseball entrepreneurs had to be enterprising in marketing and promoting their clubs. Winning games by scores of 20–1 or 16–2 detracted from fan interest. Thus, the Cubans and Gorhams created an alternative playing style when games became too one-sided. Their clowning antics on the diamond served to entertain the fans in the stands, but when the situation called for it, both clubs could also be fierce competitors.

By the late 1880s, White players' hostility towards Blacks had gain wider acceptance and resulted in club owners scheduling fewer games with Black teams. This circumstance was more symptomatic in the minor leagues because their White stars threatened to jump other circuits. The players' revolt of 1889, and the subsequent war with the American Association the following year, led to the AA folding. Their demise led to the National League absorbing the Association's four best franchises, and with several minor leagues collapsing, fewer games were scheduled against Black teams.[1]

Yet Black baseball clubs continued their symbiotic business relationship with White semiprofessional teams. Semiprofessional clubs emerged in the 1870s. They were called semiprofessionals or semipros to distinguish them from their professional counterparts. Semipros generally belonged to no league but paid their players and charged admission. Semipros often signed their players to one-year contracts that rarely contained a reserve clause for the following season. At the beginning of each season, players had to make new arrangements. Semipro teams, particularly in Chicago, attempted to form leagues and associations patterned after the National League. Although these leagues and associations were ineffective, they did lead to the creation of rivalries between Black and White clubs. Maintaining this business relationship resulted in Black baseball entrepreneurs making concessions to operate in the White semipro world. Black baseball magnates accommodated racial prejudices by marginalizing the effects of any potential conflict with racist overtones. They had a vested interest in downplaying any possible racial conflicts to sustain their business ties. This assertion is not to suggest that some conflicts that occurred did not have racial implications, but to these late-nineteenth century Black baseball entrepreneurs, such compromises were necessary to advance their economic interests.

Black baseball experienced tremendous growth and expansion in the opening decade of the twentieth century. Several Black teams, as well as Cuban squads, emerged to challenge established teams like the Philadelphia Giants, the Leland Giants, and the Cuban X Giants for players and gate receipts. Black team owners confronted challenges similar to those that conventional Black businesses faced, most notably the ways in which a separate Black economy was being imposed on them. Ballpark ownership remained the biggest obstacle to the Black game's growth and development. Owners of teams in the American and National Leagues enjoyed the advantage of being able to sustain a fanbase and maximize revenues that African Americans never enjoyed. This resulted in several African American club owners entering into partnership with White businessmen to gain access to suitable playing facilities and maintain business ties with White semipro teams.

The growth spurt that Black baseball experienced sparked efforts to form leagues and associations. League formation represented the overall attempt to place the Black game on a sound economic footing. Although the African American team owners used the National and American Leagues as their model for organization, they did not operate their circuits in the same manner as the White majors. Black baseball entrepreneurs did not embrace the fact although they were competitors on the field, they needed to be partners in business who had to cooperate to much greater degree than entrepreneurs in some more conventional business enterprises. Instead, they sought to maintain their symbiotic business relationship with White semipro clubs and concurrently schedule games that were regional and national in scope while ideally expanding their network internationally to Cuba. A "balanced schedule" was impossible when few clubs owned their own parks. To owners like Rube Foster, it was in his best interest to keep his ballpark busy on weekends rather than taking road trips that would increase travel expenses.

The early efforts to form leagues and associations produced several teams that were Black-owned and operated and functioning as full-time enterprises. Five teams—the Bacharach Giants, Chicago American Giants, Hilldale Athletic Club, Indianapolis ABCs, and the St. Louis Giants—utilized the same mode of operation that Black baseball entrepreneurs had employed in the late nineteenth century to transform their clubs into top independent teams. They began by assembling and sustaining a team of talented players, then gaining access to a ballpark within close proximity to a large urban area in order to build a fanbase. To sustain rivalries that would stimulate spectator interest, these Black clubs began to scheduled more games among themselves than with other White semipros and Cuban teams. Scheduling exhibition games with all-star teams composed of major and minor league players served to heighten a Black team's prestige. Embarking on extended barnstorming tours elevated a Black team to the ranks of an elite touring team; the tours also served as a means of market expansion.

Efforts at market expansion illustrated that Black baseball clubs did not rely solely on a separated Black economy for their economic viability. The Chicago American Giants and the Indianapolis ABCs tapped into their respective consumer markets while maintaining their business ties with White semipros that allowed them to exploit the White baseball market. Access to ballparks allowed the American Giants club owner Andrew "Rube" Foster and ABCs magnate Charles Isham "C.I." Taylor to develop and maintain fanbases in Chicago and Indianapolis, respectively, and to expand into new markets in the West and South nationally and internationally to Cuba.

As the United States entered World War I, the Great Migration—the mass movement northward of African Americans—dramatically expanded the Black consumer market, particularly in large urban centers in the North. Several Black baseball magnates attempted to tap into this growing market by creating civic ties with the Black middle class and developing a business relationship with the Black press. They used the race rhetoric of self-help and racial solidarity and racial uplift to sustain press and community relations. Race rhetoric served, in fact, to promote a sense of heightened prestige for their respective communities.

By the end of the 1910s, Rube Foster had emerged as the premier Black baseball owner, and his Chicago American Giants became the benchmark that African American team owners attempted to emulate. Operating in the largest market in the Midwest allowed Foster to develop a booking service to maximize revenues and heighten his prestige. He created a barnstorming network that enabled him to book games for midwestern Black clubs throughout the Midwest and East. Creating this network was plausible because several Black teams operated on a full-time basis, and in many ways these barnstorming tours represented a dry run for the formation of a Negro League.

In the 1920s, several forces combined to make league formation plausible. The Great Migration dramatically expanded the Black communities where several Black baseball teams resided. The expansion of the Black press provided the means for these club owners to tap into this growing market. League formation coincided with the remarkable economic growth of the United States. Baseball's market expanded through the accelerated growth of cities and small towns as the US changed from a rural society to an urban one. Combined, these factors allowed Rube Foster to form the Negro National League (NNL), and led Hilldale club owner Ed Bolden—along with Brooklyn Royal Giants magnate Nat Strong—to organize the Eastern Colored League (ECL).

Throughout the NNL's and ECL's existence, Black club owners operated their respective leagues in what can best be described as the "business alliance" model. This approach was based on the supposition that Black club owners would have maximum control over their players under contract and over the franchise, meaning the team's name and logo, which could be commodified. An association with a few club owners in certain cities enabled them to collectively eliminate players jumping their contracts, giving the owners tighter control over Black baseball's player labor pool. The business alliance model allowed owners to form loose associations among themselves to ensure that their clubs secured the best playing dates and parks in which to play. This arrangement, however, came at the expense of some of the league clubs. In most cases, several of them became reliant on Rube Foster and Nat Strong to book additional games to generate gate receipts. This arrangement led to constant franchise shifting in the NNL, with the American Giants, Kansas City Monarchs, Detroit Stars, and St. Louis Stars being the only teams to operate consistently throughout the league's existence. In the East, a peculiar business arrangement evolved where Bolden sought to maintain an alliance with Strong to schedule lucrative weekend games away from their ballparks. Weaker franchises like Bacharach Giants either scheduled their own weekend games or used Nat Strong's booking agency for contests in Gotham.

By the mid-1920s, the business alliance approach had begun to unravel. Rube Foster, Ed Bolden, and Nat Strong placed their economic interests above their respective leagues' interests. From their perspective, it was not in their best economic interests to pattern their leagues after the White major leagues. They refused to recognize that their leagues' overall economic interests and their interests were one and the same. The separate Black economy being imposed on them and the decline of White semiprofessional baseball meant that these club owners were becoming more reliant on the Black consumer dollar. The illnesses of both Foster and Bolden resulted in both leagues losing what effective leadership they had. When the United States entered the Great Depression, the NNL and the ECL faded into the dustbin of history.

Despite their demise, the Negro National League and Eastern Colored League left their imprint on the African American experience specifically and American baseball in general. The Negro Leagues inform us of the ways African Americans strived to compete within the framework of the US economy, and simultaneously they represented the overall pursuit for freedom and self-determination. The Black baseball business developed into a commercial enterprise at a time when segregation shaped the relationship between Black and White people. African Americans made it clear that despite their exclusion from mainstream America, they would develop their own institutions and shape their own sporting patterns. S.K. Govern, Benjamin Butler, William Peters, and Frank Leland in the late nineteenth century—along with Rube Foster, C.I. Taylor, Ed Bolden, and to a lesser degree John Connor, Henry Tucker, and Thomas Jackson in the early twentieth century—operated by any means necessary to advance their economic interests in the national pastime. These Black baseball entrepreneurs were not merely passive participants responding to forces that affected them. They endeavored to form Black independent teams and the Negro Leagues as business enterprises in their own image. [2]

Selected Bibliography

Lanctot, Neal. *Fair Dealing and Clean Playing: The Hilldale Club and the Development of Black Professional Baseball, 1910-1932*. Jefferson, N. C.: McFarland, 1994.

Lanctot, Neal. *Negro League Baseball: The Rise and Ruin of a Black Institution*. Philadelphia: University of Pennsylvania Press, 2004.

Lester, Larry. *Black Baseball's National Showcase; The East-West All-Star Game, 1933-1953*. Bison Books: University of Nebraska Press, 2002.

Lomax, Michael E. *Black Baseball Entrepreneurs, 1860-1901: Operating by Any Means Necessary*. Syracuse, NY: Syracuse University Press, 2003.

Lomax, Michael E. *Black Baseball Entrepreneurs, 1902-1931: The Negro National and Eastern Colored Leagues*. Syracuse, NY: Syracuse University Press, 2014.

Overmyer, James. *Queen of the Negro Leagues: Effa Manley and the Newark Eagles*. Lanham, Maryland: Scarecrow Inc., 1998.

Endnotes

1.   In the 1880s, the American Association represented a major league along with the National League.

2.   S. K. Govern was a co-owner of the Cuban Giants. Benjamin Butler operated the Gorhams of New York. William Peters and Frank Leland operated the Chicago Unions. Leland broke away from Peters and formed the Chicago Union Giants. The following club owners operated the following clubs: Rube Foster (Chicago American Giants); C. I. Taylor (Indianapolis ABCs); Ed Bolden (Hilldale Athletic Club); John Connor (Brooklyn Royal Giants and Bacharach Giants); and Henry Tucker and Thomas Jackson (Bacharach Giants).

Turkey Stearnes
and the Inclusive Grand Slam

By Vanessa Ivy Rose

For most, actions speak louder than words, but in my family, home runs speak the loudest. It comes with the territory when your grandfather is Baseball Hall of Famer (and Detroit Stars legend), Norman "Turkey" Stearnes. My grandfather was a quiet and reserved man (originally from Tennessee) who could be found hitting baseballs so far they were rumored to have landed in "somebody's kitchen," making plays in center field that deserved to be on *SportsCenter's Top Ten*, or discussing baseball on any given day, but he likely never imagined reaching Cooperstown (or four other Hall of Fames). Lack of imagination or self doubt were not issues for a man who batted over .300 in 14 of 19 seasons and captured six home run titles. Turkey stepped into the batter's box confidently, even when facing aces on the mound like Satchel Paige. The elite talent pool of the Negro Leagues was undoubtedly competitive, but Jim Crow was unequivocally Turkey's greatest opponent.

Even today, it remains apparent that an era dominated by segregationist laws, lynchings, and countless attempts to dehumanize Black Americans has had lasting effects. Over the past 100 years, tremendous ballplayers from the Negro Leagues have been hidden figures. Baseball enthusiasts and historians have celebrated and discussed the accomplishments of my grandfather and his peers, but Black ballplayers before Jackie Robinson have yet to become household names—and not for lack of talent. When the Negro Leagues dissolved (as a direct result of Major League Baseball capitalizing off of integration), the rich history and impressive statistics from that time were also cast aside.

Not having one bitter bone in his body, Turkey continued to follow baseball long after he retired. Living in Detroit, he was frequently in attendance to watch the hometown Tigers. Sitting in the bleachers at Tiger Stadium (watching a team he should have been able to play for), he always hoped to see a competitive game. If they were losing, he would return home early, but he continued to attend games up until his passing in 1979. Stepping in as the designated hitter, my grandmother, Nettie Stearnes, continued to follow the Tigers faithfully and she also wrote letters (for 21 years) to the Hall of Fame advocating for Turkey's induction. In 2000, her vision became reality as she saw her husband inducted alongside another Detroit baseball legend, Sparky Anderson. Joining that class were Carlton Fisk, Tony Perez, and Bid McPhee.

Turkey Stearnes

With such an outstanding class of baseball legends, how is it that Turkey Stearnes and many other Negro Leaguers remain unknown? Quickly reviewing the year 2020 can provide us with more than enough answers to that question. With sports serving as an outlet for so many of us in need, both the pandemic and the racial crisis of 2020 caused society to endure the world's longest rain delay. In a world filled with uncertainty, sports were on pause and society (especially America) was publicly grappling with the issue of race due to the social climate. As names like Ahmaud Arbery, Breonna Taylor, and George Floyd were thrust to the forefront due to the public nature of their horrific murders, sports fans saw their favorite athletes (and their respective organizations) using their platform to address social injustice. Sports icons of the past (such as Muhammad Ali, Tommie Smith, and John Carlos) were often referenced, LeBron James was no longer expected to "Shut up and dribble" and many who were previously in strong opposition to Colin Kaepernick suddenly were able to start seeing and acknowledging what has been a systemic problem for centuries. Making an effort to repair the harm done to the Negro Leagues, Major League Baseball decided to address a longstanding problem. In December 2020, they officially recognized over 3000 Negro League players as major leaguers within the historic records. In honor of economic justice and to ensure that their efforts were more than performative, it would also be appropriate to compensate the families of the Negro Leaguers who were grossly undervalued and underpaid.

I can honestly say my family and I are thrilled to see the progress that has been made thus far. We carry the legacy of my grandfather with us each day. Turkey's daughters (my mother, Joyce Stearnes Thompson and my aunt, Rosilyn Stearnes-Brown) have spoken on behalf of Turkey for decades via interviews and at baseball events. They also have been routinely performing "The Star Spangled Banner" at Comerica Park during the weekend celebrations for the Negro Leagues—because in addition to being retired educators, they both have professional singing on their resume. Each time they have performed the anthem, I've always thought to myself, "What a sight for Grandpa Turkey to see from the heavenly bleachers, or more than likely, center field…"

These experiences (and so many more) have led me to this moment, where I'm reflecting upon how sports, history, and my grandfather are intertwined. My mind races with thoughts about the evolution of the Black athlete and what that means for me personally (as a former collegiate basketball player and currently as a coach and educator), for my family and truly for all of us globally, even beyond sports. Our perspectives and our collective understandings are constantly evolving. As we continue to grow as a society, sports and history will start to reflect that as well. The inclusion of players and statistics from the Negro Leagues in this day and age is simply an acknowledgment of the truth we have always known: The ballplayers who played in the Negro Leagues have always been worthy of the designation "major." Using this truth as a metaphor for life, we have a chance to make this more than a historic correction. Perhaps baseball can be utilized to propel us into transforming society. Now that Major League Baseball has room for both Babe Ruth and Josh Gibson, for both Ty Cobb and Turkey Stearnes, perhaps baseball can be the gift that allows us all to see each other more deeply as humans. In essence, that would take us further than any home run and that would truly be "major"!

Building the Seamheads Negro Leagues Database

by Gary Ashwill

As the founder and lead researcher of the Seamheads Negro Leagues Database, I'm thrilled and proud that our work has made its way to Baseball Reference, where players from the Negro Leagues will take their rightful place among the other major leaguers. Here are a few notes about the database, the nature of Negro Leagues statistics, and how we put the numbers together.

One thing you will find is that the statistics here show Negro League teams with fewer regular season games than the contemporary White major leagues, usually 50-100 compared to the standard 154 games in the National League and American League at the time. This is not because they actually played fewer games (in fact, as we'll see below, much of the time they played more). It's because Black baseball teams, in the days of segregation, played a more complex schedule than White major league teams, and league games formed only a part of their season—a very important part, but only a part.

There are two main reasons for this. First, home crowds for Negro League teams consisted mostly of Black fans, who were enthusiastic supporters but had limited disposable income. Second, throughout the United States there was a huge market for baseball outside of the organized major and minor leagues, and a large number of good semipro teams looking for opponents. This meant that Black team owners could maximize their profits by appealing both to their Black fanbase in their home city and to Black and White fans elsewhere, including those in smaller cities and towns with no league teams of their own, and also fans in larger cities who wanted cheaper, more accessible alternatives to league baseball.

Negro Leaguers played games against independent Black teams, interleague games against teams in the other Black major league, exhibition games against White major and minor leaguers, and many, many games against White semipro and amateur teams. Altogether a Negro League team might play as many as 150-200 games a year, with only a quarter to half being league games, depending on the season. The 1925 Hilldale Club, for example, played at least 177 games in total, but only 72 of them were Eastern Colored League games, and six more were in the World Series.

Our regular season Negro League statistics do not include games against White major or minor leaguers or semipros, or against teams we see as obviously lesser in quality. They do include league games, interleague games (there were usually two major Black leagues operating at any one time), and games against strong independent teams that we believe were comparable to league teams. Although Major League Baseball's recognition of the Negro Leagues as major leagues covers only seven leagues that existed during the years from 1920 to 1948, a number of the most important Black professional teams during this period were independent teams (or in some cases associate members of leagues that did not compete for the pennant). The Homestead Grays and Kansas City Monarchs, possibly the two most famous Negro League teams of all time, operated for years as independents. The first three seasons of Josh Gibson's professional career were spent on independent teams (the 1930-31 Grays and the 1932 Pittsburgh Crawfords).

Official statistics were sometimes published for various Negro Leagues, sometimes compiled by league officials, other times by professional statistical services. The records vary in quality and comprehensiveness, but all are (to one degree or another) incomplete, missing both players and statistical categories. The underlying documentation for these compilations no longer exists. Combined with the fact that box scores were not published for all games, this means that the official numbers can't be checked or backed up with game-level records. Moreover, the official statistics do not include interleague games (which were very important parts of the Negro League schedule, especially in the 1940s) or games against the aforementioned independent teams of major league quality.

Rather than relying on the limited official statistics that are available, we have set out to collect box scores and detailed game accounts for as many games as possible, along with the small number of scorebooks and filled-out scorecards that can be tracked down.

Our research process begins with the most important contemporary source for information on Negro League baseball, the Black press. During the 1920–1948 period, Black newspapers were weekly publications (the sole major exception being the *Atlanta Daily World*). Several of the most important—including the *Chicago Defender* and *Pittsburgh Courier*—were distributed nationally, and as such tried to cover the whole world of Black sports, not just baseball. Boxing, basketball, and college football got plenty of coverage as well, on what amounted to only two, or at best three, pages per week for all sports. In the 1920s and 1930s, the *Defender, Courier,* and other papers attempted to cover as many Negro League games as possible, cramming their pages with box scores. But there simply wasn't enough space to fit them all in.

The Black sports pages provide us with a rough outline of a given season's schedule, and supply box scores for a good portion of the games—as many as half in the 1920s. From there we go to mainstream daily newspapers located in league cities as well as neutral towns where Negro League games were played. In this era, and especially prior to World War II, newspapers tended to print large numbers of baseball box scores, well beyond the major and minor leagues. Although you usually need to consult Black newspapers if you want interviews, commentary, and context about the Negro Leagues, many White newspapers did print detailed and reliable box scores, many of which cannot be found in the Black press.

The task of collecting box scores is not a simple one. There was no centralized source for Negro League information that functioned the way *The Sporting News* did for White baseball. Neither is there currently one central depository for all the historical newspapers that need to be consulted for Negro League research. Even the Library of Congress is missing many necessary publications. Over the decades, thousands of hours have been spent at libraries all over the country spooling through reels of microfilm, searching for elusive box scores and game stories. Our burden has been somewhat eased in recent years with the rise of digitized online archives, but these are not comprehensive, and some vital newspapers have still not been digitized. We have also been able to add some material from the few scorebooks and filled-in scorecards that have survived.

Despite the efforts of our team and contributors, thousands of Negro League games still lack box scores or detailed accounts. The late 1930s and 1940s saw a general decline in the number of baseball box scores printed in newspapers (both Black and White), so coverage falls from close to 100% in the 1920s to 50% or less in the 1940s. Overall, for the 1920-1948 period, our individual player statistics cover 9,135 out of 12,608 known games between major Black professional teams, or 72.45%.

Can we expect major additions in the future? Will we ever get close to 100% coverage of Negro League games, 1920-1948? Unfortunately, the odds of anything like this being accomplished are probably close to zero. If we are lucky, we might expect to add 300–500 more games from newspaper sources. It's always possible that previously unknown materials will emerge—perhaps one day someone will find a chest in an attic or a filing cabinet in a basement filled with long-lost league records or stacks of musty scoresheets. But we can't count on such a development.

We *can*, however, look forward to concrete improvements to the Negro League record in the short term. Currently we still lack fielding statistics, complete pitching statistics, and some other secondary categories (hit by pitch, notably) for a number of seasons. These gaps will be addressed and filled in over the next couple of years. And another of our future goals is to work out ways to present the official statistics in tandem with our box score compilations, since whatever their failings, the official numbers do include games that aren't currently part of our database.

In the long run, we would like to document as much of Black baseball history as possible, including the games against White semipros and amateurs that occupied such a large portion of Negro League schedules. But our emphasis for now will be on Black major league games.

Historiography of Black Baseball & Negro Baseball Leagues

by Gary Gillette

Analogous to the lack of attention paid until recently to the game of Black baseball itself, the historiography of Black baseball and the Negro Leagues has in many ways not been adequately chronicled. A full treatment of this important and complex subject would require a weighty book, but an outline of the historiography is valuable as well. This article presents a draft of the history of scholarship of Black baseball and the Negro Leagues *before* the re-integration of the formerly White major leagues in the late 1940s.

First, however, a few words about what is not included here. There are many fine works about Integration and re-integration in baseball—a subject deserving its own historiography—but most of them deal with the long, segregated history of the game only in passing. Even with that restriction, not everything can be included, starting with the hundreds of worthy articles on the Negro Leagues published in newspapers, magazines, academic journals, and on the internet. That part of the historiography would be longer than this part. Nor are academic theses and dissertations included unless they were published in book form. With a few exceptions, biographies and team histories are not included. There are many worthy examples of both—with, thankfully, more being published every year—but unless the biographies or team histories were early exemplars or are especially significant, they are not shown. What biographies are included are of transcendent figures and which cover the full lives of their subjects, not just their playing careers or other segments of their lives.

Documentaries, television series, and movies are not included, even though the list of them is fairly short. They are a different medium than print and require different treatment. Works that do not add much to the canon because they are essentially derivative or because they have significant flaws are also not included. Nonetheless, appropriate allowances are made for works that pushed the historical envelope or were precocious in other ways. And works primarily intended for juvenile readers are not included, with two exceptions because their beautiful illustrations have made them attractive to adults as well.

Finally, while I consulted with other scholars on this compilation, the judgment calls, choices made, omissions, and mistakes made are my own responsibility.

This article is divided into three sections. The first organizes the historiography by theoretical eras and lists prominent actors in each era along with a few organizations of special import. The second is a chronological list of important written works covering Black baseball and the Negro Leagues. The third is an alphabetical list of people and organizations mentioned in the first two sections, with a brief description of why they were selected.

Historical personages represented are mostly authors, journalists, and historians. A few important ballplayers and executives are also included because of their public advocacy.

Eras of Historiography
with Prominent Figures from Each Era

Prehistory, 1858–1907

From the advent of Black baseball until publication of Sol White's "Where would we ever be without it?" *History of Colored Baseball.*
- Octavius Catto, Sol White.

Classical Age, 1908–1948

Extensive coverage in the African American press along with very spotty coverage in the mainstream press of the founding and flowering of the Negro Leagues, the Negro World Series, the East-West Classic All-Star Game, and the re-integration of so-called "Organized Baseball."
- Dave Wyatt, Rube Foster, Ed Bolden, Wendell Smith, Sam Lacy, Fay Young, Ches Washington, Joe Bostic, Rollo Wilson, Tweed Webb, Dan Burley, Ric Roberts, Mal Goode, Teenie Harris.

Dark Ages, 1949–1969

Virtual disappearance of the legacy of Black baseball & the Negro Leagues from mainstream media and White public consciousness during the struggle to truly integrate the National Pastime.
- Lacy, Smith, Doc Young, E.B. Henderson, Jack Roosevelt Robinson, Ted Williams, Shirley Povich, MLB Special Records Committee.

Middle Ages, 1970–1993

Publication of the groundbreaking Only the Ball Was White, *Negro Leaguers inducted into Hall of Fame, early oral histories, first Negro Leagues Players Reunions, Negro Leagues tribute baseball card sets, Society for American Baseball Research's (SABR) Negro Leagues Committee, founding of Negro Leagues Baseball Museum (NLBM).*

- Robert Peterson, Bob Davids, Don Lowry, Merl Kleinknecht, John Holway, Jerry Malloy, Dick Clark, Larry Lester, Phil Dixon, James Riley, Donn Rogosin, Ocania Chalk.

Renaissance, 1994–2005

Publication of seminal Biographical Encyclopedia of the Negro Baseball Leagues *and SABR* Negro Leagues Book, *Buck O'Neil emerges as the face of Black baseball via Ken Burns' PBS series* Baseball, *opening of NLBM's beautiful new facility in Kansas City, Black sportswriters finally win Spink Awards, first annual Jerry Malloy Conferences, new SABR and academic scholarship, major- and minor-league Negro Leagues tribute games.*

- Dixon, Clark, Riley, Holway, Lester, Ken Burns, Buck O'Neil, Ted Knorr, Don Motley, Leslie Heaphy, Ray Doswell, Rob Ruck, Adrian Burgos, Jeremy Krock.

Enlightenment, 2006–2019

Negro League Researchers and Authors Group and 2006 Hall of Fame elections, Seamheads.com Negro Leagues Database launch in 2011, Agate Type Blog, Baseball Reference adds HoF Negro Leagues data and Seamheads pre-league data, Hall of Fame restores periodic NLB elections.

- Lester, Heaphy, Knorr, Dixon, Gary Ashwill, Scott Simkus, Kevin Johnson, Sean Forman, Bob Kendrick.

The Promised Land? 2020–????

Pandemic submerges most NNL centennial celebrations, but MLB belatedly fully recognizes Major Negro Leagues. New MLB record book to come. Baseball Reference debuts new Negro Leagues architecture and content.

- Ashwill, Lester, John Thorn, Todd Peterson, Ben Lindbergh, Bryant Gumbel, SABR Negro Leagues Task Force.

Timeline of Important Black Baseball and Negro League Histories and Reference Works

Significant new editions noted separately. Otherwise, republication dates and earlier publication dates noted after the slash.

Sol White's Official Base Ball Guide, 1907, a/k/a *History of Colored Baseball.* The granddaddy of 'em all, a unique history of Black baseball in the nineteenth and early twentieth centuries. *Republished in 1984 and 1990; expanded editions published in 1995 and 2014, q.v.*

Henderson's *Negro in Sports,* 1939. A masterpiece of scholarship written when research was extremely difficult. A fundamental study of Black athletes. *Revised in a 2nd ed. in 1949; 3rd ed. with new preface and introduction published in 2014.*

Henderson's *The Black Athlete: Emergence and Arrival*, 1968. Henderson's belated follow-up to his 1939 masterpiece.

Peterson's *Only the Ball Was White: A History of Legendary Black Players and All-Black Professional Teams*, 1970

Holway's *Voices from the Great Black Baseball Leagues*, 1975. Popular and eye-opening; the first major set of Black baseball oral histories. *Revised edition published 1992; republished with new foreword in 2010.*

Chalk's *Pioneers of Black Sport*, 1975. According to the book's introduction, it is "A Study in Courage and Perseverance." Chalk's diligently researched work fits that billing nicely.

Chalk's *Black College Sport*, 1976. Includes a very comprehensive chapter on "Black Stars on White College Baseball Teams."

Manley's & Hardwick's *Negro Baseball Before Integration*, 1976. Effa Manley's autobiography; a trenchant look at both the success and the dysfunction of the Negro Leagues from the inside. *Republished in revised and expanded edition in 2006.*

Rogosin's *Invisible Men: Life in Baseball's Negro Leagues*, 1983. Excellent popular history of the Negro Leagues—still in-print four decades later and still holds up today.

Riley's *All-Time All-Stars of Black Baseball*, 1983. Forerunner of the now popular genre of "all-time, all-star" selections by a leading Black baseball historian.

Bruce's *Kansas City Monarchs: Champions of Black Baseball*, 1985/1987. The first book-length history of one of the trailblazing Black baseball teams.

Wilson's play *Fences*, 1985 (first performance)/1986 (published). A brilliant autopsy of the discrimination's destructive demons and the flipside of fame via the portrait of an embittered former Negro Leaguer. Indelibly etched into the American consciousness by James Earl Jones, who originated the role of Troy Maxon on Broadway in 1987. Made into a major Hollywood movie in 2016 with director Denzel Washington starring alongside Viola Davis.

Lowry's *Green Cathedrals*, 1st ed., 1986. The wellspring of ballpark history and data from which flowed the information cited by almost every other source since its publication. Lowry perspicaciously treated Negro League parks as major-league from the beginning. *Revised & updated 2nd ed. published in 1992; slightly revised 3rd ed. published in 1993. Substantial updates in 4th and 5th editions in 2006 and 2020.*

Riley's *Dandy, Day, and the Devil*. 1987. Short biographies of Ray Dandridge, Leon Day, and Willie Wells that helped all three great players get elected to the Hall of Fame.

Ashe's *Hard Road to Glory: A History of the African-American Athlete,* 1988/1993 (three volumes). Popular and influential, this inclusive set put Black sports history on the map for many Americans who knew nothing about it.

Holway's *Blackball Stars: Negro League Pioneers,* 1988. The second of Holway's popular oral histories.

Holway's *Black Diamonds,* 1989. The third set of oral histories compiled by Holway.

Tygiel's "Black Ball" article in Thorn's & Palmer's *Total Baseball,* 1st thru 7th ed., 1989–2001. Substantive article by renowned scholar Tygiel in the new king of baseball reference works. *Revised and updated* Total Baseball *2nd ed., 1991, added Lowry's "Ballparks" section that included Negro League ballparks.*

Seymour & Seymour's *Baseball: The People's Game,* Part V of which dealt with the history of Black amateur, college, and military baseball. 1990. The graphical illustration in the front matter of "The House of Baseball Before World War II" is priceless.

"Negro League Register" in Macmillan *Baseball Encyclopedia,* 8th–10th ed., 1990–1996. A selected register of great Black ballplayers of import mostly because it was published in the beloved reference work universally known as "Big Mac." *Macmillan's 8th ed. was the official MLB encyclopedia; updated 9th and 10th editions were no longer official.*

Holway's *Josh & Satch,* 1991. Early biography of the Negro Leagues demi-gods.

Dixon's & Hannigan's *Negro Baseball Leagues: A Photographic History, 1867–1955,* 1992. The first thoughtfully curated Negro Leagues photo collection worth of being paired with the word *history.*

Tygiel's "Black Ball", Gershman's "100 Greatest Players", Lowry's "Ballparks", and Clark's & Lester's "Negro Baseball Roster" in Thorn's & Palmer's *Total Baseball,* 3rd ed., 1993. A collection of articles by weighty authors that positioned Black baseball more fully in the encyclopedia's picture. *Revised and updated 4th ed., 1995, as official MLB encyclopedia. Revised & updated official 5th edition, 1997, dropped the Negro Baseball Roster.*

Ashe's *Hard Road to Glory/Baseball: The African-American Athlete in Baseball,* 1993. Synthesis of baseball-related content from the original three-volume set.

Riley's *Biographical Encyclopedia of the Negro Baseball Leagues,* 1994. *Slightly updated edition published in 2001.* This massive, 928-page magnum opus provided the base of knowledge about most Negro League players for two decades. Its research has been widely quoted and copied—too often without attribution—but never equaled. Along with Peterson's *Only the Ball Was White,* Holway's oral histories, and SABR's *Negro Leagues Book,* one of the irreplaceable, foundational works of modern Black baseball scholarship.

SABR's *Negro Leagues Book*, 1994, Clark & Lester, editors. A landmark work referenced by many who followed. Along with Peterson's *Only the Ball Was White*, Holway's oral histories, and Riley's *Biographical Encyclopedia*, one of the irreplaceable, foundational works of modern Black baseball scholarship. *Revised and updated version published as ebook in 2020 by Lester and Wayne Stivers, though it does not contain all the original content.*

Lanctot's *Fair Dealing and Clean Playing: The Hilldale Club and the Development of Black Professional Baseball, 1910–1932.* 1994/2003. The title says it all about this trailblazing work. Along with Lanctot's sequel and Lomax's two master works, one of the four indispensable books on the historical development of Black baseball and the Negro Leagues.

Malloy's edition of *Sol White's History of Colored Baseball*, 1995/1907. *Republication of* Sol White's Official Base Ball Guide with introduction by Malloy and with *"Other Documents on the Early Black Game."* Nuf 'ced.

Leonard's and Riley's *Buck Leonard: The Black Lou Gehrig*, 1995. Autobiography of one of the most famous and probably the best-liked of the titans of Black baseball and the Negro Leagues.

Ribowsky's *Josh Gibson: The Power and the Darkness.* 1996/2004. Popular biography of the almost mythical figure.

Irvin's and Riley's *Nice Guys Finish First: The Autobiography of Monte Irvin.* The story of the Negro League superstar and MLB Hall of Famer who could have been selected as the player to re-integrate the White major leagues.

White's *Creating the National Pastime: Baseball Transforms Itself, 1903–1953.* History of baseball in the first half of twentieth century that includes insightful chapter on the Negro Leagues.

Holway's & Carroll's "400 Greatest" article in Thorn's & Palmer's *Total Baseball*, 6th ed., 1999. An important piece that gave due credit by ranking many Black baseball and Negro League players alongside their White counterparts.

Total Baseball's *Baseball: The Biographical Encyclopedia*, 2000. A key step in the mainstreaming of previously ignored Black ballplayers, many of whom were included in this compendium of short baseball biographies.

Holway's *Complete Book of Baseball's Negro Leagues*, 2001. One of the few encyclopedia-caliber works on the history of Black baseball and the Negro Leagues by a top-flight expert on the subject.

Lester's *Black Baseball's National Showcase: The East-West All-Star Game*, 2001. The category-killer book covering the history of the signal sporting event on the calendar of African Americans from its inception in 1933 to its fading after re-integration. *Revised and expanded edition published in 2020.*

New Bill James Historical Baseball Abstract, 2001. Updated version of James' influential *Historical Baseball Abstract*, this time with serious treatment of Negro League stars.

Heaphy's *The Negro Leagues, 1869–1960*, 2003. Widely cited history of Black baseball and the Negro Leagues.

Lomax's *Black Baseball Entrepreneurs: Operating by Any Means Necessary, 1860–1901*, 2003. Seminal history of the challenges and triumphs of early Black baseball. Predecessor to Lomax's twentieth-century work on the same subject. Along with its sequel and Lanctot's two master works, one of the four indispensable books on the historical development of Black baseball and the Negro Leagues.

Lanctot's *Negro League Baseball: The Rise and Ruin of a Black Institution*, 2004. Extension and expansion of Lanctot's groundbreaking work on the business of Black baseball in the early twentieth century. Along with its predecessor and Lomax's two master works, one of the four indispensable books on the historical development of Black baseball and the Negro Leagues.

Neyer/James Guide to Pitchers, 2004. The two baseball analysts and authors with very large followings included many Negro League pitchers in their popular compendium of pitchers and pitching.

"Black Baseball and the Negro Leagues" section in Palmer's & Gillette's *ESPN Baseball Encyclopedia*, 2nd ed., 2005. Included Riley's Top 100 Player rankings and other features. *Updated 3rd thru 5th editions published 2006–2008.*

Hall of Fame's *Shades of Glory: The Negro Leagues and the Story of African-American Baseball*, Lawrence Hogan et al., ed., 2006. The book resulting from the NLRAG research project that set the table for the Hall of Fame's special 2006 Negro League election.

Lowry's *Green Cathedrals*, 4th ed., 2006. Significantly updated edition of the classic work. *Revised & updated 5th ed. published in 2020—though copyright date is 2019.*

Hauser's *Negro Leagues Chronology: Events in Organized Black Baseball, 1920–1948*, 2006. First detailed, comprehensive timeline for the Negro Leagues.

Chiarello's and Morelli's *Heroes of the Negro Leagues,* 2007. Handsomely illustrated book of portraits of great Black ballplayers that included a DVD of the original 1980 documentary *Only the Ball Was White.*

Heaphy's *Black Ball* journal, 2008–present. The only academic journal systematically covering Black baseball.

Nelson's *We Are the Ship: The Story of Negro League Baseball*, 2008. Gorgeously illustrated and printed history by the premier contemporary artist of Black baseball.

Swanton's & Mah's *Black Baseball Players in Canada: A Biographical Dictionary, 1881–1960*, 2009. Much-needed reference source on the exploits of Black ballplayers north of the border.

Biddle's & Dubin's *Tasting Freedom: Octavius Catto and the Battle for Equality in Civil War America*, 2010. Biography of unsung civil rights leader and Black baseball pioneer.

Alpert's *Out of Left Field: Jews and Black Baseball*, 2011. Detailed and perceptive coverage of this critical and controversial aspect of the business of Black baseball.

Ruck's *Raceball: How the Major Leagues Colonized the Black and Latin Game*. Offers insights into the symbiotic relationship between Black baseball in the US and the Latin American game.

Luke's *The Most Famous Woman in Baseball: Effa Manley and the Negro Leagues*, 2011. Biography of Hall of Famer Effa Manley, co-owner of the Newark Eagles and campaigner for civil rights and gender equality.

Burgos's *Cuban Star: How One Negro League Owner Changed the Face of Baseball*. 2011. Biography of Hall of Famer Alex Pompez, stalwart Cuban-American owner of the Cuban Stars and New York Cubans teams.

Spivey's *"If You Were Only White": The Life of Leroy "Satchel" Paige*, 2012. The best and most complete of the many biographies of the larger-than-life pitcher and immortal Black baseball star.

Newman's & Rosen's *Black Baseball, Black Business: Race Enterprise and the Fate of the Segregated Dollar*, 2014. Superb and perceptive treatment of the relationship between Black baseball and the African-American community, especially the Black business economy.

Lomax's *Black Baseball Entrepreneurs, 1902–1931*, 2014. Follow-up to Lomax's nineteenth-century book on the same subject. Along with its predecessor and Lanctot's two master works, one of the four indispensable books on the historical development of Black baseball and the Negro Leagues.

Simkus's *Outsider Baseball: The Weird World of Baseball on the Fringe, 1876–1950*, 2014. Several essays in this thought-provoking book deal with Black baseball, particularly the endlessly repeated stories of legendary feats that cry out for more scrutiny.

Ashwill's edition of *Sol White's Official Baseball Guide* (a/k/a *History of Colored Baseball*), 2014/1907. Republication of the classic history with introduction and notes by Ashwill.

Plott's *Negro Southern League*, 2015. The definitive history of the Negro Southern League, the most important minor Negro League and a major Negro League in 1932.

Brunson's *Black Baseball, 1858-1900*, 2019 (3 volumes). Magnificent three-volume history of Black baseball in the nineteenth century.

Dixon's *Dizzy and Daffy Dean Barnstorming Tour*, 2019. Not merely a colorful account of one of the most famous teams of the barnstorming era, Dixon's book is a sociological critique of the interwar game.

Sayama's & Staples' *Gentle Black Giants*, 2019/1986. History focusing on the overlooked impact of Negro Leaguers in Japan. First published in Japanese in 1986.

Beer's *Oscar Charleston*, 2019. The full biography of a player who has not received the attention he deserves, considering that many argue he is the greatest baseball player of all-time.

Overmyer's *Cum Posey of the Homestead Grays*, 2020. Biography of the Grays' owner, Hall of Famer, and one of the towering figures in Negro League history.

Peterson's *The Negro Leagues Were Major Leagues*, 2020. Collection of essays that drives home its point and was a key factor in the push to see the Negro Leagues officially recognized.

Dramatis Personae

Alpert, Rebecca. University professor and author of *Jews and Black Baseball*.

Ashe, Arthur. World-famous tennis champion and civil rights crusader whose involvement made the three-volume history of African Americans in sports possible.

Ashwill, Gary. The foremost generator of new Black baseball and Negro Leagues history in the past decade and founder of the Seamheads' Negro Leagues database. Peerless researcher into Black baseball history and author of the fascinating Agate Type blog.

Beer, Jeremy. Oscar Charleston biographer.

Biddle, Daniel. Journalist and co-author of an Octavius Catto biography.

Bolden, Ed. Visionary postal clerk who took Hilldale from a boys' club to one of the most powerful Negro League teams of the 1920s. Founder of the Eastern Colored League and its successor, the American Negro League.

Bruce, Janet. Author of first history of Kansas City Monarchs.

Brunson, James. Historian and author of the definitive history of Black baseball at all levels in the nineteenth century.

Burgos, Adrian. History professor and author of Alex Pompez biography.

Carroll, Bob. Noted baseball and pro football writer; co-author of the "Top 400" piece in *Total Baseball*.

Catto, Octavius. Late nineteenth-century civil rights champion and captain of the pioneering African-American Pythian Base Ball Club of Philadelphia. Catto publicly forced the issue of racism by the National Association of Base Ball Players.

Chalk, Ocania. Iconoclastic journalist and federal bureaucrat; author of two landmark works, *Black College Sport* and *Pioneers of Black Sport*.

Chiarello, Mark. Book and film watercolorist; illustrator for *Heroes of the Negro Leagues*.

Clark, Dick. Influential early Negro Leagues scholar and co-author of SABR's *Negro Leagues Book*. Chair and co-chair of SABR's Negro Leagues Committee from 1985 until his death in 2014.

Dixon, Phil. Top-rank historian and prolific author and speaker on Negro League history. Co-founder of Negro Leagues Baseball Museum.

Dubin, Murray. Journalist and co-author of an Octavius Catto biography.

Forman, Sean. Founder and publisher of Baseball Reference. Added Hall of Fame Negro League data (from NLRAG) to his dominant Sports-Reference.com Website in 2012.

Foster, Rube. One of the greatest pitchers of the pre-league era as well as dominant Black baseball entrepreneur and executive before 1920. Founder and owner of the Chicago American Giants and prime mover in the formation of the Negro National League. NNL president until his incapacitation by illness.

Gillette, Gary. Creator and co-editor of the *ESPN Baseball Encyclopedia*. Founder and chair of the Friends of Historic Hamtramck Stadium. Former co-chair of SABR's Ballparks and Business of Baseball Committees.

Goode, Mal. Distinguished Black journalist and barrier-breaking broadcaster. Began his career with the *Pittsburgh Courier* in 1948. Member of the original class of the National Association of Black Journalists' Hall of Fame.

Gumbel, Bryant. Emmy Award–winning television journalist and broadcaster and longtime host of HBO's *Real Sports*. Bryant's October 2020 *Real Sports* segment on recognizing the Negro Leagues put additional pressure on MLB to do the right thing.

Hannigan, Pat. Co-author of important early photographic history of the Negro Leagues.

Harris, Charles "Teenie". *Pittsburgh Courier* photojournalist for almost five decades whose portraiture of hundreds of African-American celebrities and ballplayers was impeccable. National Association of Black Journalists Hall of Fame member.

Hauser, Christopher. Author of helpful Negro Leagues chronology.

Heaphy, Leslie. University professor and Negro Leagues historian. Author of Negro Leagues history and editor of the journal *Black Ball* since its founding.

Henderson, Edwin Bancroft "E.B." Educator, coach, player, and member of the Naismith Memorial Basketball Hall of Fame. Author of pre-World War II history, *The Negro in Sports*.

Hogan, Lawrence. History professor and lead author/editor of *Shades of Glory*.

Holway, John. Author of many early books and influential articles on the Negro Leagues. Holway's 1970s and 1980s oral histories were especially important. Original chair of SABR's Negro Leagues Committee in early 1970s.

Irvin, Monte. Superstar Negro Leaguer and Hall of Fame major-leaguer who worked for decades in the Commissioner's office after retiring as a player.

James, Bill. Pioneering baseball analyst and best-selling author. James's inclusion of Black ballplayers in his revised *Historical Abstract* and *Guide to Pitchers* exposed many of his legion of fans to the greatness of Black baseball.

Johnson, Kevin. Longtime SABR Ballparks Committee co-chair, prominent ballparks expert, co-editor of *Green Cathedrals*, 5th ed., and database guru for Seamheads.

Kendrick, Bob. Executive director of Negro Leagues Baseball Museum since 2011; stabilized NLBM's finances and administration during the difficult period following Buck O'Neil's death.

Kleinknecht, Merl. Chair of SABR's Negro Leagues Committee, 1973–1979.

Knorr, Ted. Founder of SABR's visionary annual Jerry Malloy Negro Leagues Conference. Host to the first Malloy Conference in Harrisburg as well as three subsequent Malloy Conferences.

Krock, Jeremy. Founder and director of the Negro League Baseball Grave Marker Project of SABR's Negro Leagues Committee.

Lacy, Sam. Legendary Black sportswriter for the Baltimore *Afro-American* and other papers. First African American to become a member of the Baseball Writers' Association of America (BBWAA) and second winner of the BBWAA's and Hall of Fame's J.G. Taylor Spink Award.

Lester, Larry. Co-founder of NLBM. Author of many works on Black baseball, especially the SABR *Negro Leagues Book* and the history of the East-West Classic. Currently chair and previous co-chair since mid-1980s of SABR's Negro Leagues Committee.

Lanctot, Neil. History professor and author of two of the four most important histories on the development of Black baseball and the Negro Leagues.

Leonard, Buck. Hall of Fame slugger of the Homestead Grays whose long life after baseball made him probably the most recognized face of the Negro Leagues before Buck O'Neil's ascendance.

Lindbergh, Ben. Award-winning journalist whose August 2020 article on TheRinger.com initiated Major League Baseball's reconsideration and ultimate reversal of its long history of discrimination against the Negro Leagues.

Lomax, Michael. University professor and author of two of the four most important histories of the development of Black baseball and the Negro Leagues.

Lowry, Philip J. Editor/author of the watershed *Green Cathedrals* work on ballparks, published by SABR in 1986 and updated four times since. Chair of SABR's Negro Leagues Committee in mid-1980s.

Luke, Bob. Negro League historian and author of Effa Manley biography.

Manley, Effa. The most prominent female executive in Negro Leagues history as well as one of the most outspoken and most incisive.

Mah, Jay-Dell. Canadian journalist and Webmaster of AtthePlate.com, repository of the history of baseball in Western Canada that includes excellent coverage of African-American players in the North. Co-author of biographical dictionary of Black ballplayers in Canada.

Malloy, Jerry. An early author and researcher of Black baseball history, Malloy wrote many important articles and was universally recognized for his unfailing willingness to help other scholars.

MLB Special Records Committee. Convened prior to publication of the first Macmillan baseball encyclopedia to adjudicate fundamental issues in White baseball history, including which leagues constituted official cap-M, cap-L "Major Leagues." Ignorantly failed to even consider the Negro Leagues or any aspect of Black baseball history.

Morelli, Jack. Writer and artist; author of *Heroes of the Negro Leagues*.

Motley, Don. Co-founder of NLBM and its first executive director. Revered amateur baseball coach in Kansas City.

Negro Leagues Committee. One of SABR's founding research committees, the NLC and its cadre of activist chairs and members did more to advance the history of Black baseball and the Negro Leagues than any other organization, especially in the 1970s, 1980s, and 1990s. Still a force half a century after its founding: the depth, scope, and recognition of the Negro Leagues Committee's work is truly astounding.

Nelson, Kadir. Author of *We Are the Ship* and internationally renowned African American artist.

Newman, Roberta. University professor and co-author of *Black Baseball, Black Business*.

Neyer, Rob. Protégé of Bill James and very popular baseball writer in his own right, especially as an early adopter in writing for the Web. Co-author of the *Neyer/James Guide to Pitchers*.

O'Neil, Buck. Co-founder and patron saint of the Negro Leagues Baseball Museum in Kansas City. Famous player and manager of Kansas City Monarchs, 1938–1955. Media darling and the personification of Negro League Baseball after his appearances in Ken Burns 1994 *Baseball* series.

Overmyer, James. Black baseball historian and author of a biography of Cum Posey.

Palmer, Pete. The creator of the gold-standard database underpinning the historical record of traditional Major League Baseball. Palmer was co-editor of both the watershed encyclopedia *Total Baseball* and of the *ESPN Baseball Encyclopedia*.

Peterson, Robert. Journalist who wrote the groundbreaking and best-selling book about the history of Black baseball and the Negro Leagues—the first since Sol White's in 1907.

Peterson, Todd. Negro League historian and editor of *The Negro Leagues Were Major Leagues*, the best collection of evidence and arguments for the equality of the Negro Leagues ever published.

Plott, Arthur. Negro Leagues historian and foremost chronicler of the often overlooked Negro Southern League.

Povich, Shirley. Influential sportswriter, editor, and columnist for 75 years for the *Washington Post*; one of the rare White journalists who wrote about Black baseball.

Ribowsky, Mark. Author of a Josh Gibson biography.

Riley, James. Groundbreaking Black baseball scholar and author of many books; his magnum opus was the *Biographical Encyclopedia of the Negro Baseball Leagues*.

Rogosin, Donn. Public radio/TV executive and author of *Invisible Men*. Writer and co-producer on the important early Negro League documentary *There Was Always Sun Shining Someplace*.

Rosen, Joel. University professor and co-author of *Black Baseball, Black Business*.

Society for American Baseball Research (SABR). Founded in 1971 with its mission as its name, SABR has filled in thousands of gaps in baseball history while correcting tens of thousands of errors in the historical record. It's not a stretch to say that the past 50 years of baseball history are the SABR Era.

SABR Negro Leagues Task Force. Organized in 2020 by SABR president Mark Armour, this task force evaluated the historical record and decided to treat the major Negro Leagues as fully equal to the American and National Leagues. Its decision was independent of MLB's acknowledgment of its historical discrimination against Black baseball and, in meaningful ways, more significant since SABR publishes hundreds of times more historical research than MLB.

Sayama, Kazuo. Japanese baseball historian; author of the original Japanese edition of *Gentle Black Giants* and co-author of the new English edition.

Seymour, Harold. Historian and co-author of the monumental three-volume history of baseball published by Oxford University Press from 1960 to 1990.

Seymour Mills, Dorothy. Historian and originally uncredited co-author with Harold Seymour of the Oxford University Press three-volume history of baseball.

Simkus, Scott. Author of *Outsider's Baseball* and contributor to Seamheads.

Smith, Wendell. Famous African American sportswriter and columnist for the *Pittsburgh Courier* and other papers. First Black writer to win the BBWAA's and National Baseball Hall of Fame's J.G. Taylor Spink Award.

Spivey, Donald. History professor and author of a Satchel Paige biography.

Staples, Bill Jr. Chair of SABR's Asian Baseball Committee and co-author of the English-language edition of *Gentle Black Giants*.

Stivers, Wayne. Negro Leagues researcher and co-author on 2020 revised and updated edition of 1994 *Negro Leagues Book*.

Swanton, Barry. Canadian baseball historian and coach. Co-author of biographical dictionary of Black ballplayers in Canada.

Thorn, John. Editor and publisher of dozens of baseball books, including the influential *Total Baseball* encyclopedia. Official MLB Historian who supported equality for the Negro Leagues.

Tygiel, Jules. Professor of history and author whose 1983 book *Baseball's Great Experiment: Jackie Robinson and His Legacy* became an instant classic and the touchstone on that topic.

White, G. Edward. Law and history professor and author of *Creating the National Pastime*.

White, King Solomon "Sol." Titan of nineteenth century Black baseball as player and entrepreneur. Author of 1907 history of Black baseball. Inducted into Baseball Hall of Fame in 2006 as a pioneer/executive.

Williams, Ted. The superstar slugger and Hall of Famer who made pointedly advocated for the inclusion of Negro Leaguers in his 1966 induction speech in Cooperstown.

Wilson, August. A giant of the American theater whose Pulitzer Prize-winning play *Fences* won four Tony Awards in its 1987 Broadway premiere. *Fences* was the third of Wilson's celebrated American Century Cycle (a/k/a Pittsburgh Cycle) to be written and performed.

Still Standing:
Where to See Extant Negro League Ballparks

by Gary Gillette

The 1948 Negro World Series pitted 41-year-old veteran slugger Buck Leonard and his legendary Homestead Grays against the famous Birmingham Black Barons, featuring exciting 17-year-old rookie Willie Mays. The five-game segregated 1948 Fall Classic, won by the Grays, would be the last hurrah for the Major Negro Leagues (MNL).

Regrettably, almost all home parks of Major Negro League teams from 1920–1948 are now gone, existing mostly in black and white photographs and the graying memories of the remaining fans who saw games there. Yet there are still a handful of places where one can find former Negro League home ballparks. One of them, Rickwood Field, is the oldest professional ballpark still in use today. Two others are in active usage as city recreation venues. Two more are about to be rehabilitated after years of searching for funding.

The honor roll, listed by first year used as a Major Negro League home ballpark:

Rickwood Field in Birmingham, Alabama (1924)
Hamtramck Stadium in Hamtramck, Michigan (1930)
Hinchliffe Stadium in Paterson, New Jersey (1934)
J.P. Small Stadium in Jacksonville, Florida (1938)
League Park in Cleveland (1939)

Why are there so few of these historic venues still standing? The biggest reason is that the United States has little use for former ballparks—big-league or bush-league—whether they were historically associated with Black baseball teams or so-called "Organized Baseball" teams. On the traditional MLB side of the ledger, only Fenway Park and Wrigley Field remain from the first half of the twentieth century. Most big-league ballparks were demolished shortly after their replacement opened, sometimes simply to provide more parking spaces for their adjacent replacement (e.g., Comiskey Park in Chicago and Veterans Stadium in Philadelphia).

On the Major Negro Leagues side of the ledger, most prominent Black teams played in rented quarters, forced to pick their game dates around the schedule of a White minor-league or major-league club. Only a few fortunate Negro League teams owned their own ballparks or enjoyed the benefits of being the primary tenants in their home park.

Baseball fans and historians can rejoice that a few of these segregated fields of dreams survive to this day, and there has been good news in recent years about preserving them. Herewith a brief sketch of each along with links to Web sites with more information and maps of these historic sites.

Rickwood Field

Opened in 1910, Rickwood remains in use as a venue for high school and college baseball. The Double-A Birmingham Barons of the Southern League play one game per year there—the "Rickwood Classic"—as a fundraiser for the Friends of Rickwood, who do a great job with the historic site.

Rickwood was the home of the Birmingham Black Barons from the mid-1920s through 1961, the last season played by the Negro American League (NAL). (The NAL, however, is not considered a major league after 1948.) It was the home park of the minor-league Birmingham Barons of the originally segregated Southern Association and then of the Southern League through 1987.

Because most of Rickwood's historic structure remains and the park is well-maintained, it has been used as a set for the baseball scenes in many period movies, including Ron Shelton's dreadful 1994 flop *Cobb*.

Games in three Negro World Series—1943, 1944, and 1948—were played at Rickwood, with the NAL champion Black Barons losing each series to the dynastic Homestead Grays, champions of the Negro National League (NNL).

Hamtramck Stadium

Hamtramck Stadium opened in 1930 as the new home of the Detroit Stars, who were pushed out of Mack Park by hostile White neighbors on the East Side of Detroit. It was home to the Detroit Stars in the 1930s as well as the powerhouse Detroit Wolves, who played there in 1932 for half a season before folding.

Hamtramck is a small city (two square miles) about four miles northeast of downtown Detroit, surrounded by the City of Detroit. The historic Stadium is on the verge of rebirth, with an announcement expected soon that funding has been secured to rehabilitate the grandstand. The Friends of Historic Hamtramck Stadium restored the infield in 2020 and successfully petitioned Hamtramck City Council to name the field "Turkey Stearnes Field at Historic Hamtramck Stadium."

In 1930, the final three games of the NNL Championship Series were played in Hamtramck, with the Detroit Stars losing to the St. Louis Stars in seven games.

League Park [IV]
(a/k/a Dunn Field)

Opened on the city's East Side in 1910 for Cleveland's American League franchise, which would eventually be nicknamed the "Indians." From 1932 through 1946, the Indians split their home games between League Park in the Hough neighborhood and Municipal (later Cleveland) Stadium on the downtown lakefront. From 1942–1948, the powerful NAL Cleveland Buckeyes also called League Park home, sweeping the Homestead Grays in the 1945 Negro World Series but losing the World Series to the NNL New York Cubans in 1947.

Most of League Park's structure was demolished in 1951, but the two-story ticket and team offices were saved, along with part of the exterior grandstand wall on the first base side. A new community center was added and the park was reopened in 2014 by the City of Cleveland for youth baseball. However, the field was resurfaced with artificial turf. The Cleveland Baseball Heritage Museum maintains a worth-visiting set of exhibits in the former ticket offices. The field is maintained by the Cleveland Department of Parks, Recreation and Properties.

Hinchliffe Stadium

After almost two decades of advocacy and hard work, the Friends of Hinchliffe Stadium hit a grand slam home run this year when ground was broken on the $94 million Hinchliffe Stadium Neighborhood Restoration Project that includes rehabilitation of the huge Art Deco Stadium.

Just west of downtown Paterson, New Jersey, Hinchliffe dramatically sits on a bluff above the Paterson Great Falls National Historical Park and the Falls of the Passaic River. It is owned by the Paterson school district. The enormous venue was built around a 440-yard track like many sports stadia erected after World War I. Because of that design, Hinchliffe was better suited for track and field sports and football than baseball.

Hall of Famer and underappreciated pioneer Larry Doby played high school baseball and football at Hinchliffe. Negro League baseball was played there as well, mostly by the woeful New York Black Yankees in the 1930s. According to Seamheads, the Black Yankees' won-lost percentage for their lifespan was .347. Incredibly, the club was below .300 for the last six years of their existence in the 1940s.

Hinchliffe is a must-see for devotees of the Negro Leagues or baseball history. When rehabilitated, it will represent a monumental achievement although plans call for re-carpeting it with artificial turf.

J.P. Small Memorial Stadium
(a/k/a Red Cap Stadium, Durkee Field, Barrs Field)

Red Cap Stadium was home to the Jacksonville Red Caps in 1938 and the early 1940s. After multiple name changes, it still hosts amateur baseball eight decades later as part of the City of Jacksonville's Recreation Department.

James P. Small Memorial is located just west of downtown Jacksonville in the historic Durkeeville African-American neighborhood.

Criteria

In order to be included in this list, a ballpark must have been the primary home park to a Major Negro League team for at least one season from 1920–1948. Also, a meaningful and representative portion of the historic structure from that period must have survived. Finally, the baseball field must remain, even if fallow or not maintained—or, gasp, covered in artificial turf.

Based on these criteria, only five former Major Negro League ballparks survive today. Three are hosting baseball games today and plans for restoring the other two are underway. All are listed on the National Register of Historic Places.

Aside from these five Fields of Dreams, portions remain of a few other former MNL ballparks that are worth noting and worth visiting.

Bush Stadium in Indianapolis
(a/k/a Perry Stadium and Victory Field [I])

Originally known as Perry Stadium, it was home to the Indianapolis ABCs in the early 1930s, the Indianapolis Clowns in the late 1930s and 1940s, the 1937 Indianapolis Athletics, and the 1940 Indianapolis Crawfords. Several Negro League clubs from other cities also used Perry as their home parks for a season or part of a season, including Cole's (Chicago) American Giants and the Cleveland Buckeyes.

The exterior facade of the Bush Stadium grandstand was nicely rehabilitated in 2013 when the structure was converted into a residential complex called the Stadium Lofts. Unfortunately, though, the remainder of the grandstand was demolished and part of the infield was covered in concrete. A portion of the brick outfield wall also remains standing.

Cramton Bowl in Montgomery, Alabama

One of the two home fields for the Montgomery Grey Sox of the Negro Southern League in 1932, most of the historic structure was demolished during 2011 renovations. Now only a portion of the first base–side grandstand from the baseball park remains. Cramton Bowl was designed for football and the gridiron there remains in use today.

Stars Park in St. Louis

Regrettably, none of the structure of Stars Park remains, but the HBCU Harris-Stowe State University baseball team still plays on the site. Parts of the 1928 and 1930 NNL Championship Series were played here, and the storied St. Louis Stars also won the 1931 NNL pennant playing here.

Author Note: Gary Gillette is the founder and chair of the Friends of Historic Hamtramck Stadium and former co-chair of SABR's Ballparks Committee.

The Long Road to Jackie Robinson: Nineteenth Century Pioneers in Black Ball

by Ryan Swanson

For two weeks during the summer of 1870, Charles Douglass and his Washington DC Mutual Base Ball Club might as well have been the '27 New York Yankees. Or the '31 Homestead Grays. Either way, they dominated.

What started out as a friendly exhibition trip turned into baseball tour de force. The Mutuals played eight games on the trip and won them all. Among their lopsided victories, the club defeated the Baltimore Enterprise 52 to 23, the Lockport New York Artic Club 26 to 0, the Rapids Club of Niagara Falls 64 to 10, and the Mutuals of Buffalo 72 to 10. Only a Rochester All Star team offered any sort of challenge (23 to 19). The results caught the attention of the *New York Clipper,* baseball's preeminent newspaper, who referred to them as "The Mutuals, of Washington—a colored club—recently on a tour through the western part of the state of New York."

For Charles Douglass, the tour provided validation. He, too, could organize and promote and fight for opportunity. He, too, could win. Just like his famous father, Frederick Douglass.

Charles was born in 1844, the third son of Frederick and Anna Douglass. He grew up in upstate New York. In 1863, Charles joined the famous, all-Black Massachusetts Fifty-Fourth Regiment. Illness, however, kept him from seeing much action during the Civil War. After the war ended, Charles settled in Washington, DC. There he joined the throngs of former soldiers looking for employment in the ballooning federal government. For Charles—married, father of seven, son of one of the most important African American leaders of the nineteenth century—baseball became an outlet and platform.

Douglass played the infield (mostly second base) and served as a club officer with the Washington Alert Base Ball Club. In 1868, he switched to the Washington DC Mutual Club. Both clubs, as was the case for all Black baseball clubs, operated in a perilous athletic environment. They negotiated for field time. They foraged for dues in order to pay for bats and balls. And they fought for respect among their baseball peers.

During this post-Civil War period, there is no evidence of Black ballplayers clamoring to join White baseball clubs.

A strange mix of racial integration and separation paralyzed the United States immediately after the Civil War. Clearly, the Reconstruction era meant new possibilities and promises. The Freedman's Bureau, the Civil Rights Act, and the 13th through 15th Amendments made it obvious that slavery was done. The cruel institution would take no more American lives. But figuring out how the new realities of Reconstruction translated to everyday life was complicated. Charles Douglass and several other Black DC ballplayers, for example, worked in the racially integrated Treasury Department. Why then was the feared Third Auditors Office baseball nine reserved just for White men? Didn't Reconstruction extend to the ballfield?

Baseball boomed in the United States during the middle of the nineteenth century. Clubs formed by the hundreds. Teams popped up in urban areas especially, playing wherever they could find space. In Washington, DC, Black and White baseball clubs (including Charles Douglass's teams) enjoyed playing on the White Lot, a baseball field just South of the White House. The game grew in fits and starts. It almost always reflected the tensions of the times rather than transcending them. Baseball club names—the Confederate Club, the Robert E. Lee Club, the Secesh Base Ball Club, and the Ku Klux Klan Base Ball Clubs in the 1870s for example—made it clear that elements of White supremacy were never far from the game.

Then as now, baseball had a northeastern bias—the number of baseball clubs in nineteenth century New York City and Boston dwarfed that of other cities. But the game's development had no strict geographical boundaries. Clubs organized and played in urban and rural areas, and in the former Confederacy and the states of the Union.

In a nation that defined race primarily on Black and White terms, the fact that African American clubs rose up quickly was significant. The ballot, education, and land were preeminent concerns for Black Americans, yes, but so too was finding community and recreation. Baseball fit. One of the first games of baseball on record involving Black teams had occurred in New York City in 1859. The Henson Club defeated the Unknown Club, 54–43. From there, the number of Black clubs increased steadily. This growth created animosity among White ballplayers. When the press reported on games involving Black players, they often did so with only thinly veiled racism. The *Brooklyn Eagle,* a baseball-crazy newspaper, for example, said of an 1862 contest: "The dusky contestants enjoyed the game hugely, and to use a common phrase, they 'did the thing genteelly."

Baseball itself in the nineteenth century still had unresolved issues. Fundamental rules were in flux. Debates ensued, for example, over whether pitchers should be allowed to throw overhand, if a ball caught on the bounce should count as an out, and if hitting a baserunner with the ball ("soaking" the runner) should be allowed. The game featured the core competitive elements that baseball fans know today—pitcher versus batter, runner versus fielders, etc.—but without the finer details ironed out.

The National Association of Base Ball Players was founded in 1857. The group oversaw the game's early years and then its surge in popularity following the war. At the 1865 NABBP Convention in New York City on December 14, 1865, delegates altered the existing rules to state, for example, that a fair ball only resulted in an out if "caught without having touched the ground." Further, the Conventioneers made some effort at controlling who could play and under what circumstances. "In playing all matches," Sec 29 of the NABBP rules read, "nine players from each club shall constitute a full field, and they must have been regular members of the club which they represent, and of no other club… for thirty days prior to the match."

For the first few years following the Civil War, no official policy or precedent existed governing the relationships between Black and White baseball players.

Charles Douglass had a compatriot in Philadelphia: Octavius Catto. Catto played second base for the Pythians, the premier Black baseball club in Philadelphia during the 1860s and 70s. Like Douglass, Catto did his most important baseball work off the field. Catto fielded balls and hit well enough, but it was as an administrator and promoter of the club that Catto shined. For Catto, the Pythians made up just one part of a burgeoning portfolio of activism. Catto taught at the Banneker Institute, fought for the desegregation of Philadelphia's street cars, and served as a member of the Pennsylvania Equal Rights League. And he played baseball.

In the summer of 1867, the two men's clubs met on the ballfield. First, Catto and the Pythians played host. "We have secured the grounds of the Athletic Base Ball Club and all conveniences (the best in the city) have been put at our disposal," Catto wrote to his DC counterparts prior to the game. Then, a few weeks later, the Pythians traveled to DC for a rematch. For the reception after the contest in Washington, DC, Douglass organized a lavish picnic. His father contributed five dollars to the effort.

The 1867 season ended in disappointment for the Pythians and for Black baseball more broadly. This disappointment stemmed not from anything that happened on the field, but rather due to a bureaucratic decision. In October 1867, the Pythians sent a club delegate—Raymond Burr—to Harrisburg, Pennsylvania, in order to petition for official membership in the Pennsylvania Association of Base Ball Players (PABBP). This organization served as a regional arm of the National Association of Base Ball Players.

Certainly, the Pythians had a case to make. The club had just completed a successful season, winning the majority of its games. The club featured a full roster of dues-paying members. It had a suitably hierarchical slate of officers. The Pythians could even point to friendly relations with the leadership of the

Philadelphia Athletics, the most prominent of the state's White baseball clubs. A's President Hicks Hayhurst occasionally umpired Pythians games.

None of this mattered to the leadership of the PABBP. Genial, non-committal support was one thing; official recognition was quite another. The Pythians application for membership caused an immediate stir. While the Nominating Committee usually rubberstamped all applications (after all, the goal was to grow the membership ranks as quickly as possible), it set the Pythians' application aside. Burr noticed the tension growing in the room. He also realized that a vast gulf existed between the personal sympathies of his White counterparts and their willingness to take any sort of stand for the Pythians.

"The members of the convention clustered around your delegate," Burr wrote in his report back to the Pythian Club. "Whilst all expressed sympathy for our club, a few only…expressed a willingness to vote for our admission."

In the end, the White club representatives forced Burr to retreat. "As there seemed no chance for anything but being black balled," Burr wrote, "your delegate withdrew his application."

Thus, in a courthouse in Harrisburg on a cool October day in 1867, the PABBP laid the foundational stone in baseball's racial segregation.

Two months later, the National Association extended the racial demarcation line. The NABBP's nominating committee issued a statement on what clubs might apply for membership. "It is not presumed by your committee that any club who have applied are composed of persons of color, or any portion of them; an the recommendation of your Committee in this report are based upon this view, and they unanimously report against the admission of any club which may be composed of one or more colored persons." With the decision, baseball became officially segregated. The "National Pastime" shut its doors to the likes of Charles Douglass and Octavius Catto.

Four years later, Catto was murdered on his way to vote in Philadelphia.

⌒

When the National Association of *Professional* Base Ball Players formed in 1871, it did so building upon the Whites-only precedents already in place. Then, in 1876, the National League organized and followed suit. Professionalization only solidified the separation that had been established between White and Black clubs.

Historians sometimes argue about whether it was by de facto or de Jure segregation—by custom or by law—that America's Jim Crow landscape emerged. The answer, of course, is both. For baseball it all ended with the same result. As *Sporting Life* would report, "Nothing is ever said or written about drawing the color line in the [National] League. It appears to be generally understood that none but Whites shall make up the League teams, and so it goes."

Indeed, and so it went.

Practically speaking, finding field space became increasingly difficult for

Black teams. In Washington, DC, city officials closed the White Lot—a mecca for baseball activity in the District—to Black baseball clubs in 1873. "The White Lot has been closed to all ball players except the Creightons," the *Washington Herald* reported. The reason? "The gangs of lazy negroes and other vagrants infesting the grounds made this action necessary."

The White Lot closure coincided with Charles Douglass' retirement as a ballplayer and baseball club organizer. While creeping middle age probably had something to do with his leaving the diamond, the increasingly racist undertones of so-called national pastime may have as well.

The second generation of Black baseball players and leaders was noticeably thinner than the first.

Those Black men that were needed to replace the likes of Charles Douglass and Octavius Catto faced nearly insurmountable opposition during the last decades of the nineteenth century. Plessy v. Ferguson America made organizing a baseball game among Black men a Herculean task.

But Black baseball always persisted.

Black clubs played throughout the United States during the early years of the twentieth century. They secured games wherever and with whomever possible, including exhibitions with White clubs. Individual players probed at the rigid segregation of Major League Baseball. Moses Fleetwood Walker, Weldy Walker, Bud Fowler and William Edward White, among others, pushed the boundaries. They faced virulent racism in return. "My skin is against me," Fowler said. "If I had not been quite so black, I might have caught on as a Spaniard or something of that kind. The race prejudice is so strong that my black skin barred me."

Bud Fowler

The Cuban Giants organized out of Long Island and played, off and on, from 1885 until 1914. In doing so, the club created a mechanism by which to pay Black men (even if they were called "Cuban" to the press) to play high level baseball. Most historians refer to the Cuban Giants as the first professional Black baseball club. One member of the Giants, Sol White, became the preeminent historian of early Black baseball. Such accomplishments in the face of ever-escalating resistance must be appreciated as acts of persistence and social rebellion. These players and teams, from Douglass and Catto to the Cuban Giants, paved the way for the Negro Leagues.

And what, finally, about the Negro Leagues? Rebuking the racist decisions of 1867 and the "Gentleman's Agreement" of MLB owners—to say nothing of the intolerable realities of Jim Crow America more generally—the Negro Leagues emerged in earnest in 1920. Rube Foster guided the creation of the Negro National League. The Eastern Colored League later formed as worthy rival. Other circuits came and went. Far from accepting the inequities of the time, these teams and players involved pursued opportunity and autonomy. The clubs were successful Black-owned businesses. The biggest Negro Leagues stars rivaled anything that Major League Baseball could offer. Josh Gibson. Satchel Paige. Oscar Charleston. Monte Irvin. Cool Papa Bell. Buck Leonard. Smokey Joe Williams. The list goes on and on.

When Jackie Robinson broke the National League's color line in 1947, he had the opportunity to be a trailblazer because of the Black ballplayers that had preserved and grown the game over the previous ninety years. Charles Douglass had died just months after Jackie Robinson was born. The two, of course, never knew each other, but a torch had been passed nonetheless. From Douglass to Robinson, Black baseball established a stronghold in America's sporting landscape and by doing so changed the very fabric of the nation.

Latinos in the Negro Leagues

by Adrian Burgos, Jr.

W*e are the Ship, All Else is the Sea*, was a motto Negro National League (NNL) founder Rube Foster used describe the Black baseball enterprise. The NNL's successful launch in 1920 was not Foster's first attempt at organizing a national league. Several of his earlier attempts included teams composed of Cuban players. The Negro Leagues he envisioned was inclusive of Black men from across the Americas, drawing talent from Cuba and eventually from the Dominican Republic, Puerto Rico, Venezuela, Mexico, and elsewhere in Latin America.

That Latino inclusion was part of Foster's vision for Black baseball in the United States has often been underplayed in accounts of Negro League history. Latinos were not an afterthought in the Black baseball enterprise. Foster envisioned Latinos as part of the ship; To him, Latin America was not a far off land in the sea that the ship would have to navigate to arrive at its destination.

Latinos were present at the formal organization of the Negro Leagues. Their impact would be immediate on the playing field with Cubans José Méndez, Cristobal Torriente, and Bartolo Portuondo starring in the NNL in 1920. Shortly thereafter, Latinos began making contributions as managers, team owners, and league officials, aiding in the expansion of the circuit's fan base, talent pool, and impact within the baseball world.

The Making of Cuban and Latino Stars

Talent alone would not determine a successful transition for Latinos in the world Jim Crow made, however. Stardom in Caribbean or Latin American leagues did not automatically translate into success in the Negro Leagues. Success hinged not only on matching the quality of play in the Black baseball circuit, but also meeting the challenge of cultural adjustment. Jim Crow laws and discriminatory racial practices that players were unfamiliar with in their native lands made playing professionally in the United States much more stressful than playing in Latin America. The Negro Leagues were therefore a proving ground, not just of their baseball talent but also their mental fortitude.

Martin Dihigo encountered these challenges of on- and off-the-field adjustments in 1923 as an 18-year-old with Alex Pompez's Cuban Stars in the Eastern Colored League (ECL). The Cuban native developed into a star: a triple threat who could defeat opponents with his bat, his baseball intelligence in the field or on the basepaths, or as a pitching ace. His offensive prowess, stalwart pitching, and versatility would result in Dihigo becoming one of the original nine Negro Leaguers elected to the National Baseball Hall of Fame. Along with the distinction of being the first Latino from the Negro Leagues enshrined in Cooperstown, Dihigo's success in other professional leagues

Martin Dihigo

during his baseball journeys would result in his induction into halls of fame in Cuba, the Dominican Republic, Mexico, and Venezuela.

Not everyone who came north to play in the Negro Leagues enjoyed the kind of success that Dihigo did, of course. Nonetheless, it was in the Negro Leagues that Latinos found their greatest opportunities to have an impact on professional baseball in the United States during the era of affiliated baseball's color line.

Latino Roots in the Negro Leagues

Latino participation in Black baseball predated formal organization of the NNL. Cubans came first, playing on the All Cubans and Cuban Stars in the 1900s. A decade later, Cuban baseball teams were regular participants in the Black baseball circuit that operated between May and September. By the 1916 season, two teams were playing in the circuit under the Cuban Stars name—baseball historians would later designate them as Cuban Stars West and Cuban Stars East although contemporaries did not use such designations.

Cuban baseball entrepreneur Abel Linares—who had been bringing Cuban teams since the early 1900s—operated his Cuban Stars out of the Midwest (primarily Chicago and Cincinnati). Pompez ran his team out of New York City. The two squads faced off in San Juan, Puerto Rico, early in 1916. Advertisement hailed the battle as one for the legitimate claim to the Cuban Stars name. Pompez's newly formed team defeated Linares' veteran squad. Linares demanded a rematch. Pompez declined. His Cuban Stars had to set sail for New York for the start of its inaugural season in Black baseball.

The "Cuban presence" in Black baseball came even earlier than the arrival of these pre-Negro League teams from Cuba. One of the earliest Black baseball teams to gain wide attention was the Cuban Giants of the 1880s. Managed by S.K. Govern, the team entertained guests at hotels from Babylon, Long Island, down to the Breakers in Palm Beach, Florida, before becoming a fixture of the professional scene in the late 1880s.

The Cuban Giants had no Cuban-born players or Latinos for that matter, but rather its roster was composed of African American players. The team did play on a fact increasingly known among some baseball insiders: Cubans, who ranged from light- to dark-skinned in appearance, played baseball in their native island and had also played at colleges and prep schools across the Northeast and Southern US by the early 1880s. In fact, Cuban native Esteban "Steve" Bellán had already performed at the highest level of professional baseball in the States, playing in the National Association from 1871 to 1873. Even more, Cubans could be called the "apostles of baseball" for the manner in which they spread baseball wherever they migrated to during and between the three wars for independence on the island from the 1870s through the 1890s. By the time Cuba finally won its independence in 1898, baseball was already established as the Cuban national game.

Rube Foster knew about the passion for baseball among Cubans firsthand. In 1906, the Cuban professional league provided Foster an early experience in playing racially-integrated professional baseball. He witnessed Afro-Cuban ballplayers excel in the Cuban circuit. Cuban team owners operating their own league also inspired Foster. The Texas native's efforts to organize a national league for Black professional teams in the United States thereafter would typically include a Cuban team.

Latinos *Presente*

All Latinos were welcome in the Negro Leagues based on their talent and not on the basis of their skin color or racial identity. This practice was largely the result of the early Cuban Stars teams operated by Linares and Pompez, respectively. Initially they filled their rosters with talent from the Cuban league which operated as a racially integrated league. Expansion into other parts of the Caribbean and Latin America continued this practice of Negro League executives signing any Latino believed to possess the ability to make the grade in the Black baseball circuit.

The Black leagues formed after the NNL, such as the Eastern Colored League (1923-28) and the Negro American League (1937-50), would often feature teams whose roster had strong representation of Latino players. Teams like the Indianapolis Clowns, Kansas City Monarchs, and Birmingham Black Barons would join the Cuban Stars teams in drawing talent from across the Caribbean and Latin America. Collectively, these teams made the Negro Leagues a refuge for Latino players pursuing their professional baseball careers in the United States.

Latinos achieved many firsts in the US professional scene in the Negro Leagues. Latinos served as managers, team owners, and league officials in the Negro Leagues decades before these opportunities were opened to them in MLB. Cuban-native José Méndez guided the Monarchs to multiple championships as the team's player-manager in the mid-1920s. The Cuban-American Pompez made his impact as a team owner from 1916 to 1948, expanding the Negro Leagues' talent pool and helping to organize the first Negro League World Series (1924) and also East-West Classic games hosted in New York in the 1940s.

Pompez led the way in internationalizing Latino talent in the Negro Leagues. Over his four decades in the Negro Leagues, the Florida native introduced players from the Dominican Republic, Venezuela, Puerto Rico, and Panama. In so doing, he widened the reach of the Negro Leagues decades before MLB successfully scouted and developed talent from these areas. Notably, Pompez constructed a talent pipeline from the Dominican Republic in the 1930s; he later connected this pipeline to the newly desegregated major leagues in the 1950s as a scouting official for the New York/San Francisco Giants. Just as significant, familiarity with racial norms and social customs as the bilingual son of Cuban émigrés enabled Pompez to aide Latino players in their adjustment to playing professionally in Jim Crow America.

Latinos and MLB's Color Line

The Negro Leagues were where the majority of Latinos were able to perform as players, become team managers, and even umpire while the affiliated baseball color line and Jim Crow limited these opportunities throughout organized baseball. Indeed, while just over 50 foreign-born and US born Latinos played in the American and National Leagues from 1902 through Jackie Robinson's breaking of the color line in 1947, well over 240 Latinos participated in the Black baseball circuit during that same span.

Welcoming all Latinos meant that a few players originally signed by Negro Leagues teams could potentially traverse across the color line into so-called "organized baseball" and possibly the White major leagues. While Afro-Latinos encountered many of the same barriers that African Americans did, the racial ambiguity of lighter-skinned Latinos created a potential opening.

Pedro Dibut pitched for the NNL's Cuban Stars in 1923. In the following two seasons, the Cuban-born pitcher played on the Cincinnati Reds in the National League. Fellow Cuban Oscar Estrada also made the journey from the Negro Leagues to the American League, going from the ECL's Cuban Stars where he played as a two-way player in 1924 and 1925 to playing in the minor leagues and then appearing with the St. Louis Browns in 1929. A couple of Latino players even crossed the color line in the other direction. Sal "Chico"

Hernández caught for the Chicago Cubs in 1942 and 1943 before appearing with the Indianapolis Clowns in 1945. Isidore "Izzy" Leon pitched for the 1945 Philadelphia Phillies. Three seasons later, he was pitching for the New York Cubans in the Negro Leagues.

Moving across the color line involved a combination of talent level and racial ambiguity. Major-league team officials and owners like Clark Griffith would make the case that these players were Cuban and, therefore, not Black. Manipulation of racial understandings thus permitted a select group of Latinos into White affiliated baseball, while affirming the central purpose of its color line, excluding Black players.

Latino Legacy of the Negro Leagues

A significant part of the legacy of the Negro Leagues is the preparation it gave to Latinos who would participate in the racial integration of White baseball. On the same playing fields where African American greats like Monte Irvin, Roy Campanella, and Jackie Robinson performed in the Negro Leagues, Latinos such as Orestes Miñoso, Patricio "Pat" Scantlebury, and Rafael "Ray" Noble who would later perform in the integrated major leagues. These men were part of the bridge generation that brought baseball from its segregated era to its integrated era.

Miñoso easily ranked among the more talented players Pompez signed for his New York Cubans. Miñoso starred as the Cubans' starting third baseman from 1946 to 1948, appearing in East-West Classic games in 1947 and 1948. Black sportswriters lauded his playing abilities and suggested him as a potential player for a MLB club to sign as a pioneering Black player. The Cleveland Indians acquired Miñoso from the New York Cubans after the 1948 season. Miñoso would appear with Cleveland in 1949 as the first Afro-Latino in the bigs. In so doing, Miñoso joined a growing contingent of talented Black players developed by Negro League teams who would become integration pioneers in MLB.

One legacy of Latinos in the Negro Leagues is the powerful stories and memories players have shared about their experience in Black baseball. African American and Latinos developed different tactics to combat Jim Crow and racial discrimination in ways big and small. Afro-Cuban Armando Vázquez recounted how he sometimes would accentuate his Spanish accent when speaking English to convince restaurants that refused to serve "Negroes" to allow this "foreigner" to order food—while his Negro League teammates waited on this bus. This was just one of countless stories that captured ways Latinos and African Americans dealt with life in Jim Crow America.

Understanding the legacy of Latinos in the Negro Leagues illuminates the different paths available to one generation of Latinos compared to the ones that followed. Revisiting this history allows us to learn lesser known stories, such as the Chacón family from Venezuela: Pelayo Chacón first played and later managed Pompez's Cuban Stars in the Negro Leagues while his son Elio Chacón would play for the Cincinnati Reds and New York Mets in the early 1960s. It also permits us to know more fully the story of the two Luis Tiants. Both were pitching aces: the father a left-hander who starred in the Negro Leagues with the Cuban Stars and New York Cubans from 1930 through 1947. Yet his experience of dealing with Jim Crow and racial discrimination led him to discourage his son from pursuing professional baseball in the United States. Nevertheless, the younger Luis Tiant persisted and would put together a career that made him forever a fan favorite with the Boston Red Sox.

What the younger Tiant and Hall of Famer Orlando Cepeda—whose father, Pedro "Perucho" Cepeda, played with Negro League greats Josh Gibson and Satchel Paige in the Puerto Rican league—knew, and what we now recognize more fully, is that ballplayers in the Negro Leagues were always major league. Equally significant, the Negro Leagues are a key part of Latino baseball history, partly because Latinos were part of what Rube Foster had envisioned for Black baseball from the founding of the formal Negro Leagues.

The Major Negro Leagues

by Adam Darowski

At this time, Baseball Reference, SABR's Negro Leagues Task Force, and Major League Baseball are all in agreement as to which leagues currently carry the designation "major." SABR commented on the process used:

> The group's criteria in determining major-league status was: a league of high quality, containing a large number of the best available baseball players, with a defined set of teams and a defined roster of players. Teams should have played a set schedule, with the league maintaining standings and records, some of which may no longer be available.

The seven major leagues are:

NNL: Negro National League I (1920-1931)

- Formed by Rube Foster of the Chicago American Giants.
- Folded after 1931 due to financial difficulties caused by the Great Depression.
- 19 Hall of Famers: Cool Papa Bell, Oscar Charleston, Andy Cooper, Bill Foster, Rube Foster (manager/executive), Josh Gibson, Pete Hill, John Henry Lloyd, Biz Mackey, José Méndez, Satchel Paige, Bullet Rogan, Turkey Stearnes, Mule Suttles, Ben Taylor, Cristóbal Torriente, Willie Wells, Sol White (manager), J.L. Wilkinson (executive).

ECL: Eastern Colored League (1923-1928)

- Formed by Ed Bolden of the Hilldale Club to rival the Negro National League.
- From 1924 to 1927, the ECL pennant winner would face the NNL's pennant winner in the Colored World Series.
- The league started the 1928 season, but disbanded in the spring.
- 11 Hall of Famers: Oscar Charleston, Martín Dihigo, Pete Hill, Judy Johnson, John Henry Lloyd, Biz Mackey, Alex Pompez (executive), Louis Santop, Ben Taylor, Joe Williams, Jud Wilson.

ANL: American Negro League (1929)

- Formed for the 1929 season from five ECL teams—Baltimore Black Sox, New York Lincoln Giants, Hilldale Club, Cuban Stars East, and Atlantic City Bacharach Giants. They were joined by the independent Homestead Grays.
- The league lasted only a single season.
- 10 Hall of Famers: Oscar Charleston, Martín Dihigo, Judy Johnson, John Henry Lloyd, Biz Mackey, Alex Pompez (executive), Cum Posey (manager/executive), Ben Taylor, Joe Williams, Jud Wilson.

NSL: Negro Southern League (1932)

- In 1932, the Chicago American Giants, Indianapolis ABCs, and Louisville Black Caps moved to the NSL (joining a few other teams that had previously played in the NNL).
- Operated (off and on) from 1920 to 1951, but was only considered a major league in 1932.
- 4 Hall of Famers: Bill Foster, Hilton Smith, Turkey Stearnes, Cristóbal Torriente.

EWL: East-West League (1932)

- Formed by Cum Posey of the Homestead Grays.
- The league folded before the end of the season without a champion.
- 8 Hall of Famers: Cool Papa Bell, Ray Brown, Judy Johnson, Cum Posey (manager/executive), Mule Suttles, Willie Wells, Joe Williams, Jud Wilson.

NN2: Negro National League II (1933-1948)

- Formed by Gus Greenlee of the Pittsburgh Crawfords.
- Drew teams from both the East-West League (Homestead Grays, Baltimore Black Sox) and Negro Southern League (Chicago American Giants, Nashville Elite Giants, Indianapolis ABCs).
- East-West All Star Game begins in 1933.
- 19 Hall of Famers: Cool Papa Bell, Ray Brown, Roy Campanella, Oscar Charleston, Ray Dandridge, Leon Day, Martín Dihigo, Larry Doby, Bill Foster, Josh Gibson, Biz Mackey, Effa Manley (executive), Satchel Paige, Alex Pompez (executive), Cum Posey (manager/executive), Turkey Stearnes, Mule Suttles, Willie Wells, Jud Wilson.

NAL: Negro American League (1937-1948)

- The NNL became an eastern league as the Kansas City Monarchs and Chicago American Giants joined the new NAL.
- The pennant winner faced the NN2's pennant winner in the Negro World Series from 1942 to 1948.
- The league continued to operate through the 1961 season, folding in early 1962. It was only considered a major league through the 1948 season when many top players were signed by National and American League teams.
- 17 Hall of Famers: Cool Papa Bell, Ray Brown, Willard Brown, Oscar Charleston, Andy Cooper, Bill Foster, Monte Irvin, Judy Johnson, Buck Leonard, Willie Mays, Satchel Paige, Jackie Robinson, Bullet Rogan, Hilton Smith, Turkey Stearnes, Willie Wells, J.L. Wilkinson (executive).

The addition of these leagues greatly enriches our coverage of baseball history, but it is important to consider what is not included with these seven leagues:

- Henry Aaron and Ernie Banks: because they played in the Negro American League after 1948. We will not have a new all-time home run king.
- Toni Stone, Mamie "Peanut" Johnson, and Connie Morgan: because they played in the Negro American League after 1948.
- Independent clubs such as the legendary 1931 Homestead Grays and 1932–36 Kansas City Monarchs: because they were not affiliated with an official league.

Much of the history of (and statistics for) Black baseball live outside not only the 1920 to 1948 era but also outside the seven leagues. Our statistical records for players are far from complete for a variety of reasons. For example:

- Some players are missing seasons because they played where the money was. In 1935, Satchel Paige, Ted Redcliffe and Hilton Smith played for an integrated semipro team in Bismarck, ND. In 1937, Josh Gibson, Paige, Cool Papa Bell, and other Negro League stars played for Ciudad Trujillo in the Dominican Republic. Additionally, top players such as Martín Dihigo, Gibson, and Willie Wells found it more lucrative to play in Mexico.
- Our data shows just 6 major league wins and 69 strikeouts for legendary pitcher John Donaldson, but researchers have uncovered 413 wins and 5,091 strikeouts in a career that lasted from 1908 to 1940. Donaldson, the ultimate barnstormer, pitched for anyone—from famous teams like the Kansas City Monarchs to semipro teams in Minnesota or Saskatchewan.

- Similarly, our data shows a mere fraction of the "almost 800 home runs" cited on Josh Gibson's Hall of Fame plaque. The larger number includes his total in the major leagues, but also for independent teams, in foreign and winter leagues, as well as in exhibitions.

The SABR task force will continue researching additional leagues and teams from baseball's segregated era, including from before 1920 and after 1948, along with other top-level independent Black teams of the 1930s, which frequently played against White major-league players and teams. Some Black baseball teams were forced to operate independently in order to survive, as the color barrier enacted by White officials both necessitated the Negro Leagues' existence and later led to their demise.

Baseball Reference will keep a watchful eye on these developments and update the site's online coverage where appropriate.

The Negro Leagues Revisited

by Jules Tygiel

Those of us who discovered baseball during our formative years in the 1950s confronted a paradox which our youthful minds could not quite appreciate. We knew of Jackie Robinson and his heroic efforts to end segregation, and we gloried in the achievements of Black players, who only a decade earlier could never have appeared in a big league game. Yet we had no sense of where the Roy Campanellas and Don Newcombes, the Larry Dobys and Monte Irvins, had learned their craft and polished their skills while awaiting the call of the majors. For most of us, these players had materialized out of thin air, sent by the gods of baseball to thrill and delight and to usher in a golden age of brotherhood and base stealing. That there had once existed a flourishing domain in America known as the Negro Leagues had been instantly forgotten. To know that several such teams still struggled on the margins of the national pastime would have greatly surprised us.

Thus, the Negro Leagues, "invisible" during their best years, almost totally disappeared from American memory in the 1950s and 1960s. Even in the Black community, baseball fans savored the hard-won fruits of integration and turned their gaze away from the legacy of Black baseball. "The big league doors suddenly opened one day," wrote sportswriter Wendell Smith, "and when Negro players walked in, Negro baseball walked out." Not until 1970, when Robert Peterson published his path-breaking *Only the Ball Was White*, did the veil that had dropped over the Negro Leagues begin to lift. Today [1986 -Ed.], while the stars of Black baseball remain under-represented in the Hall of Fame, they have received a far fairer share of attention in the literature of the 1970s and 1980s, giving us a broad appreciation of the role of the Negro Leagues in baseball history and in the culture and community they served.

Nowhere is the neglect of the Negro Leagues more apparent than in the two primary academic histories of baseball. Both Harold Seymour and David Voigt in their multi-volume studies deal briefly with the exclusion of Black players in the 1880s. Black ballplayers then disappear from both narratives, reappearing again only in Volume III of Voigt's work in a brief prelude to the Robinson saga. The Negro Leagues fared no better in accounts of baseball integration. Most biographies of Robinson written in the 1950s, including Robinson's own *Wait Till Next Year*, co-authored with Carl Rowan, mention his stint with the Kansas City Monarchs, but provide few details other than a critique of the heavy travel schedule and loose style of play.

Those determined to learn more about the Negro Leagues in the 1950s and 1960s had to search diligently. The standard work on the topic was Sol White's *Official Baseball Guide*. White, a former professional player, chronicled the nineteenth century travails of Blacks in organized baseball, their ultimate exclusion, and the formation of the early Black barnstorming clubs. But White's book, originally published in 1907, had long since passed out of print. (Camden House in South Carolina reissued this classic in 1983.)

Brief glimpses of life in the Negro Leagues could be found in at least two of the books about the first Black players to cross baseball's color line. Although "Doc" Young's 1953 volume, *Great Negro Baseball Stars And How They Made the Major Leagues*, focused primarily on those players who had advanced from the Negro Leagues into the majors, chapters on the Black stars of the pre-integration era and those in the minor leagues offered insightful information. A skillful, perceptive writer whose talents rank him with Wendell Smith and Sam Lacy, the deans of Black sportswriting, Young provided an introduction to the stars, if not the world, of Black baseball. In 1964 Jackie Robinson provided another overview of the integration process in *Baseball Has Done It*. This wonderfully revealing collection of interviews with Black major leaguers also included reminiscences by Negro League stars Terris McDuffie and Bill Yancey.

Player autobiographies offered other information on Black baseball. Roy Campanella's *It's Good To Be Alive* (1959) gave one of the best accounts of life in the Negro Leagues. Campanella chronicled his discovery by the Bacharach Giants as a 15-year-old prospect, his later career with the Baltimore Elite Giants, and his apprenticeship as a catcher under the tutelage of Biz Mackey. Campanella's account, still fascinating reading, introduces the reader to barnstorming in the United States and winter ball in the Carribean. Intermingled with the interminable travels and poor accommodations was the special amalgam—power and speed, "spitballs, shine balls, and emery balls"—which characterized Negro League play. Campanella's frustrations of being relegated to a Jim Crow league are evident, yet he concludes, "A Negro ballplayer playing ball in the United States might not have lived like a king, but he didn't live bad either."

Far less enlightening is Satchel Paige's autobiographical effort, *Maybe I'll Pitch Forever*, published in 1962. Paige's legendary reputation had always transcended the Negro Leagues and his brief, but successful, major league stint had firmly fixed him in the public mind. Writing in a folksy style, fully in keeping with the image he had long cultivated, Paige and co-author David Lipman dwelled more on the pitcher's skills, eccentricities, and exploits than Black baseball itself. Nonetheless, the weak administrative structure of the Negro Leagues and the team-hopping habits of the players are readily apparent.

For the remainder of the sixties, books about the Negro Leagues or books even mentioning the era of Black baseball, remained rare. Both Willie Mays and Hank Aaron devoted a few pages to their brief tenures with the Birmingham Black Barons and Indianapolis Clowns respectively in their early autobiographies *Willie Mays: My Life In and Out of Baseball* (1966) and *Aaron, r.f.* (1968). Jack Orr included a chapter on the Negro Leagues in *The Black Athlete* in 1969. Little existed to sate the curiosity of those who remembered Black baseball or younger people who had seen references to it.

The long drought came to an end in 1970 with the publication of Peterson's *Only the Ball Was White*. Poring over Black newspapers and interviewing former players, Peterson painstakingly pieced together the history of Blacks in baseball from the days of Bud Fowler, a nineteenth-century second baseman, to Jackie Robinson's historic breakthrough. Peterson introduced a new generation of readers to John Henry Lloyd, "Cool Papa" Bell, Rube Foster, and a host of other Negro League stars. Appendices to *Only the Ball Was White* included capsule biographies of Negro League greats, year-by-year standings for the leagues, box scores for the East-West All Star Games, and an alphabetical listing of hundreds of players and the teams they had performed for. Peterson's book, marked a watershed in the historiography of the Negro Leagues, opening up a broader interest in the research of others and spawning a new generation of Negro League historians, most of whom had never seen a segregated contest.

Two events in 1971 further contributed to the sudden growth of interest in Black baseball. The National Baseball Hall of Fame, succumbing to pressures from fans and the media, belatedly began to recognize the Negro Leagues by admitting Satchel Paige and setting up a Negro League committee to consider additional nominees. (The Hall of Fame insensitively planned to commemorate these stars in a separate section until protests of "Jim Crow" forced full inclusion.) In August 1971 the "Cooperstown 16" launched the Society for American Baseball Research. As the organization grew, it established a Negro League committee to coordinate research and facilitate communication among members interested in Black baseball. SABR journals, most notably the *Baseball Research Journal* and later *The National Pastime*, offered a place for Negro League writers to publish their works and a forum for discussion.

The new breed of Negro League aficionados faced a difficult task in recreating baseball in the Jim Crow era. As Peterson had warned, unearthing the history of the Negro Leagues was "like trying to find a single Black strand through a ton of spaghetti." Team records were largely unavailable. Major newspapers and mainstream sports journals like *The Sporting News* had rarely covered Black games. Black newspapers like the *Pittsburgh Courier* and *Chicago Defender* offered a more promising source, but only major public and university libraries held significant collections of back issues. As a result, oral history became the primary tool of the Negro League chroniclers. The most prolific of the interviewers was John Holway, whose *Voices from the Great Black Baseball Leagues* (1975) became the model for the genre. Holway had sought out Negro

Leaguers since the 1960s and his collection includes talks with 18 players and Effa Manley, the former owner of the Newark Eagles. Using their own words, the Black athletes brought alive the itinerant lifestyle and flamboyant play of the Negro Leagues. One controversial theme ran through both the player accounts and Holway's writing: that in the age of Jim Crow the quality of Black baseball was equal, if not superior, to the major league variety. In addition to editing the colorful accounts of the long-forgotten stars, Holway compiled records of games between Black players and major league squads between 1886 and 1948. In the 445 contests which he unearthed, Holway discovered that Blacks had won 269 and lost only 172, with four ties.

In 1973 two unique and entertaining looks at the Negro Leagues appeared simultaneously. *Some Are Called Clowns* by Bill Heward is one of the most unusual and delightful baseball books ever written. Heward, an aspiring pitcher, described his three seasons in the early 1970s with the Indianapolis Clowns, the final remnant of the old Negro Leagues. Heward complements his own experiences on the barnstorming tour with a keen sense of the club's history. The result is a fine blend of entertainment and analysis, a glimpse into a dying world which has now passed into oblivion. Novelist William Brashier offered another look at Black barnstormers in *The Bingo Long Traveling All-Stars and Motor Kings*, a fictional account which became a very entertaining and underrated feature film.

By the mid-1970s national interest in Black baseball had reached a level surpassing anything that had existed while the leagues were still alive. Ocania Chalk amassed information on the *Negro Leagues in Pioneers of Black Sports* (1975). Art Rust Jr. combined his own reminiscences with those of Negro League players in *"Get That Nigger Off The Field"* (1976). *Sam's Legacy*, a second novel dealing with Black baseball appeared in 1974. By 1977, the Hall of Fame had admitted eight Negro Leaguers, before abruptly and inexplicably disbanding the special committee which considered them, effectively barring the door to future admissions [until later resumed under a new committee].

Long ignored by the media and the baseball establishment, players like Buck Leonard, Ray Dandridge, and Willie Wells found themselves besieged by amateur and sometimes professional historians armed with tape recorders. Interviews with former Negro League players began to appear in numerous regional and national periodicals and in SABR publications. In one of the best of these interviews, Pulitzer Prize winner Theodore Rosengarten teamed with Lorenzo "Piper" Davis to produce "Reading the Hops" in *Southern Exposure*. James A. Riley and Dick Clark produced additional articles based on player reminiscences. In 1983 Riley produced a Who's Who of Negro League play, *The All-Time All-Stars of Black Baseball*, which profiled several hundred athletes who had appeared during the Jim Crow era. John Holway continued his contributions with a series of short profiles including *Bullet Joe and the Monarchs* (1984) and *Smokey Joe and the Cannonball* (1985), as well as numerous articles.

Two books by Negro League participants supplemented the work of the oral historians. In 1976 Effa Manley published her own account, *Negro Baseball ... Before Integration*, which unfortunately proved far less outspoken and interesting than the author herself. The following year, Quincy Trouppe, a former catcher, who had once had a "cup of coffee" in the majors, offered his autobiography *20 Years Too Soon*, which lovingly recreated his decades in the Negro Leagues, on the barnstorming tours, in Latin America, and finally in organized baseball. Trouppe's book, generously decorated with photographs from his scrapbooks, contains a wealth of information about Black players and Black baseball.

The oral histories and autobiographies of the 1970s and 1980s capture the flavor of life in the Negro Leagues and greatly enhance our knowledge, but as analytical tools they have severe limitations. Human memories tend toward the exaggerated and romantic. They deal largely with selected moments and places rather than the broader picture. As oral history piles upon oral history, the reader often receives variations on the same theme with little focus or historical direction. Contrary to popular opinion, oral histories do not speak for themselves; they require commentary to place them into historical perspective.

Often, good biographers will provide this perspective, but book-length chronicles of Negro League stars have been rare. In 1978 William Brashler published *Josh Gibson: A Life in the Negro Leagues*, a good effort which amply demonstrates the pitfalls of books of this type. Brashler knows the Negro Leagues and writes well, but apparently could not gather enough information to fill a book about the great catcher. This slim volume includes both Brashler's personal recollections (not of Gibson, but of Ted Williams) and a chapter on what happened to Gibson's best friend, Sam Bankhead, after Gibson's death. Thus Brashler's book is pleasurable, and in spots, revealing, but ultimately unsatisfying. One author who has attempted to move beyond the usual Negro League focus is Jerry Malloy. Malloy has published two excellent articles in *The National Pastime*. In "Out at Home" (1983) Malloy gives a detailed account of the 1887 International League season: the key turning point for Black exclusion in the nineteenth century. "Black Bluejackets" [1985, and reproduced later in this book -Ed] examines the history of the Great Lakes Naval Station team, which included numerous Negro League stars and future major leaguers Larry Doby and Chuck Harmon during World War II.

In the early 1980s, academia belatedly discovered the Negro Leagues. My own volume on baseball integration, *Baseball's Great Experiment: Jackie Robinson and His Legacy*, appeared in 1983. Although primarily concerned with Black players in organized baseball, the Negro Leagues took their rightful place as an integral part of the story. In the 1940s and 1950s they became the fount of major and minor league talent, an important transitional agency in the recruitment of Black players. I chronicled their ultimate decline and the fate of the great Black stars of that age, and analyzed the manner in which Negro League playing styles transformed the national pastime and improved the game.

Baseball's Great Experiment was published simultaneously with Donn Rogosin's *Invisible Men: Life in Baseball's Negro Leagues,* the first major overview of the subject since Peterson's book. Rogosin's work derived from his Ph.D. thesis in American Studies and offered a rich cultural panorama of "The World That Negro Baseball Made." Rogosin addressed not only the activities on the field or the internal league dynamics but the importance of baseball in Black communities during the first half of the twentieth century. Rogosin stressed the origins of the players, their role in Black America, their itinerant lifestyle, and the "Latin Connection." Based on extensive interviews, Invisible Men provided a systematic and in-depth look at the Black athletic experience in the years before integration.

While both Rogosin's book and my own received widespread publicity, a more recent study, *The Kansas City Monarchs: Champions of Black Baseball* (1985) by Janet Bruce, has gone largely unnoticed. This is unfortunate, because not only has Bruce produced one of the best books about the Negro Leagues, but her work marks an important new direction for baseball history in general. Relying not only on oral histories, but local newspapers and archival sources, Bruce examines the often talked about, but seldom studied, relationship between team and community. She places the history of the Monarchs firmly within the context of the evolution of Black life in Kansas City, describing how Blacks embraced their baseball representatives and where the team itself fit into Black society. Bruce also traces the impact of the club's decline on Kansas City itself. Historians studying any baseball team, Black or White, will benefit greatly by Bruce's pioneer work.

A soon-to-be-published manuscript, Rob Ruck's *Sandlot Seasons,* takes a similar, yet equally original approach. Ruck studied the history of Black sports in Pittsburgh, the home of both the Pittsburgh Crawfords and the Homestead Grays. Ruck's emphasis, however, is not only on professional sports, but on their relationship to the games played in the city's sandlots. En route, he takes us on a tour of the Black community rarely seen in most histories, from bourgeoisie to numbers runners, and from schoolyards to stadiums. While some readers may find both Ruck's and Bruce's books too "academic," no serious student of Black baseball should bypass them.

Thus, after forty years of baseball integration, and two decades of relative obscurity, the Negro Leagues have become a fertile ground for both baseball history and broader sociological approaches. Black baseball has attracted both widespread interest among baseball "buffs" and a level of respectability in academia. Dozens of taped interviews exist as primary sources for future writers. Yet much work remains. Additional team studies, analyses of the barnstorming phenomenon, and bicultural attempts to understand Latin baseball represent but a few of the areas requiring further efforts. If indeed baseball played a significant role in the Black community, we must also assess how the disappearance of the Negro Leagues affected Black culture. No one has yet attempted a thorough analysis of how integration changed the way in which baseball is played or the large number of sons of Negro Leaguers who have reached the major leagues. In addition, evidence must continue to be amassed on behalf of the many Black athletes still unfairly barred from the Hall of Fame.

Those who tread in this arena must also bear in mind the ultimate irony of baseball integration. The Jackie Robinson saga stands as one of the most sacrosanct in our folklore. It symbolizes American fair play and the beginning of the end for the national disgrace that was "Jim Crow." The universal acceptance of Blacks in baseball stands as a testament to the achievement of Robinson and those who followed him. No one would question that the appearance of the Negro Leagues marked a step forward in our social evolution. Yet something vital and distinctively American died with the passing of Black baseball. At their height, the Negro Leagues were a $2 million empire, largely controlled by Blacks, employing hundred of players and offering a form of cultural identification to millions of fans. Today more Blacks play in the major leagues, yet fewer make their living frotn baseball. Black athletes serve as role models for both Black and White youth, but they do so in an economic and organizational context far removed from their own ethnic and racial communities. We cannot resuscitate the Negro Leagues, nor would we want to. Nonetheless as the efforts of Negro League historians demonstrate, we can honor them and utilize them as portals to our divided past.

This article was originally published in the SABR Review of Books: A Forum of Baseball Literary Opinion, Volume 1 (1986).

Negro League Bibliography

The following is a list of books and articles referred to in this review. This is by no means a complete listing of all writings on the Negro Leagues.

Aaron, Henry as told to Furman Bisher. *Aaron, r.f.* (Cleveland World Publishing, 1968).

Brashler, William. *Bingo Long and His Traveling All-Stars and Motor Kings* (New York: Harper & Row, 1973).

---. *Josh Gibson: A Life in the Negro Leagues* (New York: Harper and Row, 1978).

Bruce, Janet. *The Kansas City Monarchs: Champions of Black Baseball* (University Press of Kansas, 1985).

Campanella, Roy. *It's Good To Be Alive* (Boston: Little, Brown and Co., 1959).

Chalk, Ocania. *Pioneers of Black Sport* (New York: Dodd, Mead and Co., 1975).

Heward, Bill and Oat, Dimitri V. *Some Are Called Clowns: A Season With the Last of the Great Barnstorming Teams* (New York: Thomas Y. Crowell and Co., 1974).

Holway, John. *Bullet Joe and the Monarchs* (Washington, D.C.: Capital Press, 1984).

---- *Smokey Joe and the Cannonball* (Washington, D.C.: Capital Press, 1985).

---- *Voices From the Great Negro Baseball Leagues* (New York: Dodd, Mead, 1975).

Malloy, Jerry. "Black Bluejackets," *The National Pastime* (1985): 72-77.

---- "Out At Home," *The National Pastime* (1983): 14-28.

Manley, Effa and Leon Hardwick. *Negro Baseball ... Before Integration* (Chicago: Adams Press, 1976).

Mays, Willie and Charles Einstein. *Willie Mays: My Life In and Out of Baseball* (New York: E.P. Dutton, 1972).

Neugeborn, Jay. *Sam's Legacy* (New York: Holt, Rhinehart and Winston, 1974).

Orr, Jack. *The Black Athlete: His Story in American History* (New York: Pyramid Books, 1970).

Paige, Leroy "Satchel" and David Lipman. *Maybe I'll Pitch Forever* (New York: Doubleday, 1962).

Peterson, Robert. *Only the Ball Was White* (Englewood Cliffs: Prentice Hall, 1970).

Riley, James A. *The All-Time All-Stars of Black Baseball* (TK Publishers, 1983).

Robinson, Jackie. *Baseball Has Done It* (New York: Lippincott, 1964).

Rogosin, Donn. *Invisible Men: Life in Baseball's Negro Leagues* (New York: Atheneum, 1983).

Rosengarten, Theodore. "Reading the Hops: Recollections of Lorenzo 'Piper' Davis and the Negro Baseball League," *Southern Exposure* (1977): 62-79.

Rowan, Carl T. with Jackie Robinson. *Wait Till Next Year* (New York: Random House, 1960).

Ruck, Rob. *Sandlot Seasons* (Evanston: U. of Illinois Press, 1986).

Rust, Art, Jr. "Get That Nigger Off The Field" (New York: Delacorte, 1976).

Seymour, Harold. *Baseball. Vol. 1: The Early Years* (New York: Oxford, 1960).

---- *Vol. 2: The Golden Age* (New York: Oxford, 1971).

Trouppe, Quincy. *20 Years Too Soon* (Los Angeles: Sands Enterprises, 1977).

Tygiel, Jules. *Baseball's Great Experiment: Jackie Robinson and His Legacy* (New York: Oxford, 1983).

Voigt, David. *American Baseball, 3 vols.* (Norman: University of Oklahoma Press, 1966, 1970, 1983).

White, Sol. *Sol White's Official Baseball Guide* (Columbia: Camden House, 1983).

Young, Andrew S. "Doc". *Great Negro Baseball Stars and How They Made the Major Leagues* (New York: A.S. Barnes, 1953).

Rube Foster and Black Baseball in Chicago

by Jerry Malloy

Obviously, no history of major league baseball in Chicago could ignore the White Sox or Cubs. So, too, no account of the national pastime in Chicago would be complete if it did not include Black baseball. The central role Chicago played in the history of the Negro Leagues can be indicated by considering (1) the astonishing career of Andrew "Rube" Foster, the Father of Black Baseball, and (2) the annual celebration of Black baseball excellence that took place each year at Comiskey Park, the Negro League's East-West All-Star Game. Both are as much a part of the rich fabric of Chicago's baseball history as the "Homer in the Gloamin'" or the interminable foul balls off the bat of "Old Aches and Pains" himself.

First, there's Rube Foster. Historian John Holway is right: "White baseball has never seen anyone quite like Rube Foster," although I suspect that Al Spalding comes closest. Foster was a giant of a man who took giant steps in everything he did. He fit right into Chicago about the time that city planner Daniel Burnham was exhorting: *Make No Little Plans!* When Thomas Carlyle wrote that history is the biography of great men, he might be summing up Black baseball for the entire first quarter of the twentieth century. Rube Foster, cutting an unimaginably wide swath through Negro baseball, proved impervious to the Peter Principle; he never found a level of incompetence as a player, manager, team owner, league founder, or commissioner.

Foster's later multifarious success in baseball can obscure his talent as a player. For the first decade of the century, he may have been the best pitcher in Black (perhaps even White) baseball. He signed on with Frank Leland's Chicago Union Giants, a powerful all-Black team, in 1901, for $40 a month plus 15 cents per meal. He was a strapping, pistol-toting, 22-year-old, right-handed son of a preacher from Calvert, Texas. His chief baseball weapon was a nasty screwball thrown from a submarine delivery. Later, he pitched in Philadelphia and New York. Along the way, he met a lot of people and made a lot of fans. White sportswriters compared him with the likes of Addie Joss, Amos Rusie, Hoss Radbourne, and Cy Young. Indeed, he got his nickname by whipping the A's Rube Waddell in an exhibition game. Some say that John McGraw hired him as a pitching coach and that he taught Christy Mathewson his "fadeaway." There's no denying that he certainly could pitch. No less a hitter than Honus Wagner called him "one of the greatest pitchers of all time. He was the smartest pitcher I have ever seen in all my years in baseball."

The cleverness and guile that Wagner recognized in Rube's makeup became increasingly apparent as his baseball presence expanded into larger and more extensive realms. In 1907 he returned to Chicago, this time to stay, as player-manager of the Leland Giants. Upset at the team's share of the gate when the Giants played White teams, Foster convinced Frank Leland to let him try his hand at negotiating the split. Soon he was able to demand a 50-50 split, and never again did a Rube Foster team play for less than half the proceeds.

The Leland Giants played in Auburn Park at 79th and Wentworth (and at 69th and Halsted, and at 61st and Racine) and became a perennial powerhouse in Chicago's strong, integrated city league. This circuit included the talented semipro teams with large followings such as the Logan Squares, Gunthers, and Duffy Florals. Major leaguers such as Johnny Kling, Joe Tinker, and Johnny Evers often picked up a few extra bucks by playing as ringers on these teams. The Leland Giants (and, later, the Chicago American Giants) also had great success during the harvest season, when, for about a month each year, the best touring teams from the Midwest converged on Chicago for some ferocious baseball battles.

The 1907 Leland Giants had a record of 110-10, including 48 straight wins. Following the 1909 season, the Leland Giants played a three-game exhibition series against the Cubs, who had finished second in the National League that season. The Cubs won all three games, by scores of 6–5, 4–1, and 1–0. Mordecai "Three Finger" Brown won two games and Orval Overall won one in the hard-fought series, which was covered by the White press, including the *Tribune*'s young sportswriter Ring Lardner. Foster tried throughout the remainder of his career to get the Cubs to consent to a rematch, but never succeeded. This was partly due to Commissioner Landis, who put the kibosh in the 1920s on the annual exhibition series that the Chicago American Giants played against a team of White major leaguers put together by Harry Heilmann.

By 1910, Foster had compiled what he considered to be the greatest team of all time, Black or White. Featuring such stars as John Henry Lloyd, Pete Hill, Grant "Home Run" Johnson, Bruce Petway, Frank Wickware, and Pat Dougherty, the Leland Giants won 123 games and lost only six!

In 1911 Foster entered into a partnership with a White businessman named John Schorling. Together they bought the ballpark that Charles Comiskey was vacating as he moved his White Sox into their sparkling new stadium, Comiskey Park, on 35th and Shields. The Old Roman's old ball park, at 39th and Wentworth, thus became the first home for one of the greatest sustained success stories in the history of Negro sport in America: the Chicago American Giants. This great team would cast a giant shadow for the remaining years of apartheid baseball in the United States. So vast was this team's impact that the inclusion of the word "American" in its title, whether due to greatness or good fortune, proved apt indeed. And so clear was Rube Foster's imprint on them, that they were often referred to as simply "Rube Foster's Giants."

Like all successful Black baseball teams, the Chicago American Giants could survive only by touring extensively and abandoning the notion of an "off season." Traveling to areas as remote from Chicago as the West Coast and Cuba, Rube Foster's team created excitement and a festive carnival atmosphere wherever it played. With Foster insisting on nothing less than first-class accouterments, what a spectacle it must have been when the American Giants burst into town in the epitome of opulence: their own private Pullman coach! Dave Malarcher, Foster's star third baseman, who later succeeded him as manager of the team, recalled:

> I never shall forget the first time I saw Rube Foster. I never saw such a well-equipped ball club in my whole life! I was astounded. Every day they came out in a different set of beautiful uniforms, all kinds of bats and balls, all the best kind of equipment.
>
> The American Giants traveled everywhere, as you know. No other team travel as many miles as the American Giants. When Rube gave them the name American Giant, he really selected a name. That was a good idea, because it became the greatest ball club that ever was. That's right: the way he played, the way he equipped his team, the way he paid his men, the way he treated his men, the miles that they traveled.

As a manager, Foster's style was ruthlessly aggressive. He built his attack around relentless speed and hustle. He consistently defeated teams that hit for higher averages or more power by using bold baserunning. He was an exponent of the hit-and-run bunt, wherein a fast base runner would advance two bases on a bunt play, usually going from first to third, but often scoring from second base. All of Foster's players, even his rare power hitters, such as the Cuban Cristobal Torriente, were expected to be excellent bunters. Bunting drills included laying down bunts into Rube's own strategically placed hat. Foster's passion for the bunted ball was demonstrated in a 1921 game against the Indianapolis ABCs. The American Giants fell behind by the score of 18-0, with only two innings left. Foster signaled for bunts on eleven (11!) straight hitters. A couple of grand slams later, the Giants had scored nine runs in each inning to tie the game, 18–18. Foster often used his ubiquitous pipe to send in plays, waving it in certain ways, or sending up a couple puffs of smoke. He also used it as an implement of discipline, thumping the skull of a player who missed or played through one of his signs.

Off the field, Foster could be charming. He often entertained players, writers, and fans with stories from his colorful career, addressing everyone, male and female alike, as "Darling" in his Texas drawl. But once a game began, he was strictly business, and would not tolerate disobedience. One of Rube's players, Arthur Hardy, recalled Foster's firm manner:

> I wouldn't call him reserved, but he wasn't free and easy. You see, Rube was a natural psychologist. Now he didn't know what psychology was and he probably couldn't spell it, but he realized that he couldn't fraternize and still maintain discipline. He wasn't harsh, but he was strict. His dictums were not unreasonable, but if you broke one he'd clamp down on you. If he stuck a fine on you, you paid it—there was no appeal from it. He was dictatorial in that sense.

He was able to command the respect and admiration of his players, many of whom went on to successful careers as managers after their playing days were over. There are those who speculate that he purposely cultivated his acquaintanceships with White managers such as Connie Mack and John McGraw in the hope that one day he would be asked to form a Black major league team. Perhaps. But baseball minds surely would recognize a fellow member in the brotherhood of great managers.

As great a player, owner, and manager as he was, Rube Foster's most impressive accomplishment was the creation of the Negro National League in 1920. (An all-Negro Eastern League was formed in 1923). Among the many changes wrought by World War I was a redistribution of the Black population of the country. When Rube Foster first arrived in Chicago at the turn of the century, only about two percent of the population of the city was Black. By the middle of the century's second decade, however, black people from the South were pouring into Chicago and the other large urban centers in the North.

This great migration occurred just as Foster was in the process of establishing the Chicago American Giants. In 1917 alone, the Black population of Chicago increased by 65,000. But this unprecedented population boom was not an unmixed blessing. After the war, racial tensions throughout the nation intensified, resulting in a series of race riots, the worst one occurring in Chicago, where 23 Blacks and 15 Whites died. (Foster's team was on the road at the time and had to postpone its return home since their ballpark was occupied by soldiers.)

While the advantages of creating a Negro League were obvious to many, it had been unsuccessfully attempted several times, as far back as 1887 and as recently as 1906 and 1911. But it remained for someone of the prominence and perspicacity of Rube Foster to accomplish the Bismarkian task of pulling together the divergent independent teams into a united league. What Hulbert and Spalding did for the National League and Johnson and Comiskey did for the American League, Rube Foster alone did for the Negro National League. Created at a meeting held in Kansas City in February 1920, the NNL's charter members, besides Foster's Chicago American Giants, were Joe Green's Chicago Giants, the Indianapolis ABCs, Kansas City Monarchs, St. Louis Giants, Detroit Stars, Cuban Stars, and Dayton Marcos.

Rube Foster's 1922 Chicago American Giants.

Rube Foster was the de facto czar of this league until his disabling illness in 1926. From his office at Indiana and Wentworth, he ran the NNL as a benevolent autocrat. Realizing the need for a semblance of balanced competition, he moved players around from team to team, even depriving his own Chicago American Giants of the great Oscar Charleston, whom he sent to Indianapolis. When the Dayton franchise—which he financed out of his own pocket—failed, he moved it to Columbus, Ohio.

When teams ran out of money on the road, he wired money so they could return home. When teams ran short of dough and had problems meeting their payroll, Foster advanced loans for players' pay. Even among such energetic and successful owners as J.L. Wilkinson of the Kansas City Monarchs and C.I. Taylor of the Indianapolis ABCs, Foster was acknowledged as the undisputed kingpin of the league, overseeing matters great and small. He even composed the league's motto: "We Are the Ship, All Else the Sea," an accurate analogy for Rube's role within the league itself.

The Negro National League never totally established stability and unity over a long period of time. Compromises had to be made to accommodate more traditional forms of income (such as exhibitions and barnstorming), and teams played unbalanced schedules. The league turned out to be an aggregation of essentially independent teams. But it did succeed in giving concrete form to the model of self-help and self-reliance, free from White interference or control, envisioned by Booker T. Washington as the best hope for the well-being of the race. In forming the NNL, Foster said he wanted "to create a profession that would equal the earning capacity of any other profession," to "keep Colored baseball from the control of whites," and "do something concrete for the loyalty of the Race." The Chicago American Giants provided a paragon of Black excellence. Foster set a standard for those who followed to admire and emulate. That was his real genius.

Rube Foster died December 9, 1930, after spending the last four years of his life in an asylum for the mentally ill in Kankakee, Illinois. One of the greatest baseball minds of all time suddenly and sadly collapsed, and he was remanded to the institution by a judge. Black Chicagoans did not forget his contribution to their community. Thousands paid homage as the body of the most famous Black man in Chicago lay in state at a funeral home. Fifty-one years later, Rube Foster became the tenth veteran of the Negro Leagues to be enshrined in baseball's Hall of Fame.

Neither the Chicago American Giants nor the Negro National League as Foster built them survived long after his death. The Great Depression had a devastating impact upon the already impoverished Black baseball fans of the country. However, in the 1930s a new league was formed, largely under the leadership of Pittsburgh Crawfords owner Gus Greenlee. The Chicago American Giants were revived, and continued to play a prominent (though less opulent) role in Negro baseball through the remaining years of segregated baseball.

In the 1930s and 1940s Chicago became the mecca of Negro baseball, as Comiskey Park was the site of the most spectacular annual event in Black sports: The East-West All-Star Game. The Negro League World Series, which pitted the East Coast and Midwest champions against each other, never attained the glamour or aura of historical moment that the major league World Series did. Instead, the focal point of the season in the Negro leagues was the mid-season East-West Game. (Several times second games, usually called "All-Star Classics," were played in various eastern cities, but never achieved the heights of the annual Comiskey Park extravagance). When the current owners of the White Sox desert that fine and noble structure known as Comiskey Park [demolished in 1991 -Ed.], they will be abandoning the home of one of the most distinguished elements of the heritage of Black baseball in America.

The East-West Game originated as the brainchild of Roy Sparrow, an aide to Gus Greenlee, in 1932, a year before the major leagues' first midsummer classic, which also was played at Comiskey Park. The game quickly established itself as the undisputed centerpiece of the Black baseball season, an unsurpassed festival of Black baseball pride. Chicago's Grand Hotel became the center of the Negro League universe as thousands flocked to Chicago for the East-West Game. League cities even sent bathing beauties to represent their teams, adding to the hoopla. In 1935, the game was tied in with Joe Louis' fight with King Levinsky. Year after year, railroads added cars to all trains headed to Chicago to accommodate the fans eager to see their all-stars play. By the 1940s, the game had become such an event that the *Chicago Defender*, one of the major Negro newspapers in the country, would refer to a crowd of 35,000 as "disappointing!"

The Negro League's All-Star Game preceded the American and National Leagues' by a year. In fact, the Black event often outdrew its White counterpart's during the 1940s.

Attendance figures were regarded as omens for eventual integration by many. At a time when attendance in many major league cities was slipping, the Negro Leagues showed impressive growth. The Kansas City Monarchs regularly outdrew the Blues, the Yankees' minor league team in that city. In 1942, the Monarchs, with Satchel Paige, defeated a team of White major leaguers in Wrigley Field before 30,000 fans, while only 19,000 watched the White Sox host the St. Louis Browns on the same day. Such figures encouraged many Negro leaders to hope that this would be their entree into the major leagues. A market this vast, they calculated, would simply be too lucrative for organized baseball to ignore. And, in fact, one of the motives frequently attributed to Branch Rickey in his decision to sign Jackie Robinson was his desire to capitalize on the expanding Negro market that he was shrewd enough to notice.

And attendance figures at Comiskey Park for the East-West Games were very imposing indeed. By the time the fourth game was played, in 1936, the Negro League All-Star Game attendance exceeded that of the major league counterpart. The Black game also outdrew the White game in 1938, 1942, 1943, 1944, 1946, and 1947—with no AL-NL game held in 1945 due to wartime restraints. Attendance hit its peak in 1943, when 51,723 fans jammed into Comiskey Park. In the following year, 46,247 watched the East-West Game, while only 29,589 watched the major league All-Star game at Forbes Field.

This article was originally published in Baseball in Chicago, the 1986 SABR convention journal.

Umpires in the Negro Leagues

by Leslie Heaphy

"What about our Negro baseball umpires? They are cussed, discussed, made the subject of all sorts of fuss. They are reviled and often as not, riled as they go about their highly-sensitive calling of calling 'em right, knowing that the fans in the stands are prejudicing them from the start, and that the players are the greatest umpire "riders" in the business. ... All together, the life of the Negro umpire isn't cheese and cherries by any means."—Dan Burley[1]

Information about various aspects of Black baseball can be difficult to find, and there are still lots of gaps in the story that need to be filled in—one such is the role of umpires. Few stories in the newspapers ever said much about the umpires beyond their names unless something happened involving a bad call or a brawl. Some fans are familiar with the name Emmett Ashford as the first Black umpire in the major leagues, but what about all the men who came before him? Who were these individuals who toiled in the shadows and never got any recognition for the difficult job they had on and off the field? Why did the leagues employ White and Black umpires? How much of a difference did it make to have umpires who were White rather than Black?

When the Negro National League (NNL) was created in 1920, one of the most important issues to be hammered out was the way umpires would be chosen and paid. League President Rube Foster believed that the umpire needed to be in charge and provide order to every game. The umpire could maintain the legitimacy of the new league if he knew the rules and could command respect. There were mixed feelings among the owners about whether the umpires should be White or Black. In 1920 most games had only two umpires rather than the four we see in the major leagues today. This made the role of the umpires even harder and more important. It was not until 1923 that the NNL owners voted to hire the first all-Black crew for the league. Prior to that umpires were generally provided by the home team and were often White.

One of the earliest recorded stories of a Black umpire involves Jacob Francis, who was chosen to represent Syracuse as one of the official umpires in the newly formed New York State League. In the census records of 1870 and 1880, Francis

Umpire Emmett Ashford in action.

is listed as "mulatto." He umpired at Stars Park throughout 1885 as one member of a three-man crew, becoming the first Black umpire for an all-White league. In addition to umpiring, Francis managed the Syracuse Pastimes, a local Black team. Francis first appeared in the 1870 census in Syracuse with his wife, Sarah, having come from Virginia. Fans generally supported Francis and even booed another umpire when he subbed for Francis. One news reporter said Francis "is one of the most popular men that ever officiated as an umpire before a Syracuse audience. An instance cannot be recalled where there was any trouble or delay in a game in which Mr. Francis officiated. He possesses an excellent judgment, is quick on his feet and gives his decisions promptly."[2]

A 1909 Seattle article talked about Pete Johnson, a Black umpire in the Jacksonville area during the late nineteenth century. Johnson appeared to be a fan favorite and well respected for his calls. Reporting on one game, a writer commented that "all the hotel guests were desirous of seeing Pete Johnson umpire as they were to witness the game itself." He had a unique way of calling the game, deciding a runner who was out on the bases was "cancelled." When a runner refused to leave the field after Johnson called him out Johnson simply said the player would be a "ghost runner."[3]

Francis and Johnson were rarities: Most games involving Black teams had White umpires before 1923. That was partly due to the lack of trained Black umpires, but more importantly most teams were owned by White men. They had control of the resources and therefore Black men did not get the chance to umpire.[4] Given the nature of race relations in the 1900s and 1910s, the idea that decisions by Whites would be more accepted than those by Blacks was not a stretch, and provided an additional rationale for the owners to justify using White umpires.

As early as 1910 the question of umpires for a proposed all-Black league was being discussed. When Chicagoan Beauregard Moseley wrote about his proposed league, he noted many decisions that had to be made, but one he seemed to be adamant about was paid umpires. He said the umpires should receive $5 a game and be paid by the home team. Moseley did not comment on whether the umpires would be "race umps" or White arbiters but his proposal matched the pattern most often used by later leagues, with umpires provided by the home team. That added an extra burden to the men in Black, who had to work harder to prove their impartiality.[5]

Foster did use Black umpires for exhibition and benefit games. In 1910 he hired boxer Jack Johnson and vaudeville performer S.H. Dudley to work a benefit for Provident Hospital, a Black-owned institution. The use of such stars gave the Black community figures to look up to as role models. Foster himself umpired a benefit game in 1913, but for regular Chicago American Giants contests he used White umpires like Goeckel.[6] With the creation of the NNL in 1920, Foster recognized the importance of umpires, writing in a 1921 column, "Future of Race Umps Depends on Men of Today." He used this column to explain why the new league would be using White umpires rather than Black. Foster's basic explanation was simply that Black men lacked knowledge of the rules. Opportunities were just not present, but the NNL was not a charity; it was business.[7]

Since there were no professional schools for Black umpires, many of the best African American umps were former players who relied on their knowledge of the game from personal experience. For example, Newark Eagles first baseman-outfielder Mule Suttles umpired after he retired in the late 1940s. Pitcher Billy Donaldson turned to umpiring in the 1920s and 1930s, while second baseman Mo Harris umpired from the 1930s through the 1940s after his career with the Homestead Grays ended. Local Cleveland sports star Harry Walker umpired for the Cleveland Bears in 1939 to try to help support Black baseball in his community.

Cincinnati native Percy Reed played second base for a local athletic club and the Lincoln Giants. He started umpiring in 1929 and from 1935 to 1947 he called every Sunday game played by Black teams in Cincinnati. Reed worked as part of a local two-umpire team with Harry Ward, known locally and in the papers as Wu-fang. Reed learned his trade from Bill Carpenter, who was an umpire in the International League.[8] Hurley McNair, a pitcher and outfielder for a number of Negro League clubs, umpired after he retired as a player in 1937. He traveled for league games until his death in December 1948.[9]

The Baltimore Black Sox employed Black umpires as early as 1917 when Charles Cromwell was hired by owner Charles Spedden. Cromwell umpired in the Negro Leagues through the 1947 season. In 1923 Rube Foster tried to hire Cromwell as part of a new team of African American umpires for the NNL. Foster wanted the best umpires and felt that White umpires had provided that in the first years of the league. With the creation of the Eastern Colored League (ECL) in 1923, Foster felt the time was right to find the best Black umpires he could. His first hire was Billy Donaldson from the Pacific Coast League, and then he went after Cromwell. Cromwell turned Foster down to stay with the Black Sox after Spedden hired Henry "Spike" Spencer from Washington, DC, to join him as the team's umpires.

Spedden proved he wanted the Black Sox to succeed by spending money on the team, and so Cromwell opted to stay and umpire at the Maryland Baseball Park. By 1924 Spedden vowed to use all Black umpires for Black Sox games, a move some said "is bound to meet with favor."[10] Cromwell's choice did not turn out to be the best when the ECL decided in 1925 that teams should not hire their own umpires as had been the practice. This put Cromwell and Spencer out of work. Cromwell came back in 1926 when the ECL gave back the hiring of umpires to the teams. In 1927, when George Rossiter took over operations for the Black Sox, he fired Cromwell and Spencer. Rossiter felt that Black umpires were not yet competent and that he would use White umpires until they were. Cromwell found work in a minor Black league in the South before returning to umpire for the Baltimore Elite Giants through 1947. Cromwell's career was like that of so many of the other Black umpires, who always had to fight to prove they were as worthy as White umpires.[11]

When the Negro National League was being formed, Rube Foster talked with the press about a variety of subjects vital to the league's success. One of those topics was umpires, who Foster stated needed to be totally in charge. Their decisions would be final and then needed to be supported by the league. Foster wanted "utmost good order on the ball field." He saw the league as an investment, a business venture, and so the right arbiters would be essential to the success of the league. Foster commented, "I think an ump should be pacific but firm, positive but polite, quick but unshoddy, strict but reasonable."[12]

On the question of the use of White versus Black umpires, Foster wanted to use African American men but believed that there were not enough available and that many people would accept the decisions of White umpires more readily. Reporter Charles Marshall thought colored umpires should be given a chance but agreed with Foster about White umpires. He wrote, "Of course we know that some players as well as some managers and fans alike feel that the White umpire's decision carries more weight and generally comes closer to the right decision than the colored official. In most cases just because he is White."[13]

With the creation of the Eastern Colored League (ECL) in 1923, the leagues continued serious discussions, deciding to hire all Black umpires for the NNL. Reporter Frank Young began a campaign to hire Black umpires in 1922. He called for training of Black men and at the same time criticized the mistakes of White umpires. He tried to counter Foster's concern that Black umpires would be swayed by the cheering of Black fans rather than engage in good decision-making. Young used his column to highlight the work of men like Jamison in Baltimore and Donaldson in California to show that there were African American men capable of umpiring for the league.[14] Kansas City was the first of the cities to use two Black umpires, Billy Donaldson and Bert Gholston.

Foster hired six Black umpires for the league, with two-man crews responsible for different cities. Leon Augustine and Lucian Snaer worked around the Milwaukee area while Caesar Jamison and William Embry worked the Indianapolis region. When Foster failed to hire Charley Cromwell, he had to look harder for qualified men. Tom Johnson was the last of the original hires, being used as a rotating umpire.[15]

Finding arbiters with the necessary qualifications and abilities to control the game and the situations that could arise proved difficult from the beginning to the demise of the Negro Leagues. While owners like Foster and Kansas City's J.L. Wilkinson favored all-race crews, they also knew having qualified umpires was even more important. Foster would not even use Black umpires for Chicago American Giants games, preferring to pay White umpires while Black umpires sat idle.[16] By the end of the 1925 season, Foster released the Black umpires who had been hired by the league and went back to the practice of the home team providing the umpires.[17] At the end of the season the other owners hired back four of the six men who had been let go. These men continued to work for the league through the 1927 season without significant incident.

After Foster left the NNL in 1926, Black umpires still had a difficult time being hired. However, when the short-lived American Negro League was created in 1929, it hired Black umpires led by former players Bill Gatewood, Judy Gans, and former umpire Frank Forbes. Because of the Great Depression, pressure on the owners increased to give Black men a chance. Unfortunately, the ANL collapsed after the 1929 season, ending one of the best opportunities for Black umpires to be hired. *Chicago Defender* reporter Al Monroe stated in more than one column that Black umpires needed to take better control of the game, they need to be less tentative and show control if they wanted respect. Without control they would never find regular employment.[18]

Umpires always had a tough time with players and fans who did not want to listen, but Negro League umpires often had a tougher time without much league support. Bert Gholston believed that the umpires always worked with the fear that they would be attacked and the league would not support them. He stated, "Several of the teams of the Negro National League are still under the impression that they shouldn't take orders from the colored umpires. Several of them were threatening to jump on the umpires."[19]

In 1934 NNL Commissioner Rollo Wilson tried to improve the situation by imposing fines and suspensions. One particular target was Jud Wilson, who had a temper and a reputation for attacking umpires. Wilson's $10 fine was not much of a deterrent. By 1936 things had gotten so bad that $25 became the fine with a 10-day suspension for assaulting an umpire. New league secretary John L. Clark created a schedule for the three league umpires, Ray "Mo" Harris, John Craig, and Pete Cleague. The other umpires would still be chosen by the home team, which encouraged charges of favoritism. Unfortunately for the umpires, without strong support from league officials, they were pretty much on their own. Longtime umpire Virgil Blueitt stated, "If the club owners would order their managers and players to abide by the umpires' rulings, much of this trouble could be avoided."[20]

Another veteran umpire, Frank Forbes, was attacked on June 5, 1937, by New York Black Yankees players, and just a few games later he got into an altercation with Newark manager Tex Burnett. A month later Forbes and fellow umpire Jasper "Jap" Washington were attacked in their dressing room by Baltimore Elite Giants players. Washington resigned when nothing happened to the players involved. League honchos Gus Greenlee and Cum Posey finally responded with tougher policies, but the enforcement was lax depending on how a team's players were affected. For example, when umpire James Crump forfeited a game, manager George Scales attacked him and the league let Crump go without any hearing at all. The lack of official support made an already hard job even more difficult for umpires, who earned no real respect for just doing their job.[21]

A reporter for the *Kansas Whip* stated that the "weakest link in a game is found in the set-up of umpires, which is limited to three." He included a variety of criticism from around the league about the umpires not being harsh enough in their actions towards players who broke the rules.[22]

In 1944 Dan Burley wrote about the abuse umpires took for little pay. He reprinted a letter he received from Fred McCrary, a longtime umpire in the NNL. McCrary was upset at the lack of attention paid to umpires. For example, he worked in every East-West game from 1938 through 1944 and all the umpires got for each game was $10 and expenses. When McCrary asked for more money, the owners told him the umpire was not important for the game.[23] Not all agreed with that assessment, as there were owners and players who treated umpires respectfully. By the 1940s some were also concerned about improving the respect because they feared the violence on and off the field might hurt the increasing push for integration.

In 1945 umpire Jimmy Thompson had his nose broken by player Piper Davis and pursued legal action against him since the league did little. Thompson won his case, though Davis only paid $230 in court costs. Later, President J.B. Martin added a league fine of $250 and indefinite suspension when the true story of the fight came out. Sometimes things got so bad that the police had to be called in to restore order. While police help was necessary it did not help the umpires exercise true authority. Sadly, it happened with both White and Black umpires, as evidenced by Goose Curry harassing White umpire Pete Strauch until the police escorted Curry off the field. The Chicago Cubs finally raised the rent on Wrigley Field to keep Black teams from using it if they could not control their players.[24]

Even the minor Negro Leagues had regular discussions about umpires and their roles. The Texas-Oklahoma-Louisiana League (TOL) decided in 1929 to hire four umpires who would be paid by the league. The league officials hoped this would give the umpires more authority and lessen incidents on the field. The Florida State Negro League in 1949 followed the pattern of having the home teams provide the umpires. But at the winter meetings before the 1950 season, discussion about the umpires' situation dominated the talks. The league decided to hire two umpires, Williams Washington and Archie Colbert, and have the "balls and strikes" umpires travel around the league. At the same time, league President Skipper Holbert let two other umpires, Gus Daniels and Charles Merrit, go for inefficiency and misconduct.[25]

At the annual East-West Classic the leagues often used both Negro League and White minor-league umpires for the contest. Having a bigger pool to draw from allowed the Classic to have four umpires which often meant better control and legitimacy for the game. The only real difference in rules for the minor-league umpires was the fact that the spitball was legal in the Negro Leagues.[26]

The best-known Black umpire from the Negro Leagues was Bob Motley, who in 2016 was the last living umpire from the leagues. Motley was born in Autaugaville, Alabama, in 1923, the sixth of eight children born to parents who were sharecroppers. Motley's father died when he was 4, making it even tougher on the family to survive. Motley served in the US Marine Corps during World War II, earning a Purple Heart for a wound. While serving in the Marines, Motley umpired a few pickup games and discovered a career that would take off after the war. He umpired for over 25 years in the Negro Leagues and White minor leagues. Umpiring from 1949 to 1956 in the Negro Leagues, Motley got to see some of the best players of the day and even umpired the 1953 and 1954 East-West Classics. Motley commented on umpiring, "An umpire has got to have guts. And force right; an ump can count on being no one's friend—at least while on the diamond."[27]

Motley attended the Al Somers Umpire School twice and graduated at the top of the class each time. His high scores did not help in the face of segregation; he never umpired above the Pacific Coast League.[28] Motley recognized that umpires were not treated well by anyone. For example, he commented, "It was pretty common in the Negro Leagues, that if the catcher didn't like the way an umpire was calling balls and strikes, he would purposely let a pitch go by and let it smack the umpire right in the facemask. That happened to me at least a half a dozen times."[29] After he called Hank Bayliss out on strikes and threw him out of the game, Bayliss came after Motley with a butcher knife on the bus home. The fans were even worse than the players in their continual comments. Motley said most fans had a favorite chant, *"Kill the umpire, Kill the umpire!"* You heard the chant so often you just expected it. Fans loved to blame the umpire when their team lost.[30]

While Motley has received some attention in his later years and Emmett Ashford is known because he was the first African American umpire in the majors, Julian Osibee Jelks never really got a shot. Jelks umpired for four years in the Pacific Coast League but never got a call to the majors. Before umpiring in the minors, Jelks was discovered by Alex Pompez when he came to New Orleans with his barnstorming Negro League teams. Pompez was so impressed with Jelks that he hired him to travel with his clubs in the mid-1950s. By 1956 Jelks got his first chance in the White professional leagues and began his climb to Triple A. Jelks umpired until the assassination of Dr. Martin Luther King Jr. and then he stopped, fearing he or his family might become targets. In 2008 Jelks was invited as a guest to the major-league draft where teams symbolically selected a former player from the Negro Leagues.[31]

Throughout the history of Black baseball and the Negro Leagues, the issue of who would act as arbiters for their games was always a concern. While Rube Foster and other owners might have favored in principle hiring Black men as umpires, they were businessmen first and needed to put the best product on the field. This led to decisions to hire White umpires most of the time based on the beliefs that they knew the rules better and could control the behavior of players and fans. With that said there were still many fine Black umpires, from Jacob Francis to Julian Jelks. Sadly, good umpires rarely get noticed and their stories are not told, making it hard to track them down and give them credit for their contributions.

Endnotes

1.   Dan Burley, "Chicken-feed for Negro Umpires," in James Reisler, *Black Writers/Black Baseball: An Anthology of Articles From Black Sportswriters Who Covered the Negro Leagues* (Jefferson, North Carolina: McFarland and Company, 2007), 136.

2.   Sean Kirst, "In Syracuse, A Groundbreaking Umpire Finds Himself Called Out," syracuse.com, February 17, 2011.

3.   "Black Umpire Springs New One in Ball Game," *Seattle Times*, January 31, 1909: 14.

4.   Scott C. Hindman, "Blacks in Blue: The Saga of Black Baseball's Umpires, 1885-1951," Bachelor's Thesis, Princeton University, 2003, 18-19.

5.   "Tentative Plan National Negro Baseball League of America," *Chicago Broad Ax*, November 26, 1910.

6.   "Diamond Dashes," *Indianapolis Freemen,* August 6, 1910; "Benefit for the Old Folks Home," *Chicago Defender*, August 20, 1913.

7.   Rube Foster, "Future of Race Umps Depends on Men of Today," *Chicago Defender,* December 31, 1921.

8.   Brent Kelley, *The Negro Leagues Revisited* (Jefferson, North Carolina: McFarland, 2000), 32-35.

9.   "Hurley McNair," pitchblackbaseball.com.

10. *Baltimore Afro-American,* January 1924; "Best in League," *Baltimore Afro-American*, September 11, 1926: 9.

11. Gary Cieradkowski, "Charles Cromwell," Infinitecardset.blogspot.com; "Black Sox Want Cromwell Here," *Baltimore Afro-American*, March 30, 1923: 14.

12. Dave Wyatt, "Chairman Foster's View on Grave Subjects," March 27, 1920, paper found on negroleagues.bravehost.com.

13. Charles D. Marshall, "Will Colored Umps Be Given a Tryout?" March 27, 1920 paper found on negroleagues.bravehost.com.

14. "Demand for Umpires of Color is Growing Among the Fans," *Chicago Defender*, October 9, 1920.

15. "Seven Colored Umps Signed for League," *Kansas City Call*, April 27, 1923.

16. "Rube Foster's Sportsmanship," *Chicago Defender*, July 11, 1924.

17. "Kansas City the First City to Use Negro Umpires," *Kansas Advocate*, April 27, 1923; "Change the Umpires." *Chicago Defender*, August 19, 1922; "Foster Explains Action in Releasing Umpires," *Pittsburgh Courier*, August 22, 1925.

18. Al Monroe, "Speaking of Sports," *Chicago Defender*, July 21, 1934.

19. "Gholston Says It's Hard to Umpire in This League," *Chicago Defender*, August 28, 1925.

20. Neil Lanctot, *Fair Dealing and Clean Playing: The Hilldale Club and the Development of Black Professional Baseball, 1910-32* (Syracuse: Syracuse University Press, 2007), 176; Leslie Heaphy, *The Negro Leagues, 1869-1960* (Jefferson, North Carolina: McFarland and Company, 2003), 110.

21. Lanctot, 176-77.

22. "National Association of Negro Baseball Clubs," *Kansas Whip*, July 17, 1936.

23. Dan Burley, "Chicken Feed Pay for Negro Umpires," September 9, 1944, in Jim Reisler.

24. Lanctot, 180, 181.

25. E.H. McLin, "Official of Negro League Swinging Ax on Umps," *St. Petersburg Times*, May 30, 1950.

26. Dave Barr, "Monarchs to Grays to Crawfords," MLB.com/blogs; *Kansas Plain Dealer*, August 20, 1948.

27. Byron Motley, *Ruling Over Monarchs* (Champaign, Illinois: Sports Publishing, LLC, 2007), Introduction.

28. Sportscelebs.com.

29. Bob Motley as told to Byron Motley, " 'No, I'm a Spectator Just Like You': Umpire in the Negro American League," *Baseball Research Journal*, Fall 2010.

30. Bob Motley.

31. Bill Madden, "Black Umpire Missed his Calling in the 1960s," *New York Daily News*, February 10, 2007; Jay Levin, "Julian Osibee Jelks, 1930-2013: Pioneering Umpire Built a New Life Outside Baseball," NorthJersey.com, July 4, 2013.

The Black Press and the Collapse of the Negro League in 1930

by David Hopkins

B lack America at the end of the 1920s was a very different place than it had been just a few years earlier. The Great Migration of African Americans from the rural South to the urban centers of the North, which had initially been motivated mainly by employment opportunities in the wake of conscription of primarily White young men for World War I, had become more and more a quest for relief from the relentless racism of the South of the time. Even though the North was hardly a paradise in terms of race relations, it was widely viewed as having more opportunities for African Americans than the South, and not just economically.

Although the established Black communities of Northern cities were initially alarmed by the arrival of rural Southerners, fearing that lack of education, country manners and superstitions, and other cultural differences would reinforce White prejudices and make their own positions weaker, the arrival of the Southern African Americans created most of what we now know as Black American Culture. Certainly the Great Migration did result in increased racial tensions in the North, but it also created greater interest on the part of mainstream White America in the minority culture that grew from it.[1]

The Northern Black press was put in a difficult position. As representatives of the established, more or less bourgeois Black communities, they had as part of their mission the education and training of the new arrivals in "correct" Northern manners. Part of this mission was their basic alignment with conservative African American leaders like Booker T. Washington, who urged patience and effort as the method best suited for gaining eventual recognition in mainstream society. As such, the Black press was full of stories of "successful" assimilation by African Americans, as well as emphasis on groups, both social and educational, that derived their patterns of organization and affiliation from similar White groups. This program of "uplift" obviously separated the Black newspapers, in many ways, from the real concerns of their readers, many of whom are likely to have found more appeal in "New Negro" movements that more radically demanded immediate equal treatment (or even more radically, economic separation from the mainstream). The Black press at that time continually struggled to balance the needs of honest reporting with the need to support African American advancement into mainstream American society."[2]

As America in the 1920s began to drift toward the series of economic calamities that became the Great Depression, Black America suffered disproportionately. Declines in agricultural incomes increased pressure on small farmers to move to the cities. Decline in industrial investment meant a lack of new job openings to absorb those workers. Since much of the urban Black workforce was unskilled, they were likely to be the first fired due to any cuts in production. Clearly, the personal effects of the Great Depression were felt in African American homes before the actual events of 1929 and 1930 made them more widespread.[3]

The decline of individual prospects for African Americans is reflected in the fate of Negro League baseball in the late 1920s. The Negro National League, founded in 1920, had gradually declined to the point that in 1927 only its Detroit, Kansas City, and St. Louis franchises seemed viable. In June 1928, the Eastern Colored League's five-and-a-half-year existence ended in collapse, with several franchises having failed and with declines in attendance for all teams.

From the ashes of the Eastern Colored League, the American Negro Baseball League was formed in January 1929, made up of the surviving ECL teams with the addition of the popular Homestead Grays. While this league's first year was more successful overall than the final year of the ECL in that most teams played most or all of their scheduled games, attendance did not significantly recover. That same year the Negro National League was forced to shrink from eight to six teams. The number of games played by each team varied greatly, so much so that the meaning and purpose of league play was largely lost.

The Pittsburgh Crawfords in 1928.

The collapse of the American Negro League in February 1930 confirmed the weakness of organized play. The Negro National League would not make it through the 1931 season before it, too, gave up the ghost. Attempts to form minor leagues—the Texas-Oklahoma-Louisiana League and the Kentucky-Tennessee League—failed. While some of the popular barnstorming teams continued to draw crowds and do good business, organized baseball was at rock bottom. Apart from barnstorming, other means taken for the survival of professional baseball included winter ball in Cuba and California and tours of the Far East.

There may have been enough economically viable teams to form a truly national league, but differences and feuding between the Negro National League teams and their Eastern counterparts, as well as the difficulties and costs of travel and accommodations, made this solution impracticable. With all of this bad news for baseball, then, how was the disastrous 1930 baseball year reported in the sports pages of the *Pittsburgh Courier*, America's largest-circulation African American newspaper?

The *Courier* was published weekly and carried throughout the country by railroad workers, mainly Pullman porters who supplemented their income by distributing the paper. As a weekly, the content is more like what we are likely to associate with news magazines rather than newspapers—timely coverage of events was simply impossible. The role of the *Courier,* therefore, was more to comment on the news, and to provide coverage of news of interest to African Americans that was ignored by the mainstream press. Editorial policy was always unequivocally in favor of the complete integration of African Americans into mainstream American society, economy, and politics. Support for African American endeavor was also unequivocal (sometimes ironic, as for example, its support for the "successful" Hollywood career of Stepin Fetchit). It was extremely difficult for *Courier* reporters to deal seriously with failure in the Black community, so the tension between the hoped-for dignity and success and the disappointing reality of 1930s Negro League baseball informs all of the reporting.

The year begins with pessimistic reports about the ANL's impending collapse. On February 1, Jim (Andy) Taylor, manager of the Memphis Red Sox (Negro National League team), delineated the difficulties facing the teams in an article titled, "Future of League Baseball Doubtful, Say Cooperation, Fair Play and Publicity Needed." Emphasizing the business of baseball, Taylor argued that lack of funds was creating a situation where weaker teams were forced to play too many away games, creating an unbalanced schedule. Looking at the standings for the 1929 season, his own club played only 63 league games, while the more popular St. Louis Stars played 92. Lack of unified schedules meant that published standings had little meaning, which discouraged fans. The main problem he saw, though, was that the newspapers did a poor job of covering the season. Game results, "correct standing, batting and fielding averages" were seldom reported, even though the Black newspapers "are widely read by our fans." Unfortunately, the *Courier* continued to have this problem all season.

Rollo Wilson, the dean of African American sports columnists, in his Sports Shots column of March 1 ("Another Baseball League") reported the collapse of the American Negro League. In keeping with the paper's central philosophy, Wilson emphasized the need for continuity and gradual development. "Thousands of dollars can be made out of baseball if the men can be uncovered who will take a sporting chance." If the teams and the leagues were organized as businesses, there was more than enough talent to fill them, but if the organization didn't appear, young players wouldn't be inclined to pursue baseball and many current players would be forced "to show their skill in lines other than baseball and will be lost to the game forever." He finished by reporting that the surviving teams would be able to pick up all-star-caliber players from the collapsed teams, ensuring that baseball would still be worth watching.

William G. Nunn's "Sport Talks" column of March 22 picks up this theme when discussing the 1930 edition of the Homestead Grays. "This year, with the disbanding of the league, [manager Cum] Posey found it possible to get plenty of good material. He has refused to pay these real fancy salaries, as have other managers. No use, he contends, to keep high-salaried men, when you can get others to take their places at reduced prices." With four future Hall of Famers, the Grays continued to be a strong team, and with their strength, they were able to be a viable business concern by barnstorming, with no league support.

Responding to all of the criticism about the collapse of the Eastern league, the March 29 *Courier* reported NNL commissioner W.C. Hueston's impassioned defense of his league, particularly its financial soundness ("Our Baseball Players Rank as High as Any Others"). He pointed to success by Negro League teams in games against "all star" squads of major league players. He also complained about poor attendance, but emphasized that "There is only one thing left for me to do and that is to say, 'Play Ball.' This I will do on the 26th day of April 1930."

Once play began, the *Courier*'s coverage was spotty at best. Some weeks there were several box scores from around the country; some weeks there were none. With no league in the East, there were no standings to report, but even the NNL standings were often not reported.

At the end of April, the collapse of the formerly stable Hilldale Club of Philadelphia was reported, only to be followed by reports of Biz Mackey's return to Hilldale two weeks later. Nowhere was the discrepancy explained. (Much later in the summer was a report on August 9 that Hilldale had played its first away game of the season!)

The *Courier*, being a Pittsburgh-based newspaper, of course continued to support the success of the Homestead Grays, with reports even of games against semi-pro teams. As of June 7, their record, as reported faithfully by Cum Posey, was 46-3-1. The cheerleading for the star team couldn't make up for the overall lack of meaningful baseball news, and Rollo Wilson said as much on June 21. "Teams suffer at the gate from the lack of strong opponents.

Your true baseball bug never wants to see a lop-sided game. He wants his favorite to win, but he craves stirring opposition along the nine-inning route." Clearly 46-31 against weak teams was neither interesting nor impressive for a team with Homestead's talent.

The next week there was news that New York's Lincoln Giants were now 42-7. Obviously, all Eastern fans wanted to see a showdown between them and the Homestead Grays, now reported by Posey to be 60-5-1. (Even with possible discrepancy in the dates of the reports, it is clear that the Grays were playing about two games a day!) However, Posey writes that the Grays couldn't receive a large enough guarantee from promoters in the East and would thus not play in New York or Baltimore, instead turning their attention to the Midwest. By this time the Grays had followed the lead of the Kansas City Monarchs and begun night play under lights. As several columnists reported poor attendance at games on any day other than Sunday, this was seen as a chance to change the teams' fortunes.

On July 5, the first Black game utilizing Yankee Stadium was reportedly arranged as a benefit by the Sleeping Car Porters Union, featuring Lincoln and Baltimore. Rollo Wilson said he hoped that Lincoln would be able to use Yankee Stadium regularly in the future. The next week, the game was reported to have been a great success, with 15,000-18,000 in attendance. Much later in the fall, though, when Lincoln was denied use of Yankee Stadium, it became clear that there was much bad behavior among the fans at the game, particularly drinking and fighting, which made the Yankees organization disinclined to offer the stadium again. Once again, the need to be supportive of the effort made Wilson and his colleagues unable to discuss the unfortunate reality of the result. In other places they didn't hesitate to mention the manners of the fans, but with a matter of real pride on the line, the use of Yankee Stadium, they couldn't discuss it at this time. (On the other hand, perhaps it wasn't really a problem and the Yankees management was merely seizing a minor incident and using it as an excuse for something they wanted to avoid.)

On the 26th, in his "Ches Sez" column, Chester L. Washington, sports editor of the *Courier,* led the cheers for night baseball. Good attendance and "the long, sizzling hits, the brilliant, difficult catches, the bullet-like, accurate throws and the brainy brand of baseball set lots of bugs' tongues a-wagging" about a possible showdown series between the Grays and Forbes Field's "other" team, the Pittsburgh Pirates. He concluded that the Monarchs, the Grays, and possibly the Lincoln Giants represented the very best in baseball.

Praise for the high quality of the above three teams continued throughout August, but on the 23rd, there was troubling news that President Hueston, commissioner of the NNL, had moved to Washington to take up an appointment to a judgeship. While worried that it might signal trouble in the NNL, Rollo Wilson took the optimist's position that from Washington, Hueston would be closer to the eastern teams and perhaps able to work out a truly national league for the future. (Of course, nothing like that occurred.) Indeed, it was reported on September 13 that the NNL was looking for a new commissioner.

As the season wound down, the absolute confusion in Black baseball was typified by the *Courier* of September 20. News reports of a victory by the St. Louis Stars over the Detroit Stars in the opening game of the "Negro world series" appeared on the same page as a report in Wilson's column about a series between the Lincoln Giants and the Homestead Grays for "sundown baseball honors. This is the world's championship tussle of Negro baseball and hardly anyone can deny it."

He went on, "I have no interest in the matter other than hoping that the fans will attend in numbers befitting the importance of the series; that there will be no undue wrangling and that the players and managers will conduct themselves as gentlemen at all times." This emphasis may seem strange since he had consistently supported and praised sportsmanship, but apparently this was becoming harder and harder for Wilson to continue.

"The thing I want most of all is for the spirit of sportsmanship to be glorified by these young athletes. They are to participate in a baseball 'classic' and I want them to be worthy representatives of their group during every minute of every game. If everyone plays fair the better team will win, the fans will be satisfied and there will be no nasty aftermath of criticism from the jackals who glory in dishing the dirt." This dirt, however, did not appear in any direct way in the pages of the *Courier,* where optimism and support were the rule and criticism the exception. The intensity of this plea underscored the seriousness of the problems only hinted at in other columns and reports, that the season was characterized as much by fighting and complaining (on and off the field) as by the play of future Hall of Famers.

When the series finished, with Homestead the winners, Wilson continued the pessimistic tone in his column of October 10. "As usual, when Negro teams meet in combat there is an alibi for every defeat. To hear both sides tell it, the umps stole all of the games." Wilson himself placed the blame for defeats on "heavy bats, dumb judgement, and dumb base running," quite a contrast with the earlier praise of "brainy" baseball often heard in the same pages. He also noted, "Reports reached me that there was dissension and constant wrangling on the [Lincoln] bench." The series involved several problems in promotion, and many people who helped to bring it about were not apparently paid for their work. Although Wilson wasn't clear on his role in the promotion of the series, he said that he lost money, time and "so-called friends" over it.

The shocking ending to his report: "As far as your fat columnist is concerned, if the Grays and the Lincoln Giants never play again, that will be soon enough for him."

From our perspective, it is difficult to be too critical of anyone involved in Negro League (and independent) baseball in 1930. The social and economic problems of America were so huge as to be almost incomprehensible to us. They were merely trying to make a living in a difficult way at a difficult time.

The reporting of that year of baseball also shows deep conflicts in the African American media over its twin missions of uplift, raising the level of African Americans, and support, insisting on respect for what had already been achieved.

That winter the Cuban Winter League would fail and the Negro National League itself would go on to collapse in the middle of its 1931 season, bringing to an end the first era of baseball organized by and for African Americans. It is truly amazing that from these ashes a much more successful league was born, and such great players had more chances to show their abilities.

Bibliography

Clark, Dick and Larry Lester, eds. *The Negro Leagues Book,* Cleveland: Society for American Baseball Research, 1994.

Holway, John B., *Josh and Satch.* Westport, CT: Meckler Publishing, 1991.

Lanctot, Neil. *Fair Dealing and Clean Playing: The Hilldale Club.* Jefferson, NC: McFarland, 1994.

Peterson, Robert. *Only the Ball Was White.* New York: Oxford University Press, 1970.

Rihowsky, Mark, *A Complete History of the Negro Leagues.* New York: Birch Lane Press, 1995.

Rogosin, Donn. *Invisible Men.* New York, Atheneum, 1983.

Smith, Page. *Redeeming the Time: A People's History of the 1920s and the New Deal.* New York: McGraw-Hill, 1987.

Pittsburgh Courier, weekly national edition, various dates.

Endnotes

1. Page Smith, *Redeeming the Time, People's History of the 1920s and the New Deal* (New York: McGraw-Hill, 1987), 212.

2. Donn Rogosin, *Invisible Men* (New York: Atheneum, 1983), 87-89.

3. Neil Lanctot, *Fair Dealing and Clean Playing: The Hilldale Club* (Jefferson NC: McFarland, 1994), 142.

4. Lanctot, 152.

5. See *Fair Dealing* for details.

Pitching Behind the Color Line: Baseball, Advertising, and Race

by Roberta J. Newman

Individually and collectively, baseball and advertising may be said to hold a mirror up to America. The image in the glass, however, is not always pretty. For the first century of its history, with very few early exceptions, "American" as defined by so-called Organized Baseball, did not extend to those of African descent. As has been well documented, the emergence of Black baseball as a response to the professional game's color line certainly serves as a reflection of racial attitudes in America from the late nineteenth to the mid-twentieth century. But what of advertising? Does baseball-related advertising during this period say something larger about perceptions of race in America? One approach to answering this complicated question—really a set of questions—is to look at the print media, where there is no dearth of advertising related to Black baseball and, therefore, reflections of racial perceptions, be they direct or inferred.

Well before the Great Migration of the early twentieth century served as a catalyst for the formation of significant African American communities in Northern cities, giving rise to a lively Black press, ads for games played by "colored" teams appeared in the mainstream dailies. Contests featuring the Cuban Giants, for example, were advertised in the *New York Times* as early as 1886. In plain, straightforward language, one such ad reads, "BASEBALL. POLO GROUNDS TO-DAY. Colored Championship match. CUBAN GIANTS VS. GORHAMS, Game 4 P.M. Admission, 25 cents."[1]

According to Sol White, Black baseball's first historian and its first hagiographer, "the 'Cuban Giants' were heralded everywhere as marvels of the baseball world. They were not looked upon by the public as freaks, but they were classed as men of talent."[2]

White's statement is belied, however subtly, by this ad's placement in the newspaper. Appearing in small type at the bottom of a column of advertising under the heading "Amusements," it is the sole baseball announcement among ads for "Imre Kiralfy's latest, greatest, and supreme triumph, NERO; OR THE FALL OF ROME," complete with 2,000 performers and a Terpsichorean corps of 1,000 on the very largest stage of all time, and "Pain's '1666' GREAT FIRE OF LONDON," reenacted at Manhattan Beach on Coney Island. An ad in the same column for "THE BIGGEST SHOW ON EARTH! America's Most Mighty Exhibition. BUFFALO BILL'S WILD WEST," is even more telling.[3] Capitalizing on the popular taste for reenactments evident here, Buffalo Bill's Wild West show featured an Indian attack on the Deadwood Stage and a tableau vivant of Custer's Last Stand, among other "wonders."[4]

The "Colored Championship" match between the Cuban Giants and the Gorhams, taken in the context of its companions in the Amusements column, most particularly the Wild West show, may be seen in quite a different light. Just as Cody's spectacular offered New Yorkers a glimpse into the exotic world of "cowboys and Indians," essentially creating the popular American notion of the West, the Cuban Giants' appearance at the Polo Grounds presented spectators with the exotic spectacle of ballplayers of color engaged in an actual championship game. In fact, close scrutiny of the ad suggests that, contrary to White's assertion, embedded in the name "Cuban Giants," is the prospect of a freak show of sorts.

As if to offer an explanation, quoting a mention of the team in *The Sporting Life*, a writer for the *New York Sun* noted that the Cuban Giants were, in fact, "neither Giants nor Cubans, but thick-set and brawny colored men."[5] Certainly, baseball enthusiasts, of whom there was no shortage in New York, would have recognized the name Giants as referring to the regular tenants of the Polo Grounds, and the Cuban Giants as an African American club of some merit. This ad, however, appears neither on a sports page nor in the nascent sporting press. Baseball enthusiasts—cranks—are not its primary target. Proximity to the ad for Buffalo Bill Cody's enterprise, not to mention those for the spectacles of Nero's fiddling and London's conflagration, seems to suggest that, for at least some of the *Times'* overwhelmingly Caucasian readers, the Cuban Giants were, at best, exotic curiosities—thick-set, brawny colored men. At worst, they were freaks.

One of the earliest forms of printed advertising is the trade card. Generally associated with tobacco and candy, baseball trade cards were also distributed as souvenirs to commemorate specific events. While trade cards featuring African American players and teams, produced prior to the desegregation of the major leagues, were certainly uncommon, they were not completely unknown. A rare example of such a card features the 1897 Fence Page Giants, an African American club formed by two players who, contrary to convention, had played in Organized Baseball with otherwise White or integrated teams, Bud Fowler and Grant "Home Run" Johnson, in conjunction with two White businessmen, to advertise the Page Woven Wire Fence Company of rural Adrian, Michigan, and Monarch Bicycles. The Page Fence Company, notes Jerry Malloy,

> was not unfamiliar with inventive promotional techniques. As a permanent demonstration of the capacity of its product to contain livestock, the company maintained a park in town stocked with various animals corralled by its woven wire fencing. This

menagerie was transported by rail to nearby country and state fairs with Page Fence cages, thus displaying the strength and versatility of the company's line of goods.[6]

The team, dressed in their natty black uniforms emblazoned in large white letters with the words "Page Fence Giants," are pictured on the front of the card, along with their White manager, identified as A.S. Parsons. Printed on the reverse side is an ad for the company, reading, "Play Ball! Play Ball! Make Fence!!! Whatever your hands find to do, do it with all your might." Clearly, the language of the trade card—which would have been distributed to fans lured to games by the appearance of the luxurious private railway carriage in which the team traveled, as well as by the players themselves, who, after disembarking, paraded through town on their Monarch bicycles[7]—equates ballplaying with building fences.

According to Sol White, the notion that the team should be transported from town to town by a private train bearing the name Page Fence, affording the players the certainty of comfortable lodging in Jim Crow America, was the brainchild of Johnson and Fowler.[8] As such, it served as a sort of protective enclosure for the players on the road. At the same time, it also served to keep them at

An 1890 photo of the Page Fence Giants

a safe distance from the White people for whom they played, functioning as their own Page Fence. In this regard it bears a fairly close, though perhaps uncomfortable, resemblance to the fence separating the company's traveling menagerie that traveled the same roads to the same towns as the team separated from fairgoers. Coupled with the private railway carriage, this trade card, and the very promotional nature of the team itself seem to suggest to White spectators that colored ballplayers, while entertaining to watch, are best kept at a comfortable distance, separated from spectators by a sturdy fence, be it real or implied.

With his *Official Guide: The History of Colored Base Ball*, Sol White did more than provide a window into a past populated by teams like the Page Fence and Cuban Giants; he also provided 14 pages of baseball-related advertising. The *Guide's* ad copy differs substantially from newspaper advertising for the Cuban Giants and Page Fence's promotional baseball machine, both of which targeted predominantly Caucasian consumers. That White's *Guide*, originally published in 1907 on the cusp of the Great Migration, is aimed at African Americans is borne out in its advertising.

Some businesses, like John W. Connor's Royal Cafe and Palm Gardens in Brooklyn, make it clear in their ads that they are Black-owned. The Royal Café ad does so by specifying that the establishment serves as headquarters for the Royal Giants, owned and managed, not so coincidentally, by John W. Connor. On the facing page, Connor is pictured as a dignified, middle-aged African American with an avuncular smile.[9] Even more direct is an ad for "The Roadside," whose bewhiskered African American proprietor is pictured prominently, illustrating the minimalist copy, limited to the name and address of the establishment almost as if to say, "the only other thing you need to know about the Roadside is that it is Black-owned."[10]

A full-page ad for the *Philadelphia Tribune*, billed as "Our Only Colored Daily Paper," also features a photograph of an African American man, city editor, G. Grant Williams. Not only does this ad target potential African American readers, using the pronoun "our" to denote a connection between the publisher, the editorial staff, and Black baseball fans perusing White's Guide, but also other businesses. With a small line of type at the bottom of the page, the *Tribune* lays claim to the role of "the best Medium for advertising when you want to reach the people."[11] And who are the people? They are members of the same community at which White's *Guide* is aimed, baseball fans of color.

But not all the advertising in White's *Guide* pitches Black-owned businesses. One large ad sings the praises of promoters Schlichter and Strong, booking agents for the Philadelphia Giants, who call their outfit "the premier attraction among colored teams" whose "presence is eagerly looked for in all sections of the country."[12] That H. Walter Schlichter should advertise in White's book is hardly a surprise, given that he is billed on the title page as the original editor. Nor is the presence of Nat Strong's name unusual. Strong, a promoter based in New York, controlled booking in the majority of the area's semiprofessional baseball venues. In order to play lucrative Sunday games in the better semipro parks, it was necessary to deal with White booking agents like Strong.[13] Even though some teams, like the Royal Giants, may have been Black-owned, this ad is a reminder that African American baseball was still subject to White control, a factor which would provoke conflict and controversy at various times in its history.

The advertising in White's *Guide*, even Schlichter and Strong's ad promoting Black baseball, exhibit a certain race pride, a pride that would continue to grow in African American communities in Northern cities fueled by the Great Migration. But to suggest that these ads signal a momentous advance for African Americans would be a gross overstatement. The status of African Americans, even the sophisticated Northern readers of the *Philadelphia Tribune*, as second-class citizens with limited possibilities, is indicated, however indirectly, in two other ads in White's *Guide*. The "Headquarters for North Philadelphia Sports," the Chauffeur's Rest claims to be home to first-class pool parlors as well.[14] While the ad suggests that its patrons are the upper crust of the sporting life—that is, boxing men, vaudevillians, gamblers, even pimps, and, presumably, sporting women[15]—the name says something else, that its high-class clientele are, in fact, tired chauffeurs.

Washington's Manufactory, a dry goods emporium, advertises for sale its "High-grade Stationery, Finest Perfumes, and all kinds of Toilet Articles," but judging by its prominent place in the ad and its type size, first and foremost among the products available at Washington's Manufactory appear to be "Waiters Supplies."[16] Like the patrons of the Chauffeur's Rest, Washington's Manufactory's target consumers are service workers, not business executives. The first-class sports that use high-grade stationery and the finest perfumes are, in reality, drivers and waiters.

As the ad in White's *Guide* rightfully claims, the *Philadelphia Tribune* was an excellent medium to reach "the people," especially the people who were African American residents of large cities such as its home, Philadelphia, as well as Pittsburgh, Chicago, New York, and Baltimore. Between 1900 and 1925, the percentage of the population identified as Black in these cities increased as much as four-fold.[17] The increase led to a proliferation of a whole series of race institutions, among them businesses like the saloons, hotels, and retail shops that advertised in White's *Guide*, fraternal organizations, record labels, and, most notably, a lively Black press, intended specifically for consumption by African Americans.[18]

By this time the *Tribune*, which commenced publication in 1884, was a major voice in the political, social, and economic life of African American Philadelphia.[19] Along with the *Tribune*, weekly papers such as New York's *Amsterdam News and Age*, the *Chicago Defender*, the *Pittsburgh Courier*, and the *Baltimore Afro-American* became mainstays of their communities. The rapidly expanding African American urban population also led to the growth of Black baseball aimed, specifically, at a Black audience. According to Lawrence Hogan:

Prior to this time, Black baseball clubs played for essentially a white clientele. The rise of black enclaves in the North, however, was too important for black ball to ignore. A new generation of both black and white entrepreneurs would attempt to tap into this growing market."[20]

But how, exactly, were they to do so? In addition to the most consistently cost-effective and reliable method of marketing, word of mouth, spreading information by means of an informal network of neighborhood institutions like barbershops, beauty parlors, and social clubs, as well as displaying game placards in store windows, on taxicabs, and streetcars, Black baseball's entrepreneurs relied upon the weeklies.[21,22] Since African American ball clubs depended upon gate receipts for revenue, publicity in the weeklies was an absolute necessity.[23]

Ed Bolden's Hilldale Club, one of the very few African American teams to control its own diamond, Hilldale Park in Darby, Pennsylvania, advertised regularly in the *Tribune*. According to the team's ledgers, the Hilldales routinely budgeted between six and nine dollars monthly during the season to promote their games in the *Tribune* in the early 1920s. Although this seems like a paltry sum to dedicate to newspaper advertising, it represented a significant investment for a team that operated in the red during this period.[24] In order to ensure that Philadelphia residents would be able to find their way to Darby, a mill town close to the city, long home to a considerable African American population, many of the team's newspaper ads include specific directions to the park, via the "No. 13 Car on Walnut Street."[25]

The relationship between the Black press and the teams was reciprocal. Teams depended upon advertising on the sports pages, as well as promotion by the editorial staff, to ensure attendance, and the papers depended on teams to provide content. Directly below a series of ads for the Hilldale Club, an announcement in the *Tribune* reads "Feature your Own Ball Game—Send Snappy Accounts to the *Tribune* as soon as the game is over.—We Boost Clean Sports."[26]

As was true of the Black weeklies in general, the *Tribune* could not afford beat reporters to cover local African American teams as the mainstream press could. This made it necessary for teams to provide their own coverage. Such coverage, however snappy, was often unreliable at best. But no matter how snappy an account may have been, the *Tribune's* ad copy makes it clear that news of games tainted by gambling or other unsavory activities were not acceptable. Only "clean" games were deserving of the *Tribune's* support.

By virtue of its proximity to Hilldale ads, this notice serves yet another purpose. However indirectly, it tells readers that Bolden's team is nothing if not on the up-and-up. The connection between the *Tribune*, the Hilldale Club, and good sportsmanship was further reinforced by the relatively huge sign atop Hilldale Park's scoreboard, the only ad in the park, urging fans to "Read the Philadelphia Tribune."[27]

With the rapid increase in urban America's Black population came an increased demand for housing. In Baltimore, for example, this led to the expansion of the city itself, including the annexation of formerly rural areas like Catonsville, home to a small African American community.[28] With expansion came real estate development. And with real estate development came its natural by-product: advertising. A large ad in the *Afro American* of October 29, 1920, announces the opening of a "New Colored Development, Sale of Choice Lots, McDonough Heights, Catonsville." "Ideally situated on high, healthy ground," reads the pitch, offering prospective purchasers the opportunity to own beautiful lots, starting at 98 dollars each, which could be financed with the "Easiest of Easy Terms."

But this offer to own a prospective piece of the American Dream was not enough to lure Baltimore's Black residents to fairly remote Catonsville, only a streetcar ride away. No, for that a "special attraction Sunday," and the chance to watch the Piedmont Tigers take on the Catonsville Social Giants in a game of baseball, would be necessary.[29] That developers of a "colored" subdivision would advertise in the pages of the *Afro American,* using a game between Black ballclubs as bait, certainly points to the growth of a vibrant community, a community to which baseball was clearly important during this period. But it also points directly to the harsh realities of African American life in Baltimore circa 1920. There was strict segregation on the playing fields and strict segregation in the housing market.

Game announcements and other baseball-related advertising regularly appeared in the many of Black weeklies throughout the 1920s, despite the fact that attendance at the games themselves declined toward the end of the decade, a casualty of worsening economic conditions.[30] And baseball was not alone. Even before the crash of 1929, Black-owned businesses, a source of race pride and, more important, income, failed at an unusually high rate.[31] The last to be hired, Black workers were the first fired. By 1932 the Black urban unemployment rate stood at close to 50%. Nearly half of all African American families in Northern cities were on relief rolls by 1935.[32] Once again the economic profile of Black communities was reflected by the advertising related to baseball in the Black weeklies.

Alongside pitches for hair straighteners, pomades, and patent medicines claiming to alleviate "male problems" on the sports pages were ads for publications like *Aunt Sally's Policy Player's Dream Book, Stella's Lucky Dream Book,* and *Number Hit Forecast and Guide,* asking Black baseball fans, "Want to change your luck? Release your Lucky Number at glance."[32] Specifically, each of the publications claimed to guarantee success in playing policy or the numbers, a popular form of gambling in urban America during the Depression, especially Black urban America. According to Paul Oliver:

> Black superstition was the subject of lucrative exploitation of
> charms and philters, and cheap pseudo-religious votive ornaments
> and accessories alike, but it was in the systematic organization

of the Numbers Racket that the most relentless and deliberate exploitation took place. The policy racketeers published "Dream Books" which gave lists of numbers which were supposed to have a mystic connection with aspects of human experience, with objects natural and man-made, and with every conceivable circumstance that might occur in dreams.[34]

Among the dream symbols to which numbers were attached, several were, in fact, related to baseball.

Numbers lotteries gave impoverished African Americans—in this case, readers of baseball news in the Black weeklies—a chance to achieve social mobility, no matter how slim. With as paltry a bet as a single penny, numbers players, who had little opportunity for economic or social advancement, due in large part to race, could hope for a payoff as high as 500-1. And pay off the numbers did, particularly for the bankers who controlled the rackets. In Harlem the numbers were controlled by Dutch Schultz during the 1930s.[35] Elsewhere, numbers bankers were, in fact, race men, like Abe Manley, Alex Pompez, and, most notably Pittsburgh policy kingpin, Gus Greenlee, Negro League owners all. "Black underworld figures," writes Neil Lanctot, "long a part of the industry and seemingly impervious to Depression conditions, would provide a necessary influx of capital into the moribund enterprise" of Black baseball.

As the nation's economy improved in the late 1930s, so too did the economic circumstances of Black baseball's primary fans, urban African Americans, though more slowly than that of their White counterparts. This improvement is reflected in baseball-related advertising, particularly in the Black press. A series of ads, for example, appeared in the *Chicago Defender*, distinguishable from the paper's editorial content only by the fine print at the top reading "advertisement," with the headline "Piney Woods School Offers Youth Unusual Opportunities." "A school that is famous for its extracurricular activities," the ad touts Piney Woods' Black baseball pedigree in this way:

> Followers of the Kansas City Monarchs like to see Ivy Barnes pitch who is sometimes called a carbon copy of Satchell (sic) Paige. This year, the Homestead Grays will present to the baseball loving public three Piney Woods boys, Leroy Bass, catching; Buddy Thompson, pitching; and Luke Easterling, third base. All of those boys received training with the Piney Woods Giant Collegians who have bested some of the fastest semi-professional teams in the country, including the famous "House of David."[37]

The Piney Woods Country Life School in Mississippi's Black Belt, here offering young Chicago boys with a talent for baseball the opportunity to secure scholarships, was founded in 1909 by Lawrence C. Jones, known to his students as Professor Ed or Uncle Ed, who began his career in education teaching sharecroppers to read in a sheep shed. According to an article published in McClure's in 1922,

> at Piney Woods they learn things like these: plowing, horse shoeing, washing and ironing, sewing, cooking, basket making, carpentry; they are working with the white people and never against them.[38]

Baseball was also a major part of their curriculum, though more so in 1940 than in 1922.

To a great extent, this ad does more than try to attract prospective ball-playing boys to a traditional Black boarding school, it uses baseball in an attempt to reverse the trend of the Great Migration, to save poor young Black children from the squalor of the city by offering them an education in country life. The ad promotes the school as a sure path to the Negro Leagues, one followed by Thompson, Bass, and Easterling, but in reality, what it offers is an education in manual labor and working for White people, never against them. The ad for the Piney Woods School sends two separate messages. On one hand, it banks on race pride associated with star Negro League players to attract students. On the other, it seems to refer back to the accommodationist attitudes of Booker T. Washington, who in 1895 told African Americans to "cast down your buckets where you are," in the segregated South.[39] In this way, it expresses a conflicted attitude about race that is reflected in baseball-related advertising in general.

As America moved closer to war, more and more African Americans were attracted to urban areas by the prospect of employment in the defense industries. Increased employment meant increased disposable income, which also meant increased attendance at games and increased purchasing power. But not all baseball-related advertising during this period pitched games or products. Some baseball-related ads spoke to a more important purpose. With a drawing of a beefy ballplayer of indeterminate race and the headline, "What is SWOC's Batting Average?" the Steel Workers Organizing Committee urged readers to vote for the SWOC in the labor board election of September 25, 1941, in a nearly full-page ad on the "Afro Sports" page of the *Baltimore Afro American*. It reads:

> This is baseball season and everybody thinks in terms of batting averages. If you know a man's batting average you can tell he's a big-leaguer. If you know a team's batting average, you can tell whether that team is going places. So it's a fair question to ask the SWOC: What is your batting average.[40]

It goes on to give a series of reasons to vote the union in, each ending with the tag line, "Not a bad batting average is it?" in bold print.

Why does the SWOC use baseball language and images to promote its cause, the unionization of Bethlehem Steel's Sparrow's Point plant? After an extremely contentious three-year battle to unionize the plant, at which many African Americans were employed, the SWOC, an affiliate of the CIO, forced an election. Perhaps in order to fight charges that unionization was anti-American, the SWOC chose that most American of images, the baseball player in midstride. It is no wonder that the player bears some resemblance to Lou Gehrig, who, though no longer the Iron Horse, had come to represent not only resilience but grace under pressure.

In a very pointed way, this ad differs substantially from the majority of baseball-related advertising in the Black weeklies. While the race of the player is indeterminate, the language of the ad is not. The ad claims that if you know a player's batting average, you can tell if he's a big leaguer. Quite apart from the spotty statistical reporting for which Black weeklies were known, there is one thing that readers of the *Afro American* knew for sure in 1942, that the players on teams they followed were not big leaguers, no matter how gaudy their batting averages.

Rare for an ad in a Black weekly in 1941, this one makes no attempt to pitch its point directly to African Americans. Instead, it tries to reach the Black readership with the same ad used to appeal to White steelworkers. Although the language seems insensitive, given baseball's color line, it is, in its own way, quite the opposite. By refusing to change its language to speak specifically to one segment of its demographic, it indirectly indicates the emerging move toward equality within the union, if not within baseball or society as a whole. Editorial support of SWOC by the *Afro American* as well as the fact that it was voted in overwhelmingly by workers, African American and Caucasian alike, supports this notion.

Beginning in the 1920s, a mainstay of print advertising in the mainstream media was the celebrity product endorsement. And often the celebrities in question were baseball players. This practice proliferated in the 1940s, but not in the Black weeklies. Certainly Negro League baseball, then in its heyday, had its fair share of star power. But for all the Josh Gibsons, Cool Papa Bells, and Satchel Paiges, product endorsements were virtually nonexistent. Paige and Gibson, when mentioned in a game ad, might guarantee a good gate, but they were not paid to sell Camel cigarettes or Gillette razor blades to African American consumers.

As popular as these exceptionally talented players were, they could not hold a candle to the iconic Black athlete of this period, boxer Joe Louis. Endorsing everything from hair pomade to local tailor shops across America, he stands out as the lone African American product endorser of note during the late '30s and '40s. Even before his knockout of Max Schmeling at Yankee Stadium on June 22, 1938, made him a champion to Americans, regardless of race, Louis was featured prominently in ads in the Black press. So popular was he that he inspired the naming of the Brown Bomber Baking Company of New York City, by their own account, "The World's Largest Negro Baking Company," whose ad was illustrated with a drawing, in monumental style, of a strong Black pugilist pummeling a White boxer. Brown Bomber Bakery, pitching its product with the slogan "11 cents spent for Brown Bomber gives you double value... a loaf of tempting delicious bread plus part payment of some Negro's salary,"[41] did not rely entirely on the sweet science to promote their "soft bread."

One of the company's most notable marketing ploys was its sponsorship of a semi-professional team, the eponymous Brown Bombers. In a way, the bakery took a page from Page Fences, using a baseball team as a living promotional tool. But while Page Fences sold enclosures, Brown Bombers sold race pride.

Oddly, bread, not hair pomade, dream books, or beer, was the one of the first beneficiaries of an endorsement by an African American ballplayer in the 1940s. Though his testimonial takes a position subordinate to a large endorsement by a bathing beauty who has clearly availed herself of one of the many skin-lightening products advertised throughout the Black weeklies, praise is heaped upon Bond Bread by a proud-looking player in pinstripes, wearing the well-known interlocking NY of the lily-white New York Yankees, identified as "Walter Wright, famous 'Brick Top' of the Black Yankees." It reads, "With rationing cutting down on the muscle builders we used to get in meat, I'm mighty glad to get Bond's extra protein."

Bond bakery, unlike Brown Bomber, was not Black-owned. It did, however, advertise regularly in the *New York Amsterdam News*. While Bond routinely relied on the image of a happy African American homemaker to sell its products to New York's Black population, here the bakery capitalizes on the community's enthusiasm for baseball. Unlike so many of the other baseball-related ads, however, Bond Bread did not advertise on the sports page. This ad appeared in the retail advertising section, where products were pitched almost exclusively to women. In this regard, Bond seemed to realize that African American women were a largely untapped market of baseball fans, and one that often controlled the family's purse strings.

The dearth of product endorsements by African American baseball players in the pages of the Black weeklies did not last into the 1940s. Seemingly from the very moment Jackie Robinson stepped across the major league color line, his name and image seem to appear on virtually every page. "For a treat instead of a treatment...I recommend Old Gold Cigarettes," reads a testimonial ad by Robinson, a non-smoker, for the Brooklyn Dodgers' radio sponsor, not just in the Amsterdam News and the New York Age, but also in Black weeklies across the country. Where ads for Tuxedo Club Pomade, "the Pomade of Champions," had once featured the profile of a Black pugilist, now it sported a baseball player. And Jackie Robinson sold Bond Bread to New York City's women, too. Appearing in the *Amsterdam News* in August 1947, one Bond ad relies on one of the oldest tricks in the advertising book, hearkening back to the days of the Page Fence Giants. Depicting a trade card with an image of the Dodger, the ad reads, "Your grocer will give you a pocket-size reproduction of this Jackie Robinson photograph, free for the asking."[42] The ad also features a little cartoon baker, decidedly Caucasian, saying "Take It From Jackie Folks, Homogenized Bond Bread is Really Something: It Stays Fresh Days Longer, Too!"

Jackie Robinson's emergence as a major product endorser, coinciding with his emergence as a major leaguer, heralded a change in the connection between baseball, advertising, and race. What was once an extremely limited practice, using images of Black baseball players to sell consumer goods, appealing to a marginalized demographic, became far more widespread, appealing to a much larger segment of the American buying public. In many ways, Robinson would lead the way to changes in the way in which African Americans were perceived in the media as much through his role as pitchman as through his role as ballplayer.

As other players followed Robinson from the Negro Leagues to the majors, they also followed him into the ranks of major product endorsers, often for national advertisers like Beechnut Gum, Pabst Blue Ribbon Beer, and a variety of tobacco products, in both the Black weeklies and the mainstream media. Televised baseball, emerging, along with Robinson, as a force in 1947, contributed to the process, acclimating American consumers to the vision of baseball in Black and White. Advertisers, while hardly color-blind, increasingly recognized the power of testimonials by Black ballplayers to sell their products to a broader spectrum of potential purchasers.

The desegregation of major league baseball sounded the death knell for the organized Negro Leagues, as well as barnstorming and semi-professional African American baseball. But Black baseball's demise, and with it the demise of related advertising, was far from sudden. As the official souvenir program of the 1949 East-West Baseball Classic illustrates, Negro League baseball at its best was still popular enough to attract significant advertising dollars. With ads on virtually every page, the souvenir program attracted national advertisers like Coca-Cola, Pepsi, and Oscar Meyer, selling products associated with baseball, no matter what the race of the players and, more important, the fans might be. Longtime advertisers in the Black weeklies, it is hardly surprising to see their ads in the program.

More thoroughly represented than national advertisers, however, are local, primarily Black-owned Chicago-land businesses, courting African American consumers. Funeral homes, pharmacies, saloons, and segregated hotels make up the bulk of the program's advertising copy. In this respect, the ads in the souvenir program resemble those published in Sol White's Guide, half a century earlier. With the slogan, "For a Winning Personality," for example, an ad for the Payne School of Modeling and Charm features a photograph of an elegant African American woman, clearly a product of the South Side school's instruction in "Fashion Modeling, Photographic Modeling, Wardrobe Assembling, Body and Figure Control, Self Assurance, Corrective Make-up, and Hair Styling."[43]

But unlike the tired chauffeurs and newly supplied waiters targeted by the advertising in White's Guide, this ad is aimed at women. The women it targets, moreover, are not aiming for jobs which are functionally equivalent to those held by the original consumers of White's Guide, maids, waitresses, and the like. Nor are they housewives, looking for the extra protein in Bond Bread. Rather, they are younger women considering careers in modeling, or those presumably looking to improve their prospects, seeking professional employment or simply in search of suitable young men.

Connecting athletics with ad copy, several of the ads in the program are visually and textually tied together with a theme, "From sports to business." The enduring popularity of Joe Louis is apparent in a full-page ad for the Chicago School of Automotive Trades, Inc., with the slogan, "From the Boxing Ring to Business." Ostensibly a profile of the heavyweight, entitled "The Influence of Sports on the Life of Joe Louis," penned by sportswriter Wendell Smith, the copy reads, "He soared from the poverty-stricken cotton fields of Alabama to the heavyweight championship, like a shooting star zips across the azure skies."[44]

Following a brief, though no less hyperbolic, synopsis of the Brown Bomber's career, the profile tells consumers that since his retirement, "he has devoted all his time to his various enterprises and businesses. He is president of the Chicago School of Automotive Trades." As the producers of Brown Bomber bread knew in the 1940s, Louis's endorsement branded their product with the image of African American strength and resilience. Like Louis, the ad implies, students at the Chicago School of Automotive Trade might also ascend like a shooting star across the azure skies of success and financial security. Although its target consumer differs from that of Payne's school by gender, its message is not entirely different. In its own way, each of these ads seems to suggest that entry into the middle class, even into the elite, is hardly out of reach.

Like Joe Louis and the beautiful woman gracing the Payne's ad, a little hard work and proper training may be only a phone call away for the predominantly African American fans at the East-West game. And unlike the ads in White's *Guide*, these speak to a rising sense of African American empowerment in a still largely segregated society, rather than representing the segregated status quo.

African American empowerment is also the unspoken message in an ad for John B. Knighten Jr. and Co., a South Side, Chicago, real estate company. It features an illustration of the nearly perfect nuclear family, consisting of a pipe-smoking father, a well-coiffed mother, perhaps a graduate of Payne's school, and a little girl in pigtails, dreaming, via a balloon, of their slice of the American pie, in the form of what appears to be a spacious home, surrounded by ample open space. Outside the dream balloon, there is a nest resting on a branch, complete with chirping baby birds. The ad reads "Birds Have Nests! Do You Have a Home?" The only thing that distinguishes this ad from similar real estate advertising which might have been placed in the mainstream press, or in souvenir programs from a major league game, is the fact that the skin of the family in the illustration is shaded with crude lines. Its message seems to be, "You, too, African American baseball fan, can participate in the American Dream of Home Ownership."[45] With the appropriate training from the Chicago School of Automotive Trade and Payne's, the final step toward the post-World-War II American ideal is a visit to John B. Knighten Jr. and Co.

While, as the relatively large number of advertisers in the 1949 East-West game program suggests, African American baseball was still a going concern two years after Jackie Robinson made his debut in Brooklyn, that was not the case only a few years later. The 1952 East-West Game, for example, drew only 14,122 fans, as opposed to 46,871 nine years earlier.[46] In a sense, Black baseball ended as it began, not with organized leagues but with barnstorming teams owned by enterprising White promoters, traveling to small towns, often in the upper Midwest, playing in front of predominantly Caucasian audiences. Harkening back to the first professional African American baseball team, the latter-day Cuban Giants, were one such team, owned and promoted by former Kansas City Monarchs owner Thomas Young Baird. But the 1950s Cuban Giants, unlike their 19th-century namesake, were, in fact, Cuban.

Touring towns like Aurora, Illinois, Dubuque, Iowa, and Yankton, Nebraska, in the early 1950s, appearances by the Cuban Giants were touted in "advertorials," promotional speech masquerading as editorial content. Long a mainstay of African American baseball reporting, Baird raised the Black baseball advertorial to a high art, going as far as to pay at least one sports journalist in Texas, under the table, in order to promote an appearance by one of his teams.[47] In the St. Joseph Michigan Herald Press on June 4, 1952, for example, on the same page as a one-inch-high ad, stretching across all seven columns on the bottom of the page, is an advertorial with the headline "Baseball Blends With Dancing At Ausco Park." It reads,

> President Ty Baird of the visitors has signed up three entertainers, two musicians who play an instrument called a 'bongoe' (sic) and a dancing comedian named Peter Sel who reportedly will imitate a waltzing penguin.[48]

Taking a page from his occasional business partner, Syd Pollack—the baseball impresario responsible for keeping alive the Indianapolis Clowns—Baird insisted that good baseball was simply not enough to put fans in the seats. Competing with the same increasingly popular medium that brought Jackie Robinson into American homes—television—a crisply played, interracial, multi-ethnic ballgame was not enough. Much like the fans of the previous century, who were faced with the choice of whether to spend their precious entertainment dollars and leisure time on Buffalo Bill's Wild West Show, Nero's fiddling, or "exotic" Black baseball, residents of St. Joseph were lured to Edgewater Park in its "twin city," Benton Harbor, to see the Cuban Giants take on the team fronted by Ausco Products, Inc., a major area brake manufacturer.[49]

Fans were attracted not just with the promise of the slugging prowess of "Havana's Babe Ruth," "Bambino" Berrera, but with penguin imitators, accompanied on that most exotic of instruments, not heretofore seen in person in the upper Midwest, the bongo.[50] For the well-heeled readers of the *Herald-Press*, African Americans calling themselves Cuban would no longer be acceptable. For an audience increasingly familiar with "real" Cubans like Desi Arnaz's alter ego, Ricky Ricardo, who made his first appearance on their television screens in 1951, only authentic Cubans would do. Despite the desegregation of the major leagues and the increasing visibility of African American baseball players in advertising, racial and, in this case, ethnic stereotyping still served as popular entertainment and promotional fodder.

Although large sections of the country, South and North alike, resisted desegregation, both formal and informal, the blurring of the color line by African American baseball players did herald changes, pitifully slow, but changes nonetheless, in the way in which race was perceived in America. The legacy of Page Fence Giants, The Chauffeur's Rest, the SWOC, and Payne's School of Modeling and Charm is on display in advertising today, be it in print, on television, or online. One of baseball's ubiquitous pitchmen, Derek Jeter, may be seen as the new image of the "all-American boy," one formerly held by the likes of the blond-haired Mickey Mantle. Most tellingly, Jeter defines himself as neither Black nor White but both. This self-definition, as much an example of the social construction of reality as Effa Manley's self-definition as Black, speaks volumes about perceptions of race in America. Though, as reviled slugger with precious few endorsement opportunities, Barry Bonds, notes, race prejudice is still very much a part of American culture, its presence in advertising is conspicuous by its absence. Today, manager Willie Randolph sells Subway sandwiches in a New York Mets uniform, not Page Fences.

This article originally appeared in the SABR Baseball Research Journal, Vol. 36, 2007.

Endnotes

1. "Amusements," *The New York Times*, July 5, 1888, 7.

2. Sol White. *Sol White's History of Colored Base Ball with Other Documents on the Early Black Game, 1886-1936.* Lincoln: Univ. of Nebraska Press, 1995, 12.

3. "Amusements," 7.

4. "William F Cody, Buffalo Bill," http://www.pbs.org/weta/thewest/people/a_c/buffalobill.htm, March 9, 2006.

5. Jerry Malloy, "The Strange Career of Sol White," in *Out of the Shadows: African American Baseball from the Cuban Giants to Jackie Robinson*, ed., Bill Kirwin. Lincoln: Univ. of Nebraska Press, 2005, 64.

6. Jerry Malloy, "Sol White and the Origins of African American Baseball," in White, xxxiii.

7. White, 24.

8. White, 24.

9. White, 83.

10. White, 52.

11. White, 69.

12. White, 79.

13. Neil Lanctot. *Negro League Baseball: The Rise and Ruin of a Black Institution.* Philadelphia: Univ.of Pennsylvania Press, 2004, 24.

14. White, 116.

15. Geoffrey C. Ward. *Unforgivable Blackness: The Rise and Fall of Jack Johnson.* New York: Vintage, 2004, 67.

16. White, 7.

17.   Campbell Gibson and Kay Jung, "Historical Census Statistics on Population Totals by Race, 1790 to 1990, and by Hispanic Origin, 1970 to 1990, for Large Cities and Other Urban Places in the United States," www.census.gov/population/www/documentation/twps0076.html, March 10, 2006.

18.   Lanctot, 4.

19.   Armistead S. Pride and Clint C. Wilson. *A History of the Black Press*. Washington, DC: Howard Univ. Press, 1997, 133.

20.   Lawrence D. Hogan. *Shades of Glory*. Washington, DC: National Geographic Society, 2006, 128.

21.   Lanctot,190.

22.   Janet Bruce. *The Kansas City Monarchs: Champions of Black Baseball*. Lawrence: Univ. of Kansas Press, 1985, 45.

23.   Lanctot, 196.

24.   Hilldale Club Ledgers, 1921-1922, Cash Thompson Collection, Box 3, African American Museum, Philadelphia, PA.

25.   *Philadelphia Tribune*, May 3, 1928,11.

26.   *Philadelphia Tribune*, May 16, 1925,10.

27.   Undated photograph, Cash Thompson Collection, Box 6, African American Museum, Philadelphia, PA.

28.   Catonsville Historical Society,"Catonsville History," http://catonsvilleweb.com/history.html, September 28, 2006.

29.   *Baltimore Afro-American*, October 22, 1920,8.

30.   Hogan, 204.

31.   Lanctot, 6.

32.   Hogan, 204.

33.   *New York Amsterdam News*, September 23,1939,14.

34.   Paul Oliver. *Blues Fell this Morning: Meaning in the Blues*. London: Cambridge Univ Press, 1960, 132-135.

35.   Burton B. Turkus and Sid Feder, *Murder, Inc.: The Story of the Syndicate*. New York: Da Capo, 1992, 95.

36.   Lanctot, 9.

37.   "Piney Woods School Offers Youth Unusual Opportunity," *Chicago Defender*, April 20, 1940, 8.

38.   Alma and Paul Ellerbe, "Inchin'Along," *McClure's Magazine,* vol. 54, no. 2, April 1922, 45.

39.   Ward, 40.

40.   "What Is SWOC's Batting Average?" *Baltimore Afro American*, September 20, 1941, 22.

41.   *New York Amsterdam News*, April 6,1940,12.

42.   *New York Amsterdam News*, August 23,1947.

43.   East-West Baseball Classic: Official Souvenir Program, August 14, 1949. Collection of the National Baseball Hall of Fame Library, Cooperstown, NY.

44.   East-West Baseball Classic: Official Souvenir Program.

45.   East-West Baseball Classic: Official Souvenir Program.

46.   Negro American League Expenses from the East-West Game, 1943 and 1952, Ty Baird Papers, 414:2:2, Kenneth Spencer Research Library, University of Kansas, Lawrence, KS.

47.   Baird Papers, 414:2:4.

48.   *"Baseball Blends With Dancing at Ausco Park,"* St. Joseph Michigan Herald Press, June 4, 1953, 12.

49.   FortMiami.org, www.fortmiami.org/museum.html, October 6, 2006.

50.   "Baseball Blends With Dancing at Ausco Park."

Quebec Loop Broke Color Line in 1935

by Merritt Clifton

When Jackie Robinson joined the Montreal Royals in 1946, he became—as every baseball fan knows—the first acknowledged Black player in Organized Baseball* since Cap Anson, Tip O'Neill, and the Ku Klux Klan routed Moses and Welday Walker back in the 1880s with threats of lynching. But Robinson didn't crack the professional baseball color line in Quebec.

That distinction belongs to longtime Negro National Leaguer Fred "Sardo" Wilson, a pitcher, outfielder, first baseman, and manager, who in Quebec went by the name Alfred Wilson, Freddy for short.

Wilson joined the Granby Red Sox of the Quebec Provincial League in July 1935. The paradox that Robinson, not Wilson, re-integrated Organized Baseball is resolved by pointing out that the Provincial League then labored in the same twilight zone as the all-Black Negro National and Negro American leagues.

Just as baseball had a color line, so it also had a language line. French-speaking players weren't overtly barred from the American professional leagues, as Black players were, but they faced strong xenophobic prejudice, especially if they didn't speak good English and were born in Canada. Some weathered it, aided by US citizenship, like former Dodgers first baseman Jacques Fournier. Others, like Fournier's successor Del Bissonette, tried American baseball for a time but eventually retreated back north of the border, where French prevailed. Still others, like Roland Gladu, spent almost their whole careers in the Quebec bush leagues, becoming legends of similar order to Josh Gibson and Satchel Paige, but making only token appearances anywhere else.

The Quebec Provincial League, unlike the Negro National and Negro American leagues, was admitted to the Organized Baseball hierarchy off and on—1921–23, 1940, and 1950–55. But mostly it remained independent, from its hazy origins in the nineteenth century through dissolution in early 1970. Even Wilson may not have been the first Black participant, because in early, unstructured days the league included several teams in Missisquoi County, formerly the northern terminus of the Underground Railroad. A substantial Black population lived there until around the turn of the century when, like many of their White neighbors, most sold small farms and moved westward.

Some Black players definitely played on the Bedford town team, as verified by old photographs, although Bedford was never actually a Provincial League member. Bud Fowler, often referred to as the first Negro baseball player of note, is rumored to have appeared with several Quebec teams in the late 1870s, despite lack of written evidence.

However, once formally chartered, the Provincial League was all White. It remained all White until after restructuring in 1935 as an "independent" league, which meant that the teams supported themselves by gate receipts alone rather than through political patronage or industrial sponsorship. The team owners therefore had to stress winning and entertainment to a greater degree than ever before, and this in turn led to innovation.

Exactly who first thought of introducing Black players isn't recorded. The Granby team owner, gasoline station owner, real estate magnate, eventual mayor, and Granby Zoo founder Homer Cabana, had organized exhibition games with barnstorming Black teams in previous years and had undoubtedly been impressed with their talent. Meanwhile, Ace Corrigan, the Granby manager, had attended spring training with the New York Giants the year manager John McGraw tried to pass off Black center fielder Oscar Charleston as a White Cuban. But whoever had the idea, they agreed it was a good one and contacted Chappie Johnson of Chappie Johnson's All-Stars (the prototype of "Bingo Long's Travelling All-Stars & Motor Kings") for help in recruiting.

According to the limited biographical information that Alfred "Freddy" Wilson gave to the Granby newspapers, he was born somewhere in Alabama during 1908, believed to have been from a Cajun district, because he did speak some French as well as English. His official birth date was actually in 1909, and he was actually born in Hastings, Florida.

Wilson in Quebec was believed to have had a college education and was certainly reputed to have a good head for business despite having had some undisclosed personal financial misfortune – not uncommon for anyone during the depths of the Great Depression. Wilson was articulate, dignified, proud and an extremely hard worker who made the most of limited natural talent. He stood about six feet tall, weighing 170 pounds, medium-sized among American professional ballplayers, but a giant in Quebec, where even today few men top six feet.

While remembered in Quebec as a gentleman, Wilson by all accounts from everywhere but Quebec was a tough and nasty piece of work, if an intelligent baseball man, who was in fact doing hard time in prison, on chain gangs, during the years he claimed to have been in college. Hall of Fame outfielder Monte Irvin reputedly called Wilson "the meanest man I have ever known."

Wilson broke into the black bush leagues at age 21, rapidly acquiring the nickname "Evil." This nickname was replaced by "Sardo" when Wilson played for a time with the Ethiopian Clowns, but his evil reputation was not forgotten.

Between stints with other teams, Wilson played for the Zulu Cannibal Giants off and on, a touring team formed by Chicago entrepreneur Abe Saperstein, who also founded the renowned Harlem Globetrotters basketball team. The Zulu Cannibal Giants outwardly conformed to Jim Crow and lived up to the worst White stereotypes of Black men. But playing names like Bissagoos, Wahoo, Tanna, Rufigi, Taklooie, Kangol, Limpopo, Mofike and Ny Ass Ass concealed a hard edge of self-respect and defiance. Some of these "African" names were actually obscenities directed at White ignorance. Others harked back to actual African heritage. And the Zulu Cannibals included some outstanding players, including catcher Frank Duncan and first baseman Buck O'Neill, who were not afraid to whip the hell out of White teams by any score they could manage. While Chappie Johnson cautiously instructed his All-Stars not to exceed a two-run lead, lest White fans take violent exception, the Cannibals often won by ten runs or more, depending upon guts and luck to save their lives.

After the Cannibals dropped Wilson for reasons unknown, probably involving bootleg liquor and brawling with teammates, Johnson promptly picked him up, then dispatched him north in 1935 when Granby summoned. Wilson responded to the challenge by playing some of the best baseball of his life. He won all five of his pitching decisions while batting .392 with 20 runs batted in 79 trips to the plate.

Newspaper accounts don't record what antagonism Wilson may have faced, but one afternoon in Sorel the fans beat up the entire Granby team after a game Wilson pitched. Wilson's race may have been advanced as an excuse. However, one must note that such conduct wasn't uncommon in Sorel, a shipyard town where the umpires sometimes carried guns. On the other hand, racism was as prevalent in Quebec as in the United States. The all-Mohawk team from the Caughnawaga reserve was subjected to all manner of indignities by the team sponsored by the Montreal Police, while headlines called them the "Red Injuns" and referred to the barnstorming Hawaiian All-Stars as the "Japs."

As Sorel ran away with the 1935 pennant race, revenue from exhibitions with barnstorming teams became essential to keeping the league afloat. Wilson used his Black baseball connections to arrange tours by both Black teams and White, including the Cleveland Browns, Boston Black Giants, the House of David, the Boston ABC, the Hawaiians and, of course, his own former teams, the Zulu Cannibals and Chappie Johnson's. The Black barnstormers brought portable floodlights with them, the first time Quebec ever saw night baseball. By the end of the year, Granby had floodlights, too, and in future years night baseball became the Provincial League rule rather than the exception.

Wilson most distinguished himself in these exhibitions. He beat the ABCs with a five-hit shutout while hitting the first home run ever to clear the Granby stadium. Then he defeated the Zulu Cannibals, 7-6, before a then-league record 7,500 fans. The box score suggests the Cannibals might have given the game to him on purpose, committing several uncharacteristic errors in the last two innings. He was a brother, after all, and they wanted him to look good.

Wilson's success in that regard was fleeting, however. While Wilson returned to the U.S., Chappie Johnson dispatched Jack Wilson, no relation, to run an all-

Black Provincial League entry in 1936 and 1937. Called the Black Panthers, they replaced the Montreal Police, who were finally expelled for taking entirely too many liberties with the law. The Black Panther players were mostly teenagers from the Deep South, away from home for the first time and miserable. Their lineup changed from day to day and week to week as players steadily defected and were replaced.

Among the few players who survived both seasons was Carl Logan, who with teammates Ormond Sampson and Hank Chaffen was chosen to play in a Provincial League all-star game against the all-white Montreal Royals, owned at the time by Charlie Trudeau, father of future Canadian prime minister Pierre Elliot Trudeau. Unfortunately, the Royals refused to play if the Black players were in the Provincial League lineup, so they were excluded.

One Black player remained in the Provincial League in 1938, 17-year-old pitcher Clifford Johnston, already an imposing 6'4" and 200 pounds. Some researchers have felt this Johnston actually was Clifford "Connie" Johnson, who at age 31 joined the Chicago White Sox in 1953 to begin a six-year major league career. However, Johnson denied that, claiming he didn't play in the Provincial League until the late 1940s.

When the Provincial League rejoined Organized Baseball in 1940, it was again conformingly White. One year later, however, the league left Organized Baseball.

Fred Wilson, meanwhile, according to Pitch Black Baseball blogger Kyle McNary, ran into trouble post-Provincial League wherever he went. In 1939, according to McNary, "Wilson was serving time in prison in Miami and playing on the prison baseball team when the warden called Newark Eagles owner Abe Manley and offered to release Wilson if Manley would sign him. With Newark in '39, Wilson batted .396 in league games, out-hitting Hall of Famers Biz Mackey, Willie Wells, Mule Suttles and Monte Irvin. Wilson often exhibited bizarre behavior, possibly from some form of mental illness and definitely heightened by heavy drinking, and he regularly threatened teammates and opponents with his switchblade. And, he didn't just threaten; he stabbed teammate and star pitcher Dave Barnhill during an argument and Barnhill was out for a most of 1944," while Wilson went into the U.S. Army instead of going back to prison, spending his military hitch playing for the Army team at Fort Benning.

Looking for a place to play baseball after World War II ended and he was released from the Army, Wilson re-integrated the Provincial League in 1945, this time with Drummondville, where he mainly pinch-hit. This was still a year before Jackie Robinson's Montreal debut. Lloyd MacKeen was then teaching school in Drummondville. "When we heard the team had a Black pitcher coming with his family," he remembered in 1980, "we told the kids that they'd soon have a classmate who was a little bit different, and they should be nice to him. We shouldn't have worried. The pitcher's son was a little hooligan, and he soon was the most popular kid in the school. I shouldn't say he was a hooligan. He was a good kid, but lively. You know, the team didn't pay the players much, and when the season was over we had to take up a collection to send the family back home to Alabama."

But the Wilson home was actually in Miami, where Wilson died in a knife fight in 1950.

Post-Jackie Robinson, and of course post-Fred Wilson, the Provincial League became an entry league for Blacks gaining their first crack at White baseball. Among the graduates were Dave Pope, Ed Charles, Vic Power, Hector Lopez, Ruben Gomez and Al Pinkston, who never played in the majors but who made the Mexican League Hall of Fame after hitting a lifetime .372. Connie Johnson won 15 games and struck out a league-leading 172 batters with Saint Hyacinthe in 1951 on his way up at last.

And toward the end, after the last flirtation with Organized Baseball in 1950–55, the Provincial League harbored a new kind of proud Black ballplayer—men who knew they were good enough to play with Whites, but who felt they had nothing to prove and preferred low pay and obscurity to taking guff somewhere south of the border. Nova Scotia-born John Mentis was one of these. He hit .340 in 13 Provincial League seasons, picking up a pair of batting titles. Twice he topped .400. "I had offers to play American baseball," he remembers, but softly adds, "I wasn't ready for that, where someone else could walk on the sidewalk and you couldn't." A quiet, gentle man, Mentis preferred the Alfred Wilson role-model to Jackie Robinson's, even if it doomed him to the same fate.

Note: SABR no longer uses the term "Organized Baseball" to refer to the American and National Leagues and their affiliated minor leagues, but it was the accepted term at the time of this article's original publication in 1984. The term "Organized Baseball" was used in the mid-twentieth century by the White baseball establishment in part to imply that the Negro Leagues were disorganized.

This article was originally published in the SABR Baseball Research Journal, Vol. 13 (1984) and was updated in 2019 for the Société d'histoire de la Haute-Yamaska web site.

Black Bluejackets: The Great Lakes Negro Varsity of 1944

by Jerry Malloy

"It is always wrong to consider that something which begins in a small way cannot rapidly become important." — Plutarch

On June 5, 1942, Doreston Luke Carmen Jr. became the thin end of a very large wedge. That was the day the nineteen-year-old native of Galveston, Texas, became the first black recruit at Great Lakes Naval Training Station in Illinois. Having been jettisoned from the United States Navy during the interwar years, blacks were being allowed back into the armed forces' most exclusive white man's club.

The large scale reentry of blacks into the Navy would have far-reaching and often unforeseen consequences, not only for the Navy, but for American society as a whole. The United States' entry into World War II suddenly made the armed forces the largest employer of blacks in the country, by far. Historian Morris J. MacGregor points out that in altering race relations "... the armed forces could command where others could only persuade." And command they did, to the extent that black participation in the military during World War II became the origin of the modern civil rights movement in the nation.

In baseball, as well, World War II furnished a peek into the future. The rigid barriers of segregation gradually broke down on the fields of play as well as on the fields of war. Conflict over racial policy in the military services foretold the coming of the civil rights movement, and blacks on military service teams were unheralded and unwitting precursors of what Jules Tygiel has termed "baseball's great experiment": the breaching of the color line.

One such group of ballplayers came together to form a team at Great Lakes in 1944. The Great Lakes white team, the Bluejackets, under the direction of Mickey Cochrane, was well publicized and highly regarded. Some called it "the seventeenth major league team." This is an account of another team from Great Lakes, the all-black team created in 1944—the Great Lakes Negro Varsity, as they were called. In their own way, these "Black Bluejackets" helped clear the path for Jackie Robinson.

The Negro and the Navy

By the end of World War II, the Navy had adopted the most progressive racial policies of any of the military services. But three and a half years earlier, when the United States entered the war, it was the most blatantly racist. Black men had served with distinction on mixed crews in *every* war since the Revolution, but during the course of WWI, the "War to Make the World Safe for Democracy," they were relegated to the menial chores of the Messman's (or Steward's) Branch. During the 1920s the black man virtually disappeared from the Navy, as Filipinos and Guamanians served as "seagoing bellhops." In 1932, with the independence of the Philippines approaching, the Navy once again began to recruit blacks, but only as "chambermaids of the Navy," in the Messman's Branch. Escalating manpower requirements after Pearl Harbor changed this. Civil rights groups mounted a "Double-V Campaign" to defeat racism at home as well as fascism abroad. The Army pressured the Navy to assist in assimilating blacks into the armed forces. Franklin Roosevelt, prompted by a combination of idealism and political considerations, also played a key role in forcing the Navy to open its ranks to blacks. The Navy's initial efforts to modify its racial policies often failed because the decision to do so was thrust upon it by outsiders. Consider:

- Not only were there no black men at Annapolis (in fact, the Navy had no black officers until 1944), the Midshipmen refused to allow a black man from Harvard University to participate in a lacrosse game.
- In July 1941 a Navy commission determined that "Negro characteristics" made black recruits suitable only for messman's duty. Six months later, the Commandant of the Marine Corps viewed the inclusion of blacks in the Navy as "absolutely tragic" and said that since the Negro could serve in the Army, his desire to enter the Navy was an attempt "to break into a club that doesn't want him."
- Throughout the war, the Navy, as well as the other armed services, segregated blood banks, despite the utter lack of scientific evidence to support such a policy. Not lost upon the black press was the fact that Dr. Charles Drew, a pioneer in the development of plasma transfer techniques and the director of the first Red Cross blood bank, was a black man.
- Black recruits eventually stationed at Great Lakes were required to spend Sunday evenings singing spirituals in an ill-considered attempt to foster black pride. Many blacks, especially those from the North, found this practice repellent and demeaning.

It is little wonder that Dennis D. Nelson, one of the first thirteen blacks to become Navy officers in 1944, recalled that "Recruits who felt they had been treated as sub-citizens found it likely they would be classified as sub-sailors as well." Another one of the first black ensigns, James Hair, remembers a very hostile atmosphere at Great Lakes, as though the attitude was that "These n******s coming in is gonna change the Navy."

The rigid segregation that the Navy imposed in training, housing, and—as we shall see—sports gave many blacks a dose of government-sanctioned discrimination that they had never experienced before. The situation of Larry Doby typified that of many recruits. Doby, who had been a popular star athlete at an integrated high school in Paterson, New Jersey, looked back upon his plunge into racism in the Navy:

> "... I enlisted and wore a US sailor's uniform at Great Lakes Naval Training Station. For the first time I was conscious of discrimination and segregation as never before. It was a shock. If you've never been exposed to it from the outside and it suddenly hits you, you can't take it. I didn't crack up; I just went into my shell. ... I thought: 'This is a crying shame when I'm here to protect my country.' But I couldn't do anything about it—I was under Navy rules and regulations and had to abide by them or face the consequences."

Mickey Cochrane's Bluejackets

In the spring of 1945, *Chicago Sun* columnist James S. Kearns wrote that "the most successful producer of winning sports teams in America the last three years [has been the] U.S. Naval Training Center at Great Lakes." The following chart helps explain how he came to this conclusion:

GREAT LAKES SPORTS TEAMS
1942 to Spring 1945

Sport	# Seasons	W-L	PCT	Home Game	Attendance
Basketball	4	130-16-0	.890	58	120,000
Football	3	27-2-2	.931	14*	305,000
Baseball	3	163-26-1	.862	57	680,000
TOTALS	10	320-49-3	.867	129	1,105,000

*No home football field in 1942

In these three baseball seasons, the team was managed by Mickey Cochrane; in 1945 Bob Feller and Pinky Higgins managed it. Kit Crissey, in *Athletes Away,* has written that "The Navy scored a tremendous public relations coup when it recruited... Mickey Cochrane.... Many professional players specifically chose the Navy and Great Lakes so they could play for him, and thus he was able to field outstanding teams in 1942, 1943 and 1944." During these three seasons, Cochrane managed 39 men who played in the major leagues before, during, or after the war.

One such major leaguer was Chet Hajduk, whose career consisted of a lone, and unsuccessful, pinch-hitting appearance for the White Sox in 1941.

But Cochrane also managed two players who later would join him in the Hall of Fame: Billy Herman and Johnny Mize. Twenty-nine of these Great Lakes Bluejackets played in the major leagues for at least five years; and 18 of them played in at least eight big league seasons: Frankie Baumholtz, Tom Ferrick, Joe Grace, Billy Herman, Si Johnson, Bob Klinger, Johnny Lucadello, Johnny McCarthy, Barney McCosky, Johnny Mize, Don Padgett, Eddie Pellagrini, Frankie Pytlak, Johnny Rigney, Schoolboy Rowe, Johnny Schmitz, Virgil Trucks, and Gene Woodling. (The 1945 team, which went 25-6, included ten players with major league careers, among them: Bob Feller, Pinky Higgins, Denny Galehouse, Johnny Gorsica, Walker Cooper, Johnny Groth, and Ken Keltner.)

The 1942 team, with an overall record of 63-14, was the only one of Cochrane's Bluejacket squads to have a losing record (4-6) against major league competition. The following year, the sailors won seven of thirteen games against big league teams. However, this 1943 team, which compiled a 52-10-1 record, was 0-1 against the Negro Leagues. In the only game ever played during World War II between the Bluejackets and an all-black team, Ted "Double Duty" Radcliffe's Chicago American Giants defeated the Navy team, 7-3. With Lt. Bob Elson announcing the game, the American Giants battered Tom Ferrick and Vern Olsen for seven runs on 17 hits through seven innings. Johnny Schmitz finished up, allowing no runs on two hits in the final two

A typical military baseball team: Members of the Army Air Base, Company E team in Portland, Oregon, 1944.

innings. Ralph Wyatt, Lloyd Davenport, and player-manager Ted Radcliffe had three hits apiece for the Giants. Pitcher Gentry Jessup went the distance, despite surrendering a dozen hits and seven walks. Three double plays helped hold the Bluejackets to three runs.

Radcliffe recalls that it was only the speed of his star center fielder, Davenport, that held Johnny Mize to a double and a triple for two of his four hits. Had the ballpark been enclosed, Mize would have had at least two home runs, but Davenport was able to chase these clouts down in time to prevent Mize from scoring. The Chicago *Defender* wrote that the 10,000 fans in attendance were "startled" by the outcome. Perhaps the Navy was, too. "They wouldn't let us come back again," says Radcliffe.

The 1944 team was the best ever assembled at Great Lakes, largely due to an excellent pitching staff. Virgil Trucks went 10-0, en route to a Navy career pitching record of 28-1. His 0.88 ERA was slightly better than Bob Klinger's 0.93, but a bit behind Si Johnson's 0.73. Jim Trexler, the only member of the team who never played in the major leagues, went 14-1. The other pitchers were Lynwood "Schoolboy" Rowe and Bill Brandt. Every position player had been, or would become, a major leaguer, and none batted below .340. The lineup consisted of: Johnny McCarthy (1B), Billy Herman (2B), Albie Glossop (SS), Merrill "Pinky" May (3B), "Schoolboy" Rowe and Mizell "Whitey" Platt (platooning in LF), Gene Woodling (CF), Dick West (RF, a catcher in the majors), and Walter Millies (C). Infielder Roy Hartsfield was the only utility player on the Great Lakes squad.

They won their first 23 games of the season before losing, on July 5, to a Ford Motor Company team in Dearborn, Michigan. (The Ford team was managed by Rabbit Maranville, who had played for the Navy's Atlantic Fleet team during World War 1.) After this defeat, later avenged, they ran off a sixteen-game winning streak, before losing to the Brooklyn Dodgers on August 8. They ended the season with nine straight victories. Against major league teams, they beat the Phillies, Red Sox, Browns, Cubs, White Sox, Giants, and Indians, while losing to the Dodgers. Their overall record was a stunning 48-2.

Trucks thought this team could have won the pennant in either major league. Skipper Mickey Cochrane gave the base newspaper, the *Great Lakes Bulletin*, the following midseason assessment: "We've got a good team. Give me one more outfielder, and an extra infielder and we'd tackle them all—in the American or National League."

The Black Bluejackets

By the autumn of 1943 enough black sailors had entered Great Lakes for the Navy to begin a black sports program. The first all-Negro team to represent the base was a basketball team in the 1943-44 season. Coached by Stanford's All-American Forrest Anderson, this squad won 19 of 22 games, outscoring its opponents by an average score of 56-36. Four members of this team, Jim Brown, Larry Doby, Art Grant, and Charley Harmon, later played on the 1944 baseball team.

Many of Doby's teammates felt that he was better at basketball (and football) than he was at baseball. Later in the war, in the Pacific, Mickey Vernon first noticed Doby's great athletic ability—on a basketball court, not a baseball diamond. Harmon, whose favorite sport was basketball despite his future career in the National League, had played on the University of Toledo team that made it to the NIT final game against St. John's University in 1943.

Jim Brown's later career as basketball coach at DuSable High School in Chicago bespeaks his knowledge of the game. A powerhouse through the 1950s and 1960s, during Brown's tenure, his 1953 DuSable Panthers became the first all-black team with a black coach to play for the Illinois state high school basketball championship. So it is small wonder that the Great Lakes Negro basketball team got the base sports program off to such a successful start. DePaul University basketball coach Ray Meyer recalls the Great Lakes black team working out at DePaul. Several members of the team inquired about enrolling at the school to play basketball. Meyer had to regretfully decline the offer, since "nobody was playing black players" in those days, and he would not have been able to put together a schedule. "With three or four of them joining big George Mikan, we would have had a team nobody could have touched," recalls Meyer.

Before the 1944 baseball season began, the Navy took a new tack in addressing the problem of race relations. Focusing on the importance of White officers directly in command of Black sailors, the Navy sought to identify the more mature non-commissioned officers with experience in integrated situations. These NCOs, many of whom had been in charge of physical training and drill instruction, were commissioned as officers and assigned to Black units. The Navy adopted a new official policy which rejected all "theories of racial differences in inborn ability." To help educate these newly commissioned ensigns, the Navy published, in February 1944, an important booklet entitled *Guide to the Command of Negro Naval Personnel*. A full decade before the United States Supreme Court's historic *Brown v. Board of Education* decision, the Navy explicitly renounced segregation and Jim Crow social arrangements:

> The idea of compulsory racial segregation is disliked by almost all Negroes, and literally hated by many. This antagonism is in part a result of the lesson taught the Negro by experience that in spite of the legal formula of "separate but equal" facilities, the facilities open to him under segregation are in fact usually inferior as to location or quality to those available to others.

One of the new officers promoted from the ranks was Elmer J. ("Al") Pesek, who was commissioned on April 10, 1944. His assignment was to manage Great Lakes' first all-black baseball team, the Negro Varsity of 1944. It is unlikely that Pesek had heard of any of the players he would be managing, but he soon discovered a promising pool of talent. Some had starred in the Negro Leagues, and others would make their mark in Organized Baseball after the war.

A Navy manual published at the beginning of the season listed the players and their prior baseball affiliations (ages are shown where available):

Pitchers	Age	Prior Affiliation
John Wright	27	Homestead Grays
Herb Bracken	29	St. Louis Giants
Luis Pillot	26	Cuban All-Stars
Catchers		
Wyatt Turner		Pittsburgh Crawfords
Leroy Clayton		Chicago Brown Bombers
Infielders		
Larry Doby	20	Newark Eagles
Andy Watts	21	Glen Rogers (WV) Red Sox
Arthur Grant		Cleveland Buckeyes
Charles Harmon	18	University of Toledo
Stephen Summerow	18	Cleveland Buckeyes
Alvin Paschal	19	Columbus (OH) Buckeyes
Jim Brown	24	Birmingham Black Barons
Earl Richardson		Newark Eagles
Outfielders		
Leroy Coates	35	Homestead Grays
William Randall	28	Homestead Grays
Howard Gay		Cincinnati Ethopian Clowns
Isaiah White		Baltimore Bees
Wiliam Campbell	22	New Kensington (PA) Elks

The New Kensington Elks may not have been much of a team. But the Birmingham Black Barons, Cleveland Buckeyes, Homestead Grays, Newark Eagles, and Pittsburgh Crawfords were established members of the Negro Leagues. The future major league careers of Doby and Harmon vouch for their abilities. Brown, Campbell, Coates, Randall, and Watts all proved to be capable hitters. Herb Bracken would lead the pitching staff with a 13-1 record. And Ensign Pesek knew he had a great pitcher when he told the *Great Lakes Bulletin* prior to the season that his biggest problem would be finding a catcher able to handle the formidable stuff of John Richard Wright.

At 5'11" and 168 pounds, Wright pitched for Navy ballclubs throughout World War II. After the war, he became the second black player—after Jackie Robinson—to be signed by Branch Rickey to a Dodgers contract. Before the war, he had been an outstanding pitcher for one of the most famous teams in the history of the Negro Leagues: the Homestead Grays. His teammates there included future Hall of Famers Josh Gibson, Cool Papa Bell, and Buck

Leonard. In 1943 his record was 30-5, and he started four games in the Negro League World Series, twice shutting out the Birmingham Black Barons on the way to a 4-3 series triumph. He also pitched in the Negro League All-Star game that year, before a record crowd of 51,723 in Chicago's Comiskey Park. While players such as Richardson, Doby, and Harmon were just beginning their careers while at Great Lakes, John Wright, to those familiar with the Negro Leagues, had already arrived.

The Season

The "Negro Varsity" joined five other teams from various military bases and technical schools in the Chicago area to form the Midwest Servicemen's League (MSL). A double round-robin was scheduled, with the teams playing other, non-conference games against semipro, industrial, and independent clubs. After the first round of games in the MSL, an all-star team of league members would play against Mickey Cochrane's Bluejackets on June 17. Seven of Pesek's black players eventually would be selected to play in this game. However, at no time did the full Great Lakes Negro Varsity play the white Bluejackets. The closest the two teams came to meeting each other came in the last week of April, when rain canceled a scheduled six-inning practice game.

After a practice game in which the Negro Varsity barely defeated Waukegan (Illinois) High School, 1-0, John Wright got the team off to a propitious start, hurling a three-hitter in a 3–2 win over Chanute Field in downstate Rantoul, Illinois. After two more victories, the team lost three straight games to even its record at 3–3. One of these losses was to the Cincinnati-Indianapolis Clowns of the Negro American League. Wright pitched one of his worst games of the season in the 7–5 loss, yielding 11 hits and seven walks. After another three-game winning streak, the team missed a chance to defeat the Douglass Aircraft nine on June 6 when, as the base newspaper informed its readers, the game "was postponed because of the Invasion."

On June 14 Ensign Pesek sent John Wright to the mound against Ft. Custer in Battle Creek, Michigan. In a tough loss, Wright drove in both Great Lakes runs with a home run as the team lost, 3–2. Wright gave up only four hits, but Ft. Custer benefited from five Great Lakes errors plus some questionable umpiring. "With the bases full in the ninth inning," according to the *Great Lakes Bulletin*, "John Wright hit a pop fly to Peanuts Lowry, former Chicago Cub. The umpire refused to call it an infield fly. Lowry trapped the ball, forced Charles Harmon at home and then William Campbell was doubled." All three of Ft. Custer's runs came in the sixth inning, two of them unearned due to a throwing error by Wright. This loss dropped the black Bluejackets' record to 6-4.

Herb Bracken, Jim Brown, Leroy Clayton, Larry Doby, Charley Harmon, William "Sonny" Randall, and Wright were chosen to represent the Great Lakes Negro Varsity on the MSL's all-star team that played the white Bluejackets three days later. Tall, slender righthander "Doc" Bracken took the mound that day to face a ballclub that had mowed down every opponent in its path to that point. In a game that the soft-spoken St. Louis native modestly recalls today as "one of the better games I pitched that year," Bracken hurled a brilliant one-hitter, but lost the game, 3–0. The lone hit was a second-inning double by Johnny McCarthy, who then took third on what was ruled a passed ball. Bracken says he tried to sneak a quick-pitch by the hitter, but crossed up catcher Leroy Clayton instead. McCarthy later scored on a double-play grounder by Dick West. Bob Klinger pitched for Cochrane's team and held the all-stars to four hits. But the story of the game was Bracken. Years later Larry Doby would recall this game as proof of how the Navy's policies of segregation unfairly deprived blacks of the chance to represent the base in sports. Several members of the team recall trying to play especially well in this game, not because they were playing against White major leaguers, but because they were playing against a good team. Like athletes everywhere, they bore down whenever they faced a good opponent.

On July 8, Wright pitched a seven-inning no-hitter against the Naval Aviation School at 87th and Anthony in Chicago. He struck out ten, walked two, and drove in three runs in the 14–1 shellacking.

On July 12, the sailors avenged their earlier loss to Ft. Custer (and Peanuts Lowry) with a 1–0 victory at Constitution Field, scoring the game's only run with two out in the ninth inning. After three more wins, the team traveled to Rantoul, Illinois, and beat Chanute Field, 5–2. "Trailing 2-0 with two out in the sixth," reported the *Great Lakes Bulletin*, "the Negro nine went ahead with four successive home runs by Larry Doby, Charley Harmon, Bill Randall, and Jim Brown. Brown squeezed Harmon home for the fifth run in the ninth."

After an easy win at Urbana against the University of Illinois Signal School, the black Bluejackets clinched the MSL title by defeating Glenview NAS, 6-2, before 10,000 spectators at Great Lakes' Constitution Field. Bracken yielded six hits as he won his seventh game of the season. Larry Doby hit a home run, and Andy Watts hit a double and two singles, as the team improved its record to 20–7.

The Negro Varsity won eight of its last ten games to finish the season with a record of 32–10. They played one game in front of 25,000 fans in Cleveland's Municipal Stadium. After splitting two games against the Colored Athletics in Grand Rapids, Michigan, they defeated the Negro Leagues' Chicago American Giants, 5-2, in East Chicago, Indiana.

Other games that Pesek's black Bluejackets played in 1944 are lost from the historical record. Bracken and Watts recall the House of David as being the best team they faced that year, even better than Cochrane's. Jim Brown says that they also played a barnstorming team that included Satchel Paige and Dizzy Dean. None of these games—and who knows how many others?—were reported by the press.

The *Great Lakes Bulletin* did not print the season statistics for the Negro Varsity, as it did for the White Bluejackets. It did point out that Wright's final record was 16-4, and that Bracken led the staff with a 13-1 record. While stationed at Pearl Harbor, Bracken received a handsome trophy from the Navy for his 1944 accomplishments. Charley Harmon was the team's leading hitter. The *Navy* presented the MSL championship team members with rings. After the war, when Andy Watts showed his Cleveland Buckeyes teammate, Sam Jethroe, the Navy ring, Jethroe said it was better than the one he received for being a member of the Buckeye team that won the Negro World Series in 1945.

The winds of war dispersed the Great Lakes Negro Varsity baseball team for good shortly after the season ended. Some players never left the United States, while others were sent to the Pacific. Several played on integrated teams later in their Navy careers. Bracken, for example, was one of two black players on a team in Pearl Harbor. Watts played on an all-Black team in an otherwise White league on Guam, where he hit .519 while playing against major league veterans Pee Wee Reese, Hal White, Johnny Rigney, and Mace Brown. (One of Watts' teammates on Guam was Charley Harmon's brother, William.)

During the long decades of segregated baseball, there always remained a slender thread of contact between the races on the diamond with exhibition and training games. The military service teams during World War II continued this legacy and expanded upon it. Many major league players played with or against blacks for the first time during their military careers. By no means was integrated baseball limited to the Navy. In 1945 the Army organized a well-publicized tournament of teams representing the European and Mediterranean Theaters of Operation. Upwards of 50,000 GI's watched such Negro League stars as Willard Brown, Leon Day, and Joe Greene participate in the championship finals in Nuremberg.

Epilogue

On February 27, 1946, the Navy issued the following order:

> Effective immediately, all restrictions governing the types of assignments for which Negro naval personnel are eligible are hereby lifted. Henceforth, they shall be eligible for all types of assignments in all ratings in all activities and all ships of the Naval Service. . . . In the utilization of housing, messing and other facilities, no special or unusual provisions will be made for the accommodation of Negroes.

Nineteen days later, Jackie Robinson walked to the plate in Jersey City, New Jersey, for his first at-bat as a member of the Montreal Royals.

This article first appeared in The National Pastime, Vol. 4, No. 2, Winter 1985.

The Double Victory Campaign and the Campaign to Integrate Baseball

by Duke Goldman

The war against the forces of fascism in Nazi Germany and Japan mirrored another war fought in the trenches of American life – that between the entrenched forces of racism and its ugly operating system of segregation, and a black populace straining to achieve equal treatment in a land ostensibly promising "liberty and justice for all."

Coincidentally, the tenure of Adolf Hitler as the head of the National Socialist government in Germany—1933-1945—mirrored the time frame of an informal campaign to integrate major-league baseball. In 1933 several sportswriters began to publicly question why major-league baseball should not have black performers. Several of these writers wrote in the mainstream press—Heywood Broun of the *New York World-Telegram* and Jimmy Powers of the *Daily News* both came out against baseball's color line early that year, with other notable sportswriters such as Dan Parker of the *New York Daily Mirror* and Shirley Povich of the *Washington Post* weighing in later on during this period. The *Daily Worker*, the most prominent Communist newspaper, also produced hundreds of columns, starting in 1933, castigating major-league baseball for excluding black players. But not surprisingly, the prime participants in the battle to integrate baseball were the members of the black press, especially Sam Lacy and Wendell Smith. During his lengthy career (extending into the twenty-first century), Lacy wrote for several important black newspapers and was sports editor of the *Baltimore Afro-American*. Smith plied his trade during this time frame for the *Pittsburgh Courier*.[1] The *Courier* was the leading black newspaper of the time, reaching a high of 350,000 in circulation in 1945—in part because of the bold stands it took on the issues of the day.[2]

The *Courier*, with Smith as its sports editor, stepped up its campaign to integrate baseball in 1942, while at the same time championing a cause expressed in a letter it published on January 31, 1942, written by 26-year-old cafeteria worker James G. Thompson. He asked: "Is the kind of America I know worth defending?" His answer to this question stressed that dedication to victory abroad must be paired with a fight for victory against similar forces at home: "The first V for victory over our enemies without, the second V for victory over our enemies within. For surely those who perpetrate those ugly prejudices here are seeking to destroy our democratic form of government just as surely as the Axis forces."[3] This crusade came to be known as the Double Victory campaign.

Thompson's letter squarely addressed the "American Dilemma" examined by Swedish sociologist Gunnar Myrdal in his landmark study of America's race problem, to be published in 1944. Myrdal's study explicated what he deemed a failure of the United States to exemplify its "creed"—that of a country dedicated to equality and liberty for all—by the relegation of the black population to second-class status.[4] Thompson's letter presaged Myrdal's work by asking how America could fight a war abroad against prejudice and blind hatred while failing to address its racial issues at home.

One of those racial issues was the continuing segregation of the national pastime. As the Double V campaign swept black (and to a limited degree, even elements of white) America, especially in 1942 but to a lesser degree until V-J day in 1945, wartime Negro League baseball and some of its prominent figures championed the cause. One such champion, Cumberland "Cum" Posey, owner of the legendary Negro League powerhouse Homestead Grays, suggested in his weekly *Courier* column, called "Posey's Points," that every team in organized Negro baseball wear a Double V symbol on its uniform, stating his belief that the cause of "victory abroad and at home is more vital than any athletic victory any of us may attain."[5] Posey was prominent among those who worried about the future of the Negro Leagues if the white major leagues were integrated, so his eloquent dedication to the cause of Double Victory is noteworthy, as "victory at home" clearly would include ending employment discrimination such as the color line in baseball.

Another Negro League owner, Effa Manley, engaged in many activities supporting the war effort, including an active promotion of the Double V campaign.[6] Similarly, Satchel Paige biographer Donald Spivey indicated that Paige was a supporter of the Double V.[7] Paige was not shy in expressing his opinions, as he proved in the run-up to the 1942 East-West All-Star game, Negro League baseball's preeminent showcase.

During the heat of the summer and the heyday of the Double V campaign, Paige felt compelled to speak over the public-address system to a throng of over 48,000 attendees before he came on in relief in the seventh inning. The reason: to deny reports that he questioned whether integration of major-league baseball was possible at that time. Paige claimed he was misquoted: He merely said that he doubted that a major-league team would pay him a salary commensurate with the $37,000 he earned in 1941 and that it would be better for a team of black players to integrate baseball rather than an individual who would face Jim Crow alone.[8]

Fans watched Satchel as he "gummed up the program with a three-minute pointless statement"[9] in trying to defuse the controversy he created, and subsequently lost the All-Star game for the West, his first such loss after three earlier All-Star game wins. Meanwhile, the large crowd also saw symbols of the

Double V displayed and distributed. The front page of the August 22 edition of the *Courier* carried a photograph of a woman wearing a Double V logo on her back selling "VV" buttons at the game. Inside the edition, a picture of a woman flashing "VV" with her fingers was captioned "At Chicago East-West All-Star Game."[10]

By the time of the East-West All-Star game, the Double V campaign as covered by the *Courier* was slowing down, although it was by no means at an end. Starting with its February 7, 1942, edition through the end of 1942, the *Courier* printed 970 Double V items, peaking with 50 such items in its April 11 issue. The campaign spread throughout black America—"there were Double V dances and parades, Double V flag-raising ceremonies, Double V baseball games between professional black teams, Double V beauty contests, Double V poems, and a double V song, 'Yankee Doodle Tan...'"[11] In the June 13, 1942, issue the *Courier* reported on a Double V game in St. Louis. The thousands who attended watched as the New York Black Yankees defeated the Birmingham Black Barons, 8-4. They also saw a drum and bugle corps form a Double V on the mound, and a $50 Double V certificate being presented to the winner of a Miss Mid-West contest.[12]

The Double V campaign was also supported by other black newspapers. In another instance where Black baseball was involved, the *Atlanta Daily World* reported on what it called a "true double-V victory" by the Birmingham Black Barons winning an opening day Negro American League doubleheader over the Memphis Red Sox in late May1943. The article mentioned as well that a high-school band formed a "V" before the game—the first victory of the day.[13] All the prominent black newspapers of the day—the *Chicago Defender*, the *Baltimore Afro-American*, the *Cleveland Call and Post*, the *New York Amsterdam News*, the *World*, and many others—reported on the progress of the Double V campaign even if it was not with the sustained attention of the *Courier*.

During 1942 especially but also throughout the war, sportswriters Smith and Ches Washington of the *Courier*, Fay Young of the *Defender*, Mabray "Doc" Kountze of the *Call and Post*, Dan Burley of the *Amsterdam News*, and Lacy and Art Carter of the *Afro-American* were promoting the breaking of the color line, often invoking the theme, if not the explicit terminology, of the Double V. Washington told the story of a victorious boxer who invoked the themes of Double V. He also trumpeted the triumphs of black track stars and boxers over the "enemy abroad" while wishing that baseball stars like Josh Gibson be given a chance at home.[14] Smith used military terminology as he suggested that Negro fans organize and fight the battle for baseball integration with a "concentrated, nationwide action" much like that of the Double V campaign.[15] And on the same day, April 11, 1942, that the *Courier* provided its peak coverage of the Double V campaign, Kountze echoed the words of the American Negro Press's Claude Barnett that "if a colored man is good enough to fight for his own country, he certainly ought to be good enough to work here" as Kountze made the case that "something ought to be done. This very year. I mean, Yeah, 1942" to integrate major-league baseball.[16]

While the Double V campaign's momentum slowed down throughout the war, it did not disappear entirely from the pages of the *Courier* until victory was declared over Japan in September 1945. Until then, the *Courier* continued the practice started at the commencement of the Double V campaign of putting a "vv" at the end of each article to separate it from the article appearing beneath it. Meanwhile, the calls for baseball integration continued to build to a crescendo in the *Courier* and the other black newspapers from 1942 through the end of the war. In the summer of 1942, the black press reported that Bill Benswanger, owner of the Pirates, would be trying out Negro League stars Leon Day, Willie Wells, Josh Gibson, and Sam Bankhead. It never came to pass. At the end of 1943, the Negro Newspaper Publishers Association met with the American and National Leagues. Baseball Commissioner Kenesaw M. Landis, an ardent segregationist, went on record as not being against the move to place Negro players in the major leagues. Everyone knew otherwise. Yet *Courier* president Ira Lewis spoke at this meeting, and invoked the concept of national unity in suggesting that baseball integration would bring joy to 15 million black Americans and millions of white Americans as well.[17] Even though the *Courier* was no longer actively promoting the Double V by then, it was certainly continuing the "campaign for the integration of Negro players into the major leagues,"[18] as described by Wendell Smith in late 1943. As history would later prove, a partial victory against racism at home—the signing of Jackie Robinson by the Brooklyn Dodgers—would virtually coincide with the victory against fascism abroad in the fall of 1945.

Jackie Robinson had his own indirect connection to Double V. According to essayist and cultural critic Gerald Early, Jackie likely would not have become an officer in the Army without the publicity created by the Double V, along with a behind-the-scenes campaign started in 1937 by *Pittsburgh Courier* owner Robert Vann to start the process of getting black officers in the military.[19] Joe Louis also applied pressure on the military to commission black officers; Jackie said that without Louis "the color line in baseball would not have been broken for another ten years."[20] Louis was another supporter of the Double V campaign,[21] and his wife, Marva, was the Double V girl of the week in the *Courier* of April 11, 1942.[22]

In the end, there is a consensus among historians who have researched the Double V, the black press, and African American history. The successful campaign to integrate baseball naturally fit within the larger themes of Double Victory. As Henry Louis Gates put it, one of the two most important legacies of the Double Victory campaign is that "through the columns of its sportswriter, Wendell Smith ... it doggedly fought against segregation in professional sports, contributing without a doubt to the Brooklyn Dodgers' decision to sign Jackie Robinson. ..."[23] The other legacy was the ultimate desegregation of the US Army by Harry Truman in 1948. A double victory—integrating baseball and one year later, the military—had now been accomplished. But the larger struggle for racial justice had just begun.

The cover image of this 1944 magazine evokes the "Double V" campaign.

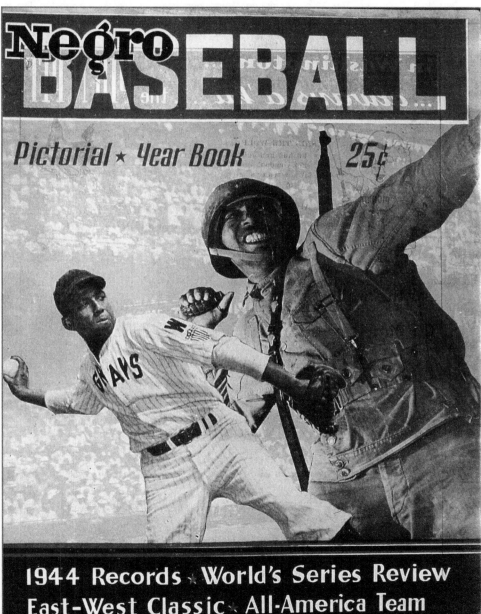

Endnotes

1.   On sportswriters supporting baseball integration, see Brian Carroll, *When to Stop the Cheering? The Black Press, the Black Community, and the Integration of Professional Baseball* (New York: Routledge, 2007), 69-87; Chris Lamb, *Conspiracy of Silence: Sportswriters And The Long Campaign to Desegregate Baseball* (Lincoln: University of Nebraska Press, 2012), 3-21; Arnold Rampersad, *Jackie Robinson: A Biography* (New York: Alfred A. Knopf, 1997), 120-121.

2.   Patrick S. Washburn, *The African-American Newspaper: Voice of Freedom* (Evanston, Illinois: Northwestern University Press, 2006), 180.

3.   *Pittsburgh Courier*, January 31, 1942.

4.   Gunnar Myrdal, *An American Dilemma Volume 1: The Negro Problem and Modern Democracy* (New Brunswick, New Jersey: Transaction Publishers, 1996 reprint of original 1944 edition), 8.

5.   *Pittsburgh Courier*, April 18, 1942.

6.   Sarah L. Trembanis, *The Set-Up Men: Race, Culture and Resistance in Black Baseball* (Jefferson, North Carolina: McFarland & Company, Inc. 2014), 118.

7.   Donald Spivey, *If Only You Were White: The Life of Leroy "Satchel" Paige* (Columbia: University of Missouri Press, 2012), 186.

8.   Associated Press, August 6, 1942, reprinted in *Chicago Defender*, August 15, 1942; *New York Amsterdam News*, August 15, 1942; *Baltimore Afro-American,* August 22, 1942; *Pittsburgh Courier*, August 22, 1942.

9.   Art Carter, "From The Bench," *Baltimore Afro-American*, August 22, 1942.

10.   *Pittsburgh Courier,* August 22, 1942: 1, 13.

11.   Patrick S. Washburn, "The Pittsburgh Courier's Double V Campaign in 1942," *American Journalism* (Vol. 74, No. 2 1986), 73, 74.

12.   *Pittsburgh Courier*, June 13, 1942.

13.   *Atlanta Daily World*, June 1, 1943.

14.   Ches Washington, "Sez Ches," *Pittsburgh Courier*, March 21, 1942.

15.   *Pittsburgh Courier*, July 25, 1942.

16.   *Cleveland Call and Post*, April 11, 1942.

17.   *Pittsburgh Courier*, December 11, 1943.

18.   *Pittsburgh Courier*, December 25, 1943.

19.   Author conversation with Gerald Early, October 11, 2012.

20.   Rampersad, *Jackie Robinson*, 92.

21.   Spivey, *If Only You Were White*, 186.

22.   *Pittsburgh Courier*, April 11, 1942.

23.   Henry Louis Gates, *What Was Black America's Double War?* the root.com/articles/history/2013/05/double_v_campaign_during_work

Contributors

Gary Ashwill is an author, researcher, and historian, primarily of Negro leagues and Latin American (especially Cuban) baseball. The Seamheads Negro Leagues Database that he co-founded was recently cited by Major League Baseball as being one of the contributing factors in their long overdue recognition of the segregated Black baseball circuits. A freelance editor residing in North Carolina, Ashwill has been writing the critically acclaimed outsider baseball blog Agate Type since 2006 and he was a contributor to the National Baseball Hall of Fame's Negro League Researchers and Authors Group (NLRAG), as well as the Baseball Think Factory's Hall of Merit.

Adrian Burgos, Jr., Professor of History, specializes in US Latino History and Sport History. He has written extensively on the history of Latinos in professional baseball, including the Negro Leagues, and was the inaugural editor-in-chief of La Vida Baseball.

Merritt Clifton, journalist, statistician, and historian, is the author of *Relative Baseball*, described by John Thorn as "a sabermetric classic self-published in 1979," as well as *Disorganized Baseball*, a three-volume history of the Quebec Provincial League and Vermont Northern League, and the novella *A Baseball Classic*. Merritt has been published in SABR's *Baseball Research Journal* and *The National Pastime* on topics ranging from Quebecois history to Japanese baseball, and has contributed work to many other publications. Merritt and his wife Beth together produce the www.ANIMALS24-7.org web site, continuing the investigative news service to the humane community that has been his full-time career since 1986.

Adam Darowski is Head of User Experience for Sports Reference, LLC (the company behind Baseball Reference and Stathead). He has been a member of the Society for American Baseball Research (SABR) since 2013. He is the co-chair of SABR's Overlooked 19th Century Base Ball Legends committee. In 2012, he created the Hall of Stats, an alternate Hall of Fame populated by a mathematical formula.

Sean Forman launched Baseball Reference in the Spring of 2000 while avoiding his Ph.D. dissertation at the University of Iowa. He eventually completed his dissertation in Applied Mathematics and taught math and computer science for six years at Saint Joseph's University in Philadelphia. In the fall of 2007, Sports Reference LLC was formed, combining baseball, basketball, and football sites, and has now grown to twenty eight employees and includes college sports, hockey, and world football. Sean was named a Henry Chadwick Award winner in 2011, 2020 SABR Analytics Conference Lifetime Achievement Award winner and continues to serve as Sports Reference's President. Sports Reference has been named a top 50 site by *Time Magazine*, won a Sloan Conference Alpha Award in 2013, and is the current statistical partner for the National Baseball Hall of Fame.

Sean Gibson is the great-grandson of Negro Leagues legend and 1972 National Baseball Hall of Fame inductee Josh Gibson. Sean has dedicated his life to the preservation of Josh's legacy and is the Executive Director of the Josh Gibson Foundation, a Pittsburgh-area non-profit organization. The Josh Gibson Foundation was established in 1994 in an effort to keep the memory of Pittsburgh's beloved Josh Gibson and the entire Negro Leagues alive. The foundation partners with the University of Pittsburgh, Duquesne University, and Carnegie Mellon University by matching up college students with elementary and middle school youth for tutoring. With a strong focus on education, the foundation currently serves roughly 300 children and plans to increase those numbers by starting new programs yearly. The foundation also sponsors the Josh Gibson Baseball Academy.

Gary Gillette is the founder and current chair of the Friends of Historic Hamtramck Stadium, a nonprofit that is working to restore the former Negro League ballpark near his home in Detroit. Gillette also served for a decade on the Tiger Stadium Conservancy's board of directors. He has four decades of baseball research, writing, and editing experience, beginning with his work with Bill James and Project Scoresheet in the mid-1980s. A contributor to six editions of *Total Baseball*, Gillette later designed and co-edited with Pete Palmer the five editions of the *ESPN Baseball Encyclopedia*. Gillette also designed the *ESPN Pro Football Encyclopedia* and served as executive editor for both editions of that reference work. A former member of the SABR's board of directors, Gillette is a past co-chair of two of SABR's major research committees—the Business of Baseball Committee and the Ballparks Committee. He was the founder and president of SABR's Detroit Chapter and is now the chair of SABR's new Southern Michigan Chapter.

Duke Goldman is a longtime SABR member specializing in the Negro Leagues, Monte Irvin, and the process of baseball integration. Duke is a recipient of the Robert Peterson Recognition Award for his *Black Ball* journal articles and other SABR publications, as well as two SABR-McFarland research awards, one of them for his article on Negro League Business Meetings that appears in *From Rube to Robinson*. Goldman roots for the Mets, Red Sox, and every New York Yankees opponent.

Leslie Heaphy was elected to the SABR Board of Directors in 2010. She has been a member of SABR since 1989 and chair of the Women in Baseball Committee since 1995. She is on the board for the International Women's Baseball Center. Leslie is an Associate Professor of History at Kent State University at Stark and publishes in the area of the Negro Leagues and women's baseball. In 2008, she became the founding editor of the journal *Black Ball*, published by McFarland. She lives in Canton, Ohio. She was the 2014 winner of the Bob Davids Award, SABR's highest honor.

David Hopkins is retired from the Faculty of International Culture Studies at Tenri University in Nara, Japan. His main field of research is comparative popular culture, including music, film, comics, radio and baseball. Since 2015, as Kato David Hopkins—his name since acquiring Japanese citizenship—he has been the main actor in Public Bath Press, a publisher focusing on underground music of Japan.

Adam Jones is a 14-year MLB veteran. A native of San Diego, Jones was drafted by the Seattle Mariners in the 1st round (37th) of the 2003 MLB June Amateur Draft from Samuel F. B. Morse HS (San Diego, CA). He came up in the Mariners' minor league system as a shortstop before transitioning to the outfield. He made his MLB debut with the Mariners on July 14, 2006, and played with them during the 2006 and 2007 seasons. Jones was traded to the Baltimore Orioles in 2008 and spent the bulk of his career there (2008–18) before he signed with the Arizona Diamondbacks as a free agent for the 2019 season. Jones is a five-time MLB All-Star, a four-time Gold Glove winner, and a Silver Slugger winner. He currently plays for the Orix Buffaloes of Nippon Professional Baseball in Japan. An avid history buff and a longtime supporter of the Negro Leagues Baseball Museum in Kansas City, Jones is committed to educating others about the game and sharing his passion. Jones and his wife Audie have two sons, August and Axel.

Bob Kendrick is the President of the Negro Leagues Baseball Museum (NLBM) in Kansas City, Missouri. He is also the host of the Black Diamonds podcast on SiriusXM. Kendrick has been responsible for the creation of several signature museum educational programs and events, including Buck O'Neil's Birthday Bash and the Hall of Game, which honors former MLB greats who played the game in the spirit and signature style of the Negro Leagues. Kendrick has been associated with the museum for nearly three decades, beginning as a volunteer during his 10-year newspaper career at the *Kansas City Star*. He was appointed to the museum's Board of Directors in 1993, became its first Director of Marketing in 1998, and was named Vice President of Marketing in 2009 before accepting his current position as president in 2011.

Larry Lester is co-founder of the Negro Leagues Baseball Museum and serves as chairman of SABR's Negro League Research Committee. Since 1998, he has organized the annual Jerry Malloy Negro League Conference, the only scholarly symposium devoted exclusively to Black Baseball. He is the author of *Rube Foster* *in His Time, Black Baseball's National Showcase: The East-West All-Star Game 1933–1953, Baseball's First Colored World Series: The 1924 Meeting of the Hilldale Giants* and *Kansas City Monarch*s, and *The Negro Leagues Book* (with Dick Clark), which has been updated in a second volume (with Wayne Stivers) available on Kindle. Lester lives in Raytown, Missouri. Lester is winner of the 2016 Henry Chadwick and 2017 Bob Davids awards.

Michael E. Lomax is a retired associate professor of health and sport studies at the University of Iowa and the author of *Black Baseball Entrepreneurs, 1860-1901: Operating by Any Means Necessary.*

Jerry Malloy (1946–2000) was a pioneer researcher who has been honored by the creation of an annual Negro League Conference named for him, as well as a book prize. His first great contribution to baseball history was *Out at Home: Baseball Draws the Color Line, 1887*. This monumentally important essay, published in *The National Pastime in 1983*, transformed our understanding of Black baseball and won commendation from C. Vann Woodward, the preeminent historian of American race relations. Malloy's subsequent work included a contextual republication of *Sol White's History of Colored Baseball with Other Documents on the Early Black Game, 1886–1936*. The late Jules Tygiel, also a Chadwick Award recipient, said of him, "His articles for SABR were pathbreaking and exceptional and rank among the very best this organization has ever published. Even more so, I doubt that the best among us have ever been as generous with their research and support as was Jerry."

A cultural historian, **Roberta J. Newman** focuses on the intersections of baseball, the media, and popular culture. Her most recent book, *Here's the Pitch: the Amazing, True, New, and Improved Story of Baseball and Advertising (2019)*, was the recipient of a SABR Research award, among other honors. She is also co-author of *Black Baseball, Black Business: Race Enterprise and the Fate of the Segregated Dollar (2014)*. Her work has appeared in *NINE: A Journal of Baseball History and Culture, Cooperstown Symposium* volumes, *The National Pastime, Baseball Research Journal*, and other publications. Newman is a Clinical Professor of Liberal Studies at New York University.

Visual artist, historian, and teacher **Todd Peterson** lives in Overland Park, Kansas. He is a two-time winner of the Normal "Tweed" Webb Lifetime Achievement Award for outstanding research, and was a contributor to and editor of *The Negro Leagues Were Major Leagues (2019)*. Peterson is currently working on a book about the Negro League playoffs.

Joe Posnanski is the #1 *New York Times* bestselling author of six books, including *Paterno, The Secret of Golf,* and *The Baseball 100* (out September 28). He has written for *The Athletic, Sports Illustrated, NBC Sports* and the *Kansas City Star.* He has been named National Sportswriter of the Year by five different organizations and is the winner of two Emmy Awards. He lives in Charlotte, North Carolina, with his family.

Vanessa Ivy Rose is an author, educator, storyteller, activist, basketball coach and creative from the metro Detroit area. In honor of her grandfather's baseball legacy, Vanessa has been interviewed by various newspapers, podcasts and was featured on Fox Sports Detroit's "Inside the Tigers: Stars Forever". She also creates (and hosts) webinars and has spoken at several baseball conferences including the "Detroit Negro Leagues Baseball Centennial" and "Women in Baseball."

Ryan Swanson is an Associate Professor of history, in the Honors College at the University of New Mexico. He also serves as the Director of the Lobo Scholars Program. He earned his Ph.D. in history from Georgetown University 2008. His latest book, *The Strenuous Life: Theodore Roosevelt and the Making of the American Athlete,* came out in 2019. He is also the author of *When Baseball Went White: Reconstruction, Reconciliation, and Dreams of a National Pastime,* which won the 2015 Society for American Baseball Research (SABR) research award, and co-editor of *Separate Games: African American Sport Behind the Walls of Segregation,* which received a North American Society for Sport History (NASSH) book prize in 2017, and *Philly Sports: Teams, Games, and Athlete's from Rocky's Town.* Swanson has published a wide variety of articles, book chapters, and editorials on the role of athletics in the United States.

Cecilia M. Tan has been writing about baseball since a fourth grade book report about Reggie Jackson. She has written for *Yankees Magazine,* Baseball Prospectus, and *Gotham Baseball.* Her editing skills have been applied to many baseball publications ranging from the 2012-2013 *Baseball Prospectus Annuals* to the *Baseball Research Journal.* She has been Publications Director for SABR since 2011.

Jules Tygiel (1949–2008) was a historian and college professor at San Francisco State University, best known for his 1983 book on the evolution of baseball's integration, *Baseball's Great Experiment: Jackie Robinson and His Legacy,* which received a Robert F. Kennedy book award, and a place among *Sports Illustrated*'s greatest sports books. Tygiel wrote several other baseball books, including *Past Time: Baseball as History,* which received SABR's Seymour Medal as the best baseball book of 2000. His other baseball contributions included monographs, book reviews, frequent appearances on television discussing Robinson and baseball's integration, and a significant role in promoting the fiftieth-anniversary celebration of Robinson's career.

◄STATHEAD

Please enjoy this copy of *The Negro Leagues Are Major Leagues: Essays and Research for Overdue Recognition*, produced by Sports Reference LLC and the Society for American Baseball Research, Inc. We at Sports Reference are very proud of this project and are giving complimentary copies to currently active Stathead subscribers.

In June of 2021, we dramatically expanded our coverage of the Negro Leagues and historical Black major league players on Baseball Reference. But the history of the Negro Leagues is far more than its statistical record. Many of the articles found in this book were commissioned as part of that update to provide additional context for the Negro League statistics. They have been combined with some significant past articles from the SABR archives in this book.

We hope that you will enjoy learning more about the Negro Leagues as much as we did as a team. We hope this information will enrich your experience of scrolling through Josh Gibson's page with awe, compiling Negro League WAR leaders in Stathead, or simply falling into that Baseball Reference rabbit hole we've all grown comfortable in.

Thank you—from all of us at Sports Reference LLC.

Sincerely,

Sean Forman
President
Sports Reference LLC

SABR BOOKS ON THE NEGRO LEAGUES AND BLACK BASEBALL

FROM RUBE TO ROBINSON:
SABR'S BEST ARTICLES ON BLACK BASEBALL

Brings together the best Negro League baseball scholarship that the Society of American Baseball Research (SABR) has ever produced, culled from its journals, Biography Project, and award-winning essays. The book includes a star-studded list of scholars and historians, from the late Jerry Malloy and Jules Tygiel, to award winners Larry Lester, Geri Strecker, and Jeremy Beer, and a host of other talented writers. The essays cover topics ranging over nearly a century, from 1866 and the earliest known Black baseball championship, to 1962 and the end of the Negro American League.

Edited by John Graf
Associate Editors Duke Goldman and Larry Lester
$24.95 paperback (ISBN 978-1-970159-41-7)
$9.99 ebook (ISBN 978-1-970159-40-0)

PRIDE OF SMOKETOWN:
THE 1935 PITTSBURGH CRAWFORDS

The 1935 Pittsburgh Crawfords, one of the dominant teams in Negro League history, is often compared to the legendary 1927 "Murderer's Row" New York Yankees. The squad from "Smoketown"—a nickname that the *Pittsburgh Courier* often applied—boasted four Hall-of-Fame players in James "Cool Papa" Bell, Oscar Charleston, Josh Gibson, and William "Judy" Johnson. This volume contains exhaustively-researched articles about the players, front office personnel, Greenlee Field, and the exciting games and history of the team, as well as historical photos of every subject in the book.

Edited by Frederick C. Bush and Bill Nowlin
$29.95 paperback (ISBN 978-1-970159-25-7)
$9.99 ebook (ISBN 978-1-970159-24-0)

THE NEWARK EAGLES TAKE FLIGHT:
THE 1946 NEGRO LEAGUE CHAMPIONS

The Newark Eagles won only one Negro National League pennant, but the 1946 squad that ran away with the NNL and then triumphed over the Kansas City Monarchs in a seven-game World Series was a veritable "Who's Who in the Negro Leagues," including Leon Day, Larry Doby, Monte Irvin, and Max Manning. Day, Doby, Irvin, and player/manager Raleigh "Biz" Mackey, as well as co-owner Effa Manley have been enshrined in the National Baseball Hall of Fame in Cooperstown.

Edited by Frederick C. Bush and Bill Nowlin
$24.95 paperback (ISBN 978-1-970159-07-3)
$9.99 ebook (ISBN 978-1-970159-06-6)

BITTERSWEET GOODBYE:
THE BLACK BARONS, THE GRAYS, AND THE 1948 NEGRO LEAGUE WORLD SERIES

The last Negro League World Series ever played was in 1948 between the Birmingham Black Barons and Homestead Grays. This volume presents biographies of every player on both teams, as well as managers, owners, and home ballparks. Also included: recaps of the season's two East-West All-Star Games, NNL and NAL playoffs, and World Series, plus essays about the effects of baseball's integration, the exodus of Negro League players to Canada, and the signing away of top Negro League players, specifically Willie Mays.

Edited by Frederick C. Bush and Bill Nowlin
$21.95 paperback (ISBN 978-1-943816-55-2)
$9.99 ebook (ISBN 978-1-943816-54-5)